CA/£25

Especially autographed for [barcode: D1467812] still

and devotion to my ailment is much appreciated.

With kind regards

Edmund ashov inll

_____

March 1998

EDMUND DE ROTHSCHILD

EDMUND DE ROTHSCHILD

A GILT-EDGED LIFE

Memoir

With a foreword by
Leopold de Rothschild

JOHN MURRAY
Albemarle Street, London

A catalogue record for this book is available from the British Library

ISBN 0-7195-5471 3

Typeset in 12¼/13¼pt Garamond MT by Servis Filmsetting Ltd

Printed and bound in Great Britain by The University Press, Cambridge

*To all those who have made
my life so happy and interesting*

Contents

Illustrations

Acknowledgements

Among the many people who have assisted me in one way or another in writing this memoir, I owe a particular debt of thanks to my wife Anne and to my curator Michael Hall, without whose encouragement I doubt I should have embarked on the undertaking at all. I am also greatly indebted to various members of my family, especially my son Lionel and my brother Leo, who have made many invaluable suggestions and have helped to correct my mistakes and hazier recollections. Leo also kindly agreed to write a short foreword.

My thanks are also due to everyone at the Rothschild Archive in London, in particular Victor Gray, Melanie Aspey, Tamsin Black and Mandy Bell, who have dug out old papers and photographs, cheerfully replied to scores of queries, and have in every way been as obliging as they could. My two secretaries, Frances Lamden at N.M. Rothschild, and Jean Weedall at Exbury, have, as always, supported and helped me in every way possible – not least of all by putting up with me from day to day.

Of the many others who were contacted or who got in touch with me in the course of writing, I should like particularly to thank Peter Barber, Laura Bartlett, Chaim Bermant, the Gellert family, Stanley Meeks, Sir Martin Le Quesne, Douglas Stirrat, Sir Lawrence Verney, Philip Warner and Roland Williams. Roland has been tremendously helpful in reading and rereading the passages about N.M. Rothschild before and after the war, and in supplementing my own recollections with his. I also have to thank my excellent, patient editors at John Murray, Caroline Knox, Gail Pirkis and Howard Davies, and also Douglas Matthews for undertaking to compile the index. But for

Caroline Knox's guidance and unfailing reassurance, there have been occasions when I might well have lost heart.

Above all, though, my thanks are due to George Ireland, without whom this book would not have been written. George has transcribed and made sense of many hours of my random and hotchpotch recollections on tape, ploughed through mountains of dusty old files and deed boxes, looked things up for me, interviewed old friends, and helped me to put my thoughts and memories in order and on to paper. Indeed, this book could fairly be said to be as much the product of George's work as mine.

The author and publishers wish to express their thanks to William Heinemann, for permission to quote from *Requiem for a Nun* (1955), by Nevile Shute; and to Weidenfeld & Nicolson, for permission to quote from *Return to the Forest* (1962), by Eric Bessborough.

Foreword

Twelve years separate my brother from me: in many ways the life he describes in this very personal memoir is familiar, in other ways so remote as to belong to, as he entitles his first chapter, another world. Eddy was born into an age of affluence only to see it spirited away by the war and death duties, and so realised perhaps even more the worth of what in my youth I had taken for granted. We shared many of the same things, but viewed them differently: he is an exuberant extrovert, a sportsman, and a visionary blessed with confidence in whatever project currently occupies him.

The reader will find much of interest in this book: what, mercifully, is missing is the malice with which so many spice their autobiographies. Instead, we have a series of journeys, both literal and metaphorical, including a long extract from the earlier memoir *Window on the World* which makes particularly fascinating reading. Eddy was probably one of the last people to have been 'sent round the world' by parents anxious to increase their offspring's knowledge of how others live outside their own country – all, of course, in comparative comfort.

Like his father, Eddy had two careers – banking and gardening. The part he played in helping to shape the bank's renaissance after the war is graphically and anecdotally described, as is his spearheading of the transformation of the garden at Exbury from a private wonderland of horticultural excellence into a major public attraction enjoyed by thousands of visitors annually. It is a jewel of which the country can well be proud.

On a personal note, I would like to pay tribute to Eddy for being such a generous and affectionate elder brother: I am sure that these qualities will impress the reader no less than they have his family.

LEOPOLD DE ROTHSCHILD

xi

I

Another World

My earliest memory is of being put to bed for the night in a bath during a Zeppelin raid in the First World War. The bath was in the basement of our London home in Park Street, just behind Park Lane, and my elder sister Rosemary and I were being tucked in for the night by our nannies. Frantic with excitement, we were engaged in heated debate as to which of us had the better right to sleep without the bath taps overhead.

I was born at No. 46 Park Street on 2 January 1916, and at the age of a few weeks was taken on my first major outing: a visit to see my grandparents at Gunnersbury, near Acton. My grandfather was Leopold de Rothschild, and during the summer and autumn months he and my grandmother lived at Gunnersbury Park in the house, known as the Large Mansion, at the centre of a small estate acquired in the 1830s by Leopold's own grandfather, Nathan Mayer Rothschild. 'NM' was the founder of the English branch of the Rothschild family, and of the family bank N.M. Rothschild & Sons, at New Court, just off St Swithin's Lane, in the City of London.

I was the first grandson – the latest addition to the fifth generation of the family in England – and my grandfather had expressed the wish to see me before he died. History does not relate how I comported myself during the visit, and sadly my grandfather died the next year.

By all accounts my grandfather – 'Leo' to the family – was an affable, large-hearted man, and of all my forebears he is the one with whom I feel I should have got on best. With his elder brothers Nathaniel – 'Natty', the first Lord Rothschild – and Alfred, Leo was a partner of N.M. Rothschild, where he was a great favourite with the staff. All of them were deeply shocked when, one March day in 1912, he was shot at in St Swithin's Lane by a demented young man called William Tebbitt, to whom my grandfather had previously done some kindness. Although the shots were fired at quite close range, through the window of his motor car, my grandfather was unharmed. Afterwards he discovered that one of the bullets had lodged in a pack of cards he happened to be carrying in his overcoat pocket.

Leo's real interests lay away from the world of business – in the hunting field and above all on the Turf, where he regularly headed the list of winning owners. He was once described as 'a perfect type of the high-minded, generous, straight-going English sportsman – *sans peur et sans reproche*'. He married Marie Perugia, the younger daughter of Chevalier Achille Perugia, of Trieste. Her elder sister Louise was already married to his friend Arthur Sassoon, and Leo is supposed to have said that he would only consent to marry when he found someone as beautiful and accomplished as Mrs Sassoon – whereupon Mrs Sassoon produced her sister Marie, my grandfather's junior by sixteen years.

My grandmother Marie's first public appearance with Leo was at a meet of the Rothschild Staghounds, near Leo's country house at Ascott, in the Vale of Aylesbury. The couple were married at the Central Synagogue in London, on 19 January 1881. Uncle Arthur and Aunt Lou Sassoon gave a dance for them at their home, No. 2 Albert Gate, near Hyde Park, and the Prince of Wales attended the wedding. It was the first time that the Prince had attended a Jewish ceremony, and he signed both the marriage contract and the register. The wedding breakfast was held at 148 Piccadilly (next door to Apsley House), the home of Leo's widowed mother Charlotte Baroness Lionel de Rothschild.

My father Lionel, Leo's eldest son, was born the next year. He was educated at Harrow and Cambridge, and when he came of age in 1903, the London omnibus drivers who plied the Piccadilly route sported my family's blue and yellow colours on their whips; and, as at every Christmas, each of them received a brace of pheasant from my grandfather's country estates.

At the time of my birth, my father was a junior partner of NMR (he had joined the bank in 1903, becoming a partner in 1915), and since 1910 had sat in the House of Commons as the Unionist (Conservative) Member for Aylesbury. But, like father like son, Lionel's real interests lay elsewhere, though in his case neither on the racecourse nor in the hunting field. As a young man he was addicted to motoring, while in later life he used to describe himself as 'a banker by hobby, a gardener by profession'. He has sometimes been called the greatest amateur horticulturist of his generation.

My mother, Mlle Marie-Louise Beer when my father met her, was a great-great-niece of the composer Giacomo Meyerbeer, whose delightful operatic compositions Schumann is said to have considered more suitable for performance in the circus big top than in the opera house. Giacomo changed his surname from Beer to Meyerbeer in deference to a legacy he inherited from a certain Mr Meyer. Despite his Italian-sounding first name (also adopted), the Beers were originally a German-Jewish banking family from Frankfurt, who later moved to France.

Lionel and Marie-Louise were introduced to one another by my father's cousin, Baron Robert de Rothschild, a grandson of James Mayer de Rothschild (the youngest brother of NM), who founded the French branch of the family and established the bank which became de Rothschild Frères in Paris. In 1907 Robert had married my mother's beautiful elder sister Nelly. The two sisters were very close, and my mother used to recount an incident from her childhood when she and Nelly were on a family holiday in Holland. Standing among a crowd of well-wishers cheering President Kruger, who was there on a visit from South Africa, my mother was suddenly knocked to the ground as the crowd surged forward. Nelly picked up her little sister and sat her safely on her shoulders.

My mother's father, Edmond Beer, owned a small estate on the outskirts of Paris, at Saint-Germain, and it was there that my parents' wedding took place on 8 October 1912.

My father's interest in motoring dated back to his student days. His first self-propelled conveyance was a motorised tricycle, which he owned as a Cambridge undergraduate at the turn of the century; he kept it chained to a lamp-post outside his lodgings in Jesus Lane. Later on, he and his mechanic, Martin Harper (recruited from the garage my father used to haunt in Cambridge), went on regular motoring trips to the Continent, and sometimes even further afield, to test out the latest motor car that had taken my father's fancy. For a time my father sat on the board of Wolseley, where his friend J.D. Siddeley (later Lord Kenilworth) was managing director, and he took several of their Edwardian models on extensive continental test-runs.

One year, accompanied by my father's friend Vere Ponsonby (later Lord Bessborough), they drove a Rolls-Royce across North Africa.

When one of the wheels gave out they sent a telegram to the Rolls-Royce motor works at Crewe, and a mechanic was despatched with a replacement wheel. When the man had fitted the wheel, my father gave him a £10 tip and enough money to make his way home.

On another occasion, a motor car-mad cousin, Baron Henri de Rothschild, challenged my father to a race from Paris to Monte Carlo, each of them at the wheel of a new 60-hp Mercedes Benz. Starting and finishing times were verified by the proprietors of the Elysée Palace Hotel in Paris, and the Hôtel de Paris in Monte Carlo – and my father won the race in eighteen hours.

I only ever met Henri once, when he was an old, sick man, but he had been a remarkable and versatile character in his day. When my father knew him before the First World War, he lived in an immense house on the Faubourg Saint-Honoré; according to his son Philippe, the street door was big enough to admit four tall giraffes walking abreast. There Henri wrote plays under the pen name André Pascal, as well as short stories and medical treatises. He owned his own theatre, the Théâtre Pigalle, sponsored Diaghilev's Ballets Russes, and at the same time kept a distant eye on the fortunes of the Unic motor-car factory, which he had set up to make custom-built vehicles. He was said by my father never to have attended a board meeting, and eventually he sold Unic to Renault. Henri also owned the most splendid, by far, of all the family's yachts, the *Eros*.

For my parents' honeymoon, my father had planned a leisurely motoring trip through France and Italy. A new Siddeley saloon had been acquired and shipped out to France, and after their wedding my parents set out from Saint-Germain accompanied by Martin Harper and an extra driver-mechanic, Richard Miller.

The first leg of the journey proved to be one of the most eventful. Not far outside Paris, on the road to Fontainebleau, the steering system of the new car failed, causing it to crash into the kerbstone and turn over. Fortunately, except for a few bruises, no one was hurt; and as the honeymoon couple sat at the roadside wondering what on earth to do next, a heavily-bearded French motorist, gesticulating and calling out my father's name, pulled up alongside. He turned out to be Monsieur Daladier, for many years one of my grandfather's chauffeurs in England, and he obligingly drove Harper back to Paris to collect another car.

An amusing vignette of the honeymoon couple's overdue arrival in Fontainebleau that evening is related by Harper in a memoir he wrote of his motoring adventures with my father. My parents were greeted on the steps of their hotel by my father's unflappable manservant, Arthur Bloxham – who, as was usual in those days, had gone on ahead by train with my mother's maid and the luggage. Bloxham, Harper recalled, showed not the faintest flicker of surprise at my parents' late arrival, nor at the unfamiliar car in which they drove up. 'Not for him any show of surprise,' observed Harper, 'particularly in front of Continentals.'

No. 46 Park Street remained our London home until 1928, by which time Rosemary and I had been joined by Naomi, in 1920, and Leo, in 1927. The house was arranged with the dining-room on the ground floor, the drawing-room and boudoir on the first floor, my parents' bedrooms and dressing-rooms on the second floor, and the nurseries on the third. Unmarried, live-in staff had their bedrooms on the fourth floor, while the kitchens and other utility rooms were all in the basement. From the nurseries we had a good view into the high-walled gardens of the Duke of Westminster's town-house, Grosvenor House (now the site of the well-known hotel).

Rosemary and I were friends, but like most children we squabbled and fought a good deal. When I was three or four, and we had just returned home from a walk with our mother in Hyde Park, we had a great argument on the doorstep of No. 46. Each of us was determined to ring the front door bell first. My mother gave us a light tap across the shoulders with her parasol, whereupon, much to her surprise, it broke in two. Unseen, Rosemary and I had had a tug-of-war with it, but rather than own up to this we preferred to tease my unsuspecting, kindly Mama for her terrible severity.

In 1928, the year in which my father left the House of Commons, we moved from Park Street to the Kensington end of Hyde Park. My father had acquired a lease, from Lord Lee of Fareham, of No. 18 Kensington Palace Gardens. I remember going there for the first time, and being rather impressed by the silk-hatted gatekeepers who were on duty at the entrance to the road.

As young children, though, my sisters and I lived mostly with our nannies in the country – at Inchmery House, on the edge of the New Forest in Hampshire, overlooking the Solent, close to the mouth of the Beaulieu River. My father had bought Inchmery shortly before he married my mother, as a consequence of his friendship with a fellow motoring enthusiast, Lord (John) Montagu of Beaulieu. John Montagu, the father of my neighbour Edward, the present Lord

Montagu of Beaulieu, was the man with whom King Edward VII made his first ever trip in a motor car.

Besides motoring, my father and John Montagu also shared a passion for power-boat racing, for which the Solent offered excellent conditions, and the two friends commissioned a number of boats for their joint use. These were built either in the boatyard at Buckler's Hard, on the Beaulieu River, or by Mr Samuel Saunders of Cowes, on the Isle of Wight. The engines for the craft were specially built by Napier, at their factory at Acton, or by Daimler. In 1906 my father and John Montagu broke the world water speed record – at the then staggering speed of 28.8 knots – and the next year they went to France and won the Perla del Mediterraneo, a splendid silver-gilt and enamel trophy designed by René Lalique, which I still possess. The trophy is in the form of a bas-relief plaque, and shows a view of the Côte d'Azur with a speedboat, in gold and enamel, crashing through the waves. Inset at the centre is a large baroque pearl, held in the mouths of three fish.

Inchmery House, a few miles across the Forest (or a shorter distance by Beaulieu river-boat) from Lord Montagu's Palace House, was originally built as a seaside villa for a Dowager Countess De La Warr. It had begun life as a small Georgian house with a wide veranda offering splendid views across the mouth of the Beaulieu River and the Solent, and to the Isle of Wight beyond. At some point in the nineteenth century a new dining-room, library and conservatory had been added and, on the second floor, a nursery with views up and down the Solent from Cowes almost to the Needles. One of my favourite childhood haunts was a long corridor, the walls of which were hung with colourful pictures of racing-cars, motor boats and early aeroplanes. At one time my father had wanted to race cars as well as boats, but he had given in to some stiff opposition from his parents.

From the garden at Inchmery there was a pleasant walk, known to us as the Green Walk, along a low cliff, shaded by Scots pines, towards Lepe House, once the Ship Inn but in my youth the home of our nearest neighbours, Lord (Harry) and Lady Forster. Nearer to the beach there was another path, the Lower Walk, where we were always warned to watch out for adders. Below the cliff, in front of the house, there were tidal saltings, teeming with bird life of all kinds, and in the summer months we would go there to gather samphire, a delicious cross between asparagus and seaweed. There was no village at Lepe, just a few cottages and a coastguard station.

We moved from Inchmery House when I was five, but I still have one or two vivid recollections of my happy life there. During the summer months my father would sometimes take us in his motor launch *Cautious Clara* for a picnic at Alum Bay, near the Needles on the Isle of Wight. There, Rosemary and I would collect the different coloured sands with our buckets and spades, and I remember sitting on the lawn at Inchmery on a blazing hot summer's day, playing with a pile of the sands that I had brought home. Another, perhaps even earlier, memory of life at Inchmery is of attending a bonfire party and fireworks display to mark the end of the First World War. It was given by an elderly gentleman, Mr Haig, who lived at Woodside, a house in the neighbourhood, and during the course of the evening he showed me a glow-worm, which intrigued me more than anything I had ever seen before.

We left Inchmery after my father came into his inheritance from Uncle Alfred, my grandfather Leo's elder, bachelor brother, and the last surviving male Rothschild of that generation. When Uncle Alfred died, aged 75, in January 1918, he left my father his 3,000-acre estate of Halton, near Wendover, on the Hertfordshire border with Buckinghamshire. This included the grandiose house which had been built for him by the firm of William Cubitt, together with its fabulous contents.

'Nature,' an obituarist wrote of Uncle Alfred, 'had endowed him with the artistic temperament. He studied painting and music so assiduously during early manhood that he thoroughly mastered both arts before he made his début in the great world where his taste and judgement with respect to pictures and china, singing and playing, porcelain, faïence, gems, and other varieties of *objets d'art* soon came to be regarded as infallible.' And at Halton Alfred had amassed a collection of furniture, paintings and works of art which filled the house to overflowing.

The picture collection included works by such masters as Cuyp, Hobbema and Jan van Huysum, Boucher, Watteau and Lancret, Gainsborough and Reynolds. There were sculptures by Canova, French furniture by the greatest *ébénistes* of the eighteenth century, and the finest examples of French and German porcelain. In his heyday, Alfred had also kept, and conducted, his own orchestra, making it a rule that all the musicians should be the same height and wear moustaches.

Uncle Alfred's London house, No. 1 Seamore Place (since demolished to make way for Park Lane), was, if anything, an even greater treasure-house than Halton, but he bequeathed both house and contents to the Countess of Carnarvon, together with a substantial slice of the remainder of his estate. Lady Carnarvon (born Almina Wombwell) was reputed to be Uncle Alfred's illegitimate daughter, and it was with the money she inherited from his estate that Lord Carnarvon was able to finance the excavations in Egypt which led to Howard Carter's discovery of the tomb of Tutankhamun in the Valley of the Kings in 1922.

During the First World War, Halton had been occupied by the Royal Flying Corps. As my father had no desire to move there from Inchmery, he sold the whole estate to the Air Ministry for £112,000, a figure well below its probate valuation. With part of the proceeds he acquired the Exbury estate, next door to Inchmery, from his friend Harry Forster, the Conservative MP who had served as Financial Secretary to the War Office and a member of the Army Council during the war. Harry Forster – who was created Lord Forster of Lepe just prior to taking up his appointment as Governor-General of Australia in 1920 – lost both his sons, as well as a son-in-law, in the Great War.

The purchase of the Exbury estate, for £60,000, comprised some 2,600 acres (approximately four square miles), including several farms, Exbury House and the tiny hamlet of Exbury. The farmland was a mixture of pasture and arable, and there was also a good-sized acreage of woodland and foreshore. To the east, the estate is bounded by the Dark Water River, with Southampton Water beyond; to the south and west by the Solent and the Beaulieu River, and to the north and north-west by Lord Montagu's Beaulieu estate and the New Forest.

Exbury's recorded history dates back to the tenth century, when it was part of the Hundred of Waltham, which in 904 was acquired by the Bishop of Winchester from King Edward the Elder. In the Domesday Book, Exbury, then called Teocrebarie, is recorded as being held by two Anglo-Saxons, Bolla and Wulfgeat, who had three hides of land 'where it is now forest' worth 40 shillings. By the thirteenth century the name had evolved to Ekeresbur, and by the fourteenth century, Eukeresbury. During the fifteenth century, the manor of Exbury belonged to the Berkeley family; and in the early sixteenth century, it passed into the hands of the Comptons, of Compton Wyniates, in Warwickshire, who held it for two hundred years. In 1718, the Comptons sold it to William Mitford, whose descendant Henry Reveley Mitford, father of the 1st Lord Redesdale, sold it to Harry Forster's father in 1879. Sydney Bowles, who married the 2nd Lord Redesdale and was to become the mother of Nancy and the other celebrated Mitford sisters, was born in Inchmery House.

Before the First World War, my father had had great plans drawn up for the extension of Inchmery. The proposed scheme would have entailed rebuilding the house, laying out an elaborate garden, and the construction of a model village, hospital and golf course. The house was to have been transformed into a rectangular Italianate building round a courtyard – not unlike Osborne on the Isle of Wight – with formal gardens and a long carriage-drive. The construction of the carriage-drive would have entailed re-routeing the nearest road and – crucially, as it turned out – re-siting a letter box. Failure to obtain permission from the authorities to move the letter box prevented the start of work, and the war then intervened.

With the acquisition of Exbury, the plans for Inchmery were naturally shelved, and instead my father embarked upon an extensive remodelling of his new house and estate. The modest eighteenth-century brick manor house was greatly extended, upwards and outwards – eastwards, in fact, because my father insisted that the extensions must allow for the preservation of a magnificent magnolia which grew up the south-west corner of the old house. During building operations, the magnolia was carefully laid down on the ground, and then later re-erected. Sadly, it has since lived out its span.

An extra storey was added, a portico was built along the length of the south front, and the whole, enlarged structure was encased in honey-coloured limestone. The work was carried out by William Jenkins, an architect employed by Cubitts, and the resulting house, in the Georgian style, was completed in 1923. During the building works, Rosemary and I used sometimes to be taken over to Exbury for a picnic tea organised by Deeks, my parents' butler, in the hall of the new house, with scaffolding all around us.

The finished house is an odd shape, but it follows the configuration of the residence originally built for Colonel Henry Mitford in about 1725. Notes on Mitford's plan explain that he wanted to have the benefit of the morning sun in his dining-room, good light in his drawing-room in the evening, but no sun at all in his library. The house was therefore designed as a triangle, with a large circular hall in the centre, and this shape has been retained, except that my father's rebuilding has rather blunted the points of the triangle at one side. All that remains of the body of the eighteenth-century house are the brick-vaulted cellars, though these have since been considerably extended.

One somewhat intangible feature of the old house seems also to have been done away with in my father's rebuilding: the ghost of William Mitford, author of a celebrated *History of Greece*. In his *Memories* (1915), the 1st Lord Redesdale recounts that as a young man he was once woken up in the dead of night at Exbury by an uncanny noise coming from the locked and empty room above. 'Someone,' he wrote, 'was dragging a very heavy weight up and down the floor; then I heard the door open, and the footsteps came down the stairs pulling the weight, bump, bump, bump, until whoever it was reached my door. Then there was silence for a minute or two, and presently the weight was dragged up again bumping as before, and the door of the upstairs room was opened, the weight was dragged across it and all was still.' When Lord Redesdale's father Henry Mitford was told of these events, he was considerably shaken – because he remembered that his grandfather, after a long day's literary labour, would go into an empty upstairs room and pull a heavy trunk about for exercise.

Exbury – free of ghosts since I have known it – is the last substantial old-fashioned country house to have been built by my family in England, and it is still my home today. It stands two miles back from the Solent, commanding a wonderful, uninterrupted view to the sea and the Isle of Wight. A gently curved eighteenth-century ha-ha separates the south lawn from the park, where plantations of trees are arranged so as to extend and give greater depth to the view; the clumps nearest to the house are the largest, gradually receding in size as they get nearer to the Solent shore. Viewed from the south, the house looks rather like a smaller version of Carton, the former seat of the Dukes of Leinster in Ireland.

Besides the rebuilding of Exbury House, a 200-strong force of workmen more than doubled the size of Exbury village, just beyond the house gates. The new cottages were built of red brick, with tiled roofs and oak doors and window frames. Hundreds of thousands of bricks and tiles were imported for their construction, and a traction engine was used to haul the loads along tracks over the New Forest from Beaulieu Road railway station to Exbury, via Beaulieu bridge.

More than once, Lord Montagu aired his fears about the damage this was doing to his somewhat decrepit bridge, until one day the bridge finally collapsed under the traction engine's weight. My father then entered into a long argument with the chief engineer of the Joint

Roads Committee in London about the vehicle's weight. The engineer maintained that the traction engine weighed 14 tons, my father said five – and Lord Montagu guessed eight. Eventually, an amicable arrangement was reached, and the Treasury made a grant towards the construction of a new road from Beaulieu Road railway station to Exbury which followed a more direct route over the Forest.

Largely thanks to Uncle Alfred, our new home was furnished in considerable splendour. The ground-floor rooms were hung with seventeenth-century Dutch landscapes, French and English eighteenth-century portraits, and were filled with French furniture, clocks, garnitures and porcelain in a profusion that nowadays would certainly be thought overdone. One of the rooms on the south front was panelled with a set of eighteenth-century French *boiseries*, bought by my grandfather in Paris and originally made for Madame de Pompadour's music room at the Château de Bellevue. In another room my father installed a set of panels said to have been designed by Nicolas Pineau for the Parisian hôtel of the Master of the Royal Hunt, the duc d'Ecrivillion. The staircase hall was hung with a set of enormous Beauvais tapestries.

Besides providing us and all these things with a new home, Exbury offered my father the opportunity for which he had been yearning to create a garden. Even as a small boy, he had been more interested in tending his little garden than visiting the stables, and as he grew older he abandoned country sports altogether in favour of horticulture. At Inchmery, the grounds had been too small to satisfy his gardening ambitions, and he told my mother that for him the real attraction of Exbury lay in its surroundings. When they first looked over the property together, the garden consisted of little more than a grassy walk and a glade overhung by two huge cedars of Lebanon. But at the end of the glade they were excited to discover the two tall cypress trees (*cupressus sempervirens*) mentioned in Lord Redesdale's *Memories*, which had been grown from seed from a wreath that had fallen from the Duke of Wellington's funeral carriage in 1852, and which still bore their original labels.

Otherwise, almost the whole area between the house and the Beaulieu River was woodland. When my father mentioned to Mr Cyril Potter, who was then Harry Forster's tenant at Exbury, that he had plans to lay out a more elaborate garden scheme than existed, Mr Potter declared to him severely that it would be a grave sin indeed to spoil the best pheasant wood in the district.

Ericaceous shrubs – azaleas, camellias and, above all, rhododen-drons – were already my father's great passion. It was the era when many new species of rhododendron were being discovered in far-off places, and my father, besides his love of gardening, had (in common with many other members of the family) a strong urge to collect. Once in possession of Exbury, therefore, he commenced the clear-ance of undergrowth and the preparation of about 250 acres, right up to the east bank of the Beaulieu River, for planting. The light acid, lime-free loam of the area is just right for growing rhododendrons and, until recently, it seemed that a tiny finger of the Gulf Stream touched the coast of the Solent, giving Exbury its own warm micro-climate, virtually free from frost. The Gulf Stream must since have shifted, as nowadays Exbury is not altogether frost-free.

Manpower in those days was in ready supply, and my father had an army of men working full-time on the garden construction project. He preferred, I remember, to resist my mother's enquiries as to the exact number of labourers he employed, but the workforce, at its peak, was in the region of four hundred.

Two stories often told about my father give a flavour of the world he inhabited, and of what now seems its somewhat restricted outlook. Although they are probably too good to be true, I have frequently retold the stories myself. One concerns a remark he is alleged to have made when addressing the City Horticultural Society: 'No garden, however small, should contain less than two acres of rough wood-land.' The other records his reaction to a canteen of cutlery which had been bought as a wedding present for a young clerk at New Court. 'That's no good,' my father is supposed to have said. 'He won't be able to have more than twelve people to dinner.'

My father and his two brothers, Evelyn and Anthony (always known as Tony), were brought up between the four large homes their parents maintained. In London, they lived at No. 5 Hamilton Place (now a private club), which my grandfather Leo had inherited on his father's death. Having initially planned to rebuild the house, my grandfather settled for alterations, again carried out by Cubitts. These included the addition of two storeys, the construction of a conservatory to the whole height of the north front, and open arcades along both sides of the ground floor. Inside, Leo engaged forty Italian craftsmen for two years to complete a magnificent set of panelling, hand-carved in maple and mahogany, for the library. There was a sweeping serpentine stair-case, and in the kitchen a spit on which a whole ox might be roasted.

At Hamilton Place, they were right at the heart of the Rothschild family in London. The house was a stone's throw from No. 148 Piccadilly, by then occupied by Natty (Lord Rothschild), and from Uncle Alfred's house in Seamore Place. Lord Rosebery, the Liberal Prime Minister who was married to a Rothschild, had his London house just around the corner in Berkeley Square.

Out of London, when not at Gunnersbury, my grandparents and family lived principally at Ascott, in Buckinghamshire, between Leighton Buzzard and Wing, though Leo also owned Palace House, near Newmarket, close by the stables of his trainer Mr Alfred Hayhoe. A force of between fifty and sixty full-time indoor servants was employed between my grandparents' four households, together with numerous chauffeurs and temporary and outdoor staff.

Ascott was one of the network of Rothschild houses in Buckinghamshire – or 'Rothschildshire', as the county was sometimes dubbed. These included Tring Park, Natty's country seat; Mentmore, built by my grandfather's uncle Baron Mayer and left to his only daughter Hannah (Lady Rosebery); Waddesdon Manor, the palatial home of our cousin Baron Ferdinand de Rothschild and his formidable sister Miss Alice; and later on Halton, belonging to Uncle Alfred. All these houses, built or rebuilt in the nineteenth century, were fitted out on a sumptuous scale, as one can still see at Waddesdon today. Lady Eastlake, a much-quoted visitor to Mentmore, famously remarked that she 'did not believe that the Medici were ever so lodged at the height of their glory'.

Ascott is the house with which I have had the closest associations, and it is outwardly the least imposing of them all. It was built around the core of an early seventeenth-century, black and white timber-framed farmhouse, which, with about 100 acres of farmland, was bought (together with a number of other properties in the neighbourhood) by Baron Mayer, when Joseph Paxton was building Mentmore for him a few miles away. My grandfather eventually took it over to use as a hunting-box, but then proceeded to extend it, in the same style, to plans by the architect George Devey. The gardens, with broad expanses of lawn and parterres, were laid out for my grandfather by Sir Harry Veitch, the well-known Chelsea nurseryman. From its high vantage point, the house commands sweeping southerly views across the Vale of Aylesbury to the Chilterns.

Inside, by the time I knew it, Ascott was furnished with eighteenth-century French and English pieces, and a tremendous collection of pictures. My grandfather had inherited a share of the Old Master painting collection formed by his father – always known as Baron Lionel – including a large number of Dutch seventeenth-century works from the Van Loon Collection, one of the most spectacular collections of the Dutch school ever assembled, which Baron Lionel bought *en bloc* in 1878. One picture, which was added to the collection by my father's brother Tony, and which dominated one wall of the dining-room (the picture is more than six feet wide), was a *View of Dordrecht* by Aelbert Cuyp. The experts say that it is one of the finest of Cuyp's works, and even as a philistine schoolboy I remember gazing at it with pleasure.

Besides extending the house at Ascott, my grandfather built hunt kennels for the Rothschild Staghounds, and a model stud-farm called Southcourt. The staghounds had been formed in the 1830s by Baron Lionel and his three brothers Nathaniel, Mayer and Anthony. They were all passionate about hunting in the Vale of Aylesbury, but sought an alternative to the Royal Buck Hounds, from whom I should guess they experienced a certain amount of condescension; and so they decided to establish their own hunt. Previously at Mentmore, the hunt kennels were moved to Ascott after Baron Mayer's death in 1874. After the First World War, the pack switched to fox-hunting and merged with the Whaddon Chase, as the two hunts covered much the same country. A splendid pictorial record of the four Rothschild brothers hunting their staghounds survives in Sir Francis Grant's painting *Full Cry*, a copy of which now hangs at New Court.

Southcourt superseded a stud-farm which my grandfather, as a young man, had established at Gunnersbury, and which produced the 1879 Derby winner Sir Bevys for 'Mr Acton', the racing pseudonym Leo used during Baron Lionel's lifetime. Southcourt thoroughbreds included the 1904 Derby winner St Amant, of which a bronze model by Sydney Marsh now stands in the hall at Exbury – next to a photograph of my grandfather leading him into the winners' enclosure on Derby Day. It rained very heavily that day, and one mischievous commentator attributed St Amant's victory to the fright he took at an opportune clap of thunder. My grandfather caught a bad dose of pneumonia, but survived.

In his second volume of autobiography, *The Second Burst*, Sir Alfred Munnings evokes an idyllic picture of a visit to Southcourt in the early 1920s, when my uncle Tony had commissioned him to paint some of the horses. 'Throughout April and May,' Sir Alfred wrote, my daily routine was as follows. After breakfast to the stables in a car, where Kent, the stud-groom, made everything, bar painting, as easy as possible. We became the best of friends; a kinder man than Kent never lived. He would see me settled in a peaceful paddock with tall elm trees, painting in the company of well-bred mares and foals, a stud-helper holding one of the mares whilst another held a little foal. And so the hours would fly, with blackbirds and thrushes trilling their songs in every tree and fence. Lunch hour came with a surprise packet of wonderful sandwiches – never the same from day to day. In the afternoon I resumed work again to the sound of bird-song and the foliage of elms rustling in the breeze; at 4.30 Kent would appear with a silver teapot, sugar-bowl and cream-jug on a silver tray, which he placed on the grass with a smile. 'There, sir, that should help you to keep going!'

Most members of my family have been considerate hosts, and at Ascott my grandparents' guests sat down to gargantuan, hours-long meals. One not infrequent guest was King Edward VII, with whom my grandfather and his brothers had been friends since their days together at Cambridge, and my father had a favourite story about one of the King's visits. The guests placed to either side of my father were engrossed in conversation with their other neighbours, when suddenly Sir Edward Grey (the Foreign Secretary), who was seated on one side, turned to my father and asked, peremptorily, 'Do you whistle in your bath?' My father, who was suffering from acute indigestion that day, was pondering the remark when a stentorian voice at the far end boomed out, 'Is there a parrot in the house?' 'No, your Majesty,' came my grandmother's reply, 'it is a young man.' Suddenly my father realised that he was whistling to himself aloud.

After dinner everyone played billiards or cards. Once, during a game of bridge, my great-aunt Louise Sassoon was very surprised to hear Mrs Keppel turn to the King and ask, 'Well, what have you got in your hand, old cock?' Aunt Lou and her husband knew the King well, and he was a regular guest at their house at Hove, especially when he was suffering from one of his bouts of bronchitis in the winter months. He also used to stay with them at Tulchan, in Scotland, during his annual summer tour of Speyside. There, Arthur Sassoon had a special concrete barrage built out into the river on the best beat, so that the Royal feet need never get wet.

Another visitor to Ascott in those days was Sir Douglas Haig, whom my grandfather had got to know when the two men were taking a cure at a spa on the Continent. On one occasion, when Sir Douglas and his wife Dorothy were staying with my grandparents during army manoeuvres near Leighton Buzzard, my grandparents were asked to entertain the Military Attaché from the German Embassy in London and a party of German officers. At dinner, Dorothy Haig had been asked to make herself agreeable to one of the officers, which she did – with the consequence that he took a great fancy to her. My grandmother remembered him, rather the worse for wear, making open (and unwelcome) advances to Dorothy on the sofa after dinner; and I was told that when the officer left Ascott he signed his name through hers in the visitors' book. Dorothy Haig writes about the incident at some length (though not about the visitors' book) in her memoir *The Man I Knew*.

A footnote to the story is that when Sir Douglas Haig was appointed to succeed Sir John French as Commander-in-Chief of the British forces in France in 1915, it is said to have been from my grandfather, who liked to keep *au courant* with affairs, that he first learned the news of his appointment. And that Christmas, my grandfather sent a consignment of fur-lined gloves to France to be distributed among Sir Douglas's staff.

My own life as a small boy was, of course, a world apart from such exciting goings-on. Occasionally, we children stayed in London during the week, but mostly we lived with our nannies at Exbury. We saw our parents at the weekends, in a rather formal way, and from time to time we went to stay with various Rothschild cousins, most often with my widowed grandmother Marie.

My earliest memory of Gunnersbury, which in those days still had a small estate farm, is of standing by a stile leading into a field of wheat, and looking up to see the wheat-ears waving in the breeze above my head. Gunnersbury was also the scene of my most exciting early adventure. The grounds there contained several large ponds, including one known as the Horseshoe Pond and another called the Potomac. The latter was reputed to contain a gigantic pike, and all of them were strictly out of bounds to children. But at the age of four or five, in the company of my nanny, I was allowed to try my hand at fishing – and, wild with excitement, I caught my first fish, a small perch.

Colour photographs of Gunnersbury taken by my father as a young man confirm that gardening was in the family blood. There was a

Japanese Garden, an Italian Garden and a Heath Garden, hothouses for delicate flowers and fruit, a splendid orangery, and specially heated tanks for the cultivation of the unusual blue hybrid water lilies for which my grandfather had a passion. Growing orchids was another of my grandfather's (and later one of my father's) specialities, and on Coronation Day in 1911 he presented King George V with a display of blooms from the Gunnersbury orchid house, contained in a crystal vase made by Fabergé.

On my grandfather's death in 1917 Gunnersbury was left to my father. In his young days, Leo had used to enjoy a morning ride over the fields, through Ealing and by Hanger Hill, Greenford or Perivale; but by the time he died the surrounding area was becoming very built-up. So in 1925 my father agreed to sell the house and estate to the town councils of Acton and Ealing. The property changed hands on Christmas Day that year, and in May 1926 it was opened for use as a public park by Neville Chamberlain, then Minister of Health. Some of the old buildings at Gunnersbury now house a local history museum, which contains several mementoes of Rothschild family life, including the large black carriages, known as 'berlins', in which the family travelled to and from London in the nineteenth century. From time to time, I have been able to help with the planting-out of the grounds there, and my daughter Charlotte, who is a professional singer, has occasionally given recitals in our old home.

After the sale of Gunnersbury, my grandmother lived mainly at Ascott, and every Christmas holiday we went there to stay. Except for the tall Christmas tree standing in the billiard-room surrounded by a tempting mass of presents, the house was a gloomy, forbidding place to a child – a maze of long corridors and stairways lit by flickering gas lamps. At night the plumbing emitted strange sounds, and I used to lie awake in bed counting the chimes of the stable clock. Most terrifying of all was the journey we had to make from the nursery to the drawing-room on dark afternoons – by several long passageways and flights of stairs, and finally – at a run – past a ferocious-looking stuffed bear holding a staff in the hall.

In grown-up company we were invariably first of all told not to make such a noise, after which we would be asked a few perfunctory questions – 'What does the cow say?' or 'What does a pig do?' – before being despatched back to the nursery for a bath. There were hip-baths at Ascott, and hurrying along the corridors I remember peering through the open doors of the bedrooms to see the baths, silhouetted by the light of the log fires, ready for use after a day's hunting. And I can still feel the sensation of the warm water being poured over my back from a jug.

My grandmother lived at Ascott with my uncle Tony, my father's youngest brother. Evelyn, the middle of the three brothers, had died in action in Palestine in November 1917, from wounds sustained in the Royal Bucks' cavalry charge against the Turks at El Mughar. His cousin Neil Primrose (with whom my father had shared a twenty-first birthday party at Ascott in 1903) was also serving with the Bucks in Palestine, and was killed at Gaza on the same day that Evelyn died at a military hospital in Cairo. Neil was the younger son of the 5th Earl of Rosebery, who married Hannah, the only daughter and heiress of Baron Mayer, the builder of Mentmore. Tony, who rose to be a major in the Bucks during the war, served at Gallipoli, where he was wounded and mentioned in despatches, and afterwards in France, on the General Staff.

In France, Tony made friends with General Adrian Carton de Wiart, whose heroism and dashing appearance, enhanced by an eye-patch and the loss of a hand, earned him the nickname 'Nelson'. When Tony's son, my cousin Evelyn, was born in 1931, General Carton de Wiart consented to be his godfather.

My great-aunt Louise Sassoon – Aunt Lou to us children – was already a widow when I knew her, and she was usually at Ascott, too. She was a most attractive and entertaining character, and was someone we liked very much to see. Once she took me out on some errand in the neighbourhood in a magnificent old-fashioned car with a tall, two-piece windscreen and running boards. It was unusual, even then, in having solid tyres, which made driving along the unsurfaced roads around Ascott a memorable experience.

Other regular Ascott guests, each of whom had their own small suite of rooms, included my grandmother's friend Grace Countess of Wemyss. She was the widow of the much older Earl of Wemyss (he had been born in the reign of King George III) who was a Lord of the Treasury in Lord Aberdeen's administration. To Rosemary and me she was known as 'Grouse Lady Wemyss'. Often there was also in residence a redoubtable, straight-backed old lady called Countess Hochberg, always referred to as 'the Contessa', but what her precise connection with the family was, I do not know.

Permanent residents included the elderly Miss Monaghan, my father's old nanny, whom Rosemary and I used always to visit in her room. She would regale us with sweets and cakes and tell us fairy tales and stories of the past. There was also my grandmother's efficient secretary, Miss Nelly Craston, and Miss Moorhouse, her lady's maid of many years' standing. To us, Miss Moorhouse was fierce and aloof, but she was continually being chided by my grandmother. And Granny had a little café-au-lait bitch, of unknown parentage, called Shousha, which always yapped. Shousha had been sent to Ascott by my uncle Evelyn from Libya, when he was serving with the Bucks in the Senussi campaign. She was treasured by Granny as a living relic of Evelyn, and lived to be nearly twenty years old.

John Tarver, who had at one time been my father's tutor, was the Head Agent at Ascott, and later – during the Second World War – at Exbury, too. The Tarvers had a son called Anthony with whom I was allowed to play in the garden, in a brooding and rather sinister spot overhung by great elm trees. One dark winter's afternoon, on a nearby road, Anthony and I shone our torches through the windscreen of an oncoming car. The driver pulled over and threatened us both with a good hiding.

On Christmas Day, all the family staying at Ascott went over to Tring for lunch with my great-aunt Emma, Lady Rothschild, the widow of my great-uncle Natty. Emma was a Rothschild by birth as well as marriage, and she lived at Tring Park with her bachelor son Walter, the 2nd Lord Rothschild and celebrated zoologist, whose life and achievements have been so well described by his niece, my cousin Miriam, in her book *Dear Lord Rothschild*. All the children had to go up to Great Aunt Emma in her chair to receive a present, and Rosemary and I dreaded her tart remarks.

Christmas lunch was a lengthy affair, eleven or twelve courses long; and it was one of the most notable events of the year. Older members of the family, including Uncle Walter, were seated at one end of the table; the children, including Miriam and her brother Victor, sat at the other end. Miriam wrote in her book that Uncle Walter liked his nieces, but suspected that his nephews made fun of him, and I remember that in the middle of lunch every year Victor would always call up the table, 'Uncle Walter, Uncle Walter, we're having a great argument down here. What's the difference between an alligator and a crocodile?' Upon which Uncle Walter would obligingly rise to the bait, and proceed to stammer a long and inaudible explanation into his beard, ignoring our childish giggles.

Uncle Walter was a highly original character, famous for driving his carriage with a team of zebra in Hyde Park. In the park at Tring, there were wallabies and South American rheas (relatives of the ostrich) roaming free, as well as, at one time, giant tortoises from the Galapagos Islands. There is a photograph of Uncle Walter astride one of the tortoises, called Rotumah, which lived to be more than 150 years old. Poor Rotumah had no mate, and, according to Miriam, eventually died from an excess of sexual frustration.

There was also a museum at Tring containing Uncle Walter's extensive collection of stuffed mammals and birds, reptiles and mounted insects. Including the basement, its floor space covered something like an acre and a half, and it provided Uncle Walter with his chief occupation in life.

He had begun his collection as a small boy, with butterflies and moths, and had gradually built it up into one of the greatest in the world, spanning butterflies, moths, birds, mammals and parasites. He planned the collection so as to include not simply a single specimen of each creature, but several specimens of every kind. Exhibits traced the development of species and included examples of extinct and disappearing animals. Uncle Walter had, for instance, the only six specimens of an extinct pigeon from the Solomon Islands, which, he used to say, had become extinct 'owing to the natives eating them'.

One special display included specimens of all the birds and beasts named in honour of my family – Rothschild's Giraffe, Zebra, Wallaby, Albatross and Grackle (a white mina bird with blue rings around the eyes). The butterfly collection included examples of Rothschild's Birdwing, a gorgeous species from New Guinea. When I began to show a little interest in butterflies, Uncle Walter gave me a wonderful collection of South American specimens, housed in a special collector's cabinet. His younger brother Charles, who died young, was an authority on fleas – an area in which Miriam, Charles's eldest daughter, has since become a great expert.

Shortly before his death in 1937, Uncle Walter gave his collection to the Natural History Museum. It constituted the museum's greatest ever accession, even though some exhibits, including many of the stuffed birds, had been sold to collectors in America before Walter made his generous gift. The collection can still be seen on display at Tring today.

On Boxing Day at Ascott, all the family, including my grandmother, went out with the Whaddon Chase. We children were accompanied by Richard ('Bill') Holland, the stud-groom (the head of the stables) at

Exbury, who taught us to ride and always came to Ascott with us. In his youth, Holland had helped to train Lord Rosebery's racehorses, including the one which won the Derby in 1894, and before coming to Exbury he had worked for my grandmother in the stables at Ascott. Every year, a week or two before Christmas, he and his men would ride our horses to Beaulieu Road station, load them into special horse-boxes on a goods train, and accompany them on the journey to Buckinghamshire.

On other days during the Christmas holidays we might go over to Mentmore or back to Tring; but more often, we would be marched off on a long, cold walk. When I was seven, my governess, Miss Eve Frayling, described me in a report as 'rather tiresome, both during his lessons and out for his walks', and I certainly remember finding our walks extremely dull. Sometimes the huntsman, Will Boddington, would take me to see the hounds at the hunt kennels or, if I was very lucky, I would be allowed to go after rabbits with one of my grand-mother's old keepers and his ferrets.

Although Waddesdon, too, was quite close by, I have no recollection of going there as a child. Looking back, the explanation for this may lie in the ill-feeling caused within my branch of the family by the circumstances surrounding the will of the redoubtable Miss Alice de Rothschild – dubbed 'The All Powerful' by Queen Victoria – who had inherited Waddesdon from her brother Ferdinand. It had always been understood in the family that Alice was going to leave Waddesdon to my uncle Tony. But, or so the story goes, not long before she died, during a trip to the Continent in 1922, she had received a visit from our cousin Jimmy de Rothschild, and had changed her will in his favour. Jimmy, who had a house a few doors down from us on Park Street, at No. 34, came from the French branch of the family, and Alice was said always to have favoured him. But she is supposed also to have made it known that she would only leave Waddesdon to a Rothschild with British nationality. Consequently, according to family lore, when Jimmy eventually obtained his British nationality (for which he had applied in 1919), he hastened to inform Miss Alice.

At our own homes, my father was very much in charge of all the household arrangements. My mother was often said to be unwell, and even when well enough her role was practically confined to entertaining the lady guests after dinner, while the gentlemen enjoyed their port and cigars. I have always imagined that this situation must have arisen at the start of my parents' marriage, when my mother was neither fluent in English nor familiar with English ways, and my father had not wanted to overburden her. Whether or not that was the real reason, my father was the one who dealt with the staff, ordered all the meals from the chef, and who would even visit the kitchens when the preparations for a meal were under way. More conventionally, he also enjoyed sitting in his study leafing through the cellar-book with his butler, deciding which wines to drink.

Emile Gallois, the French chef, together with the valet, the lady's maid and four footmen, moved with my parents between London and Exbury. My father's valet was a charming man called James King, who always made us children laugh, and my mother had a French maid called Camille. Once, when King was on holiday, my father was looked after by one of the footmen, Stanley Meeks, who still remembers my father teaching him the particular way in which he liked his shoe-laces to be tied. On King's return from holiday, my father gave Meeks a large, white £5 note – with which he bought a gold watch that he used for forty years.

Between the wars my mother took Camille with her when she was invited to join a trip to Egypt organised by Major-General Sir Charles Grant, who was married to Lord Rosebery's daughter Sybil. One day they returned to their Nile steamer from a sightseeing excursion, without Sir Charles, to find that the bottom of the boat's gangway lay some distance from the river bank, in deep mud. The only immediate solution seemed to be for the Egyptian guides to carry the two women over the mud, so they threw my mother and Camille over their shoulders. Alarmed by the potential indignities of the situation and by Camille's shrieks, my mother was much relieved when a group of German tourists appeared round a bend in the river and volunteered to give them assistance. Never before or afterwards in all her life, my mother used to say, had she been so pleased to see a party of Germans.

Except for the group of servants who accompanied my parents, the houses in London and at Exbury were manned by separate staffs, each led by a superb butler. Arthur Bloxham, formerly my father's valet, presided in London, first at Park Street and later at Kensington Palace Gardens; William Witts, who had succeeded Bloxham as valet, took over from Deeks not long after we moved into Exbury House. When my parents had a weekend house party, the indoor staff at Exbury numbered around thirty, temporarily swollen by the presence of the footmen from London. Frank Hagues, John White, Percy Hobbis and George McCrindle were the footmen who 'lived in' at Park Street in the early days. A later addition, Ernest Hicks, served as my batman during the Second World War, while Henry Southgate, the under-butler at Kensington Palace Gardens, spent part of the war on fire-watch duty at the bank's premises at New Court, putting out the incendiaries which landed on the roof.

Good French chefs were always at a premium, and Monsieur Gallois – whom I believe my father had enticed away from the Ritz Hotel in Paris – was a figure of great importance in the staff hierarchy; in 1919 he was being paid £48 9s a quarter, while Bloxham was receiv-ing £45. At Exbury, Gallois had his own small dining- and sitting-rooms, and he was assisted in the kitchens by a staff of five or six maids and 'kitchen boys'. The old kitchens at Exbury, unchanged though now long since abandoned, contain a great black range which must have created a fearsome heat, despite the double height of the room. Every detail was designed to the highest standards of the day; even the hatches from which the footmen collected the dishes for the dining-room were made of solid mahogany, and all the water pipes were laid in lead channels – so as to prevent flooding in case of a burst pipe.

In the days before the perils of a continuously rich diet were recog-nised, my parents and their friends ploughed their way through a very heavy bill of fare. A typical dinner consisted of soup, a fish course, meat or poultry (sometimes both), followed by pudding, a savoury and dessert. Pâté de foie gras was a regular item on the menu for luncheon, and among my father's favourite dishes were *Caneton Lamberty*, cold roast duckling stuffed with foie gras and encased in a port jelly, and (for his guests) *Barbue Richemont*, a dish of brill stuffed with a mixture of crab-meat and quenelle, garnished with crab claws.

Besides the elaborate meals he prepared for the dining-room, Gallois, assisted by a French pastry cook, used to make us children the most wonderful cakes. One of our favourites was a sponge and meringue cake in the shape of a house with a small bear standing in the doorway, and he made us birthday cakes in all manner of shapes. One year he made a memorably delicious nougat birthday cake for Rosemary in the form of a pony-trap. As well as cakes, the pastry cook made all the croissants and brioches for the adults' breakfast.

Uniformed in the family's blue and yellow livery, the footmen carried the food to the dining-room on large trays covered by great silver domes. Virtually every item used in the kitchen or dining-room was engraved with the family device, five arrows representing the five sons of Mayer Amschel Rothschild, who dispersed to the financial capitals of Europe in the early years of the nineteenth century. Nathan Mayer was the English arrow, and I am constantly reminded of him and his brothers when I see the arrows on the cutlery and the glass which we still use at Exbury today.

Gallois, unfortunately, drank, and eventually this proved his undoing. Shortly before some important dinner party at Kensington Palace Gardens, my father went on one of his visits of inspection to the kitchen – where he found Gallois lying dead-drunk under the kitchen table. Apparently, it was not the first time that this had happened, and as a result M. Emile Gallois was replaced by M. Emile Gorgeon. Dismissing Gallois so much affected my father that Rosemary afterwards found him in his study holding his head in his hands in tears.

Just by the kitchens at Exbury was the still-room, in the charge of the motherly figure of Alice Hancock. She and the girls who helped her produced quantities of delicious scones, jams and fruit preserves, as well as the tea, coffee, toast, boiled eggs, grapefruit and anything else for breakfast which did not require the chef's special attention. The ladies generally took breakfast in their rooms, and it was Alice who prepared the trays for them. Downstairs, the men tucked into huge breakfasts of eggs, bacon, sausages, haddock and whatever else my father had ordered, helping themselves from the dining-room sideboard.

During the week it was Alice Hancock who looked after my father's Aberdeen terrier Jean, and her offspring Zulu and Slip. Jean was a remarkably intelligent little dog: every Friday afternoon she could be found sitting expectantly at the front door, awaiting my father's arrival from London.

There was also an efficient Scottish housekeeper, Mrs Bisset. One of her principal tasks was to see to all the linen, which was laundered by a full-time team of five laundry maids at the laundry in the village.

The servants began work between 5.30 and 6.00 a.m. Unmarried staff at Exbury lived in the East wing at the back of the house, the men sleeping on the ground floor, the women upstairs. The East wing had been converted from the stables of the old house, a new stable-yard being built further off. Married or more senior staff were given cottages on the estate or in the village, where there was also a bothy for the labourers employed in constructing the gardens.

Laura Bartlett, our old nursery housemaid, remembered that there was always a happy atmosphere 'below stairs' at Exbury, and that the staff were well fed and looked after. They had regular Saturday night dances at the club which my father had built for them in the village; they were even at a dance when a German bomb narrowly missed the house in 1941. There was no pub in the village, but alcohol was served at the club. There was an estate bus to take staff into Brockenhurst, the nearest small town; and when Laura was old enough to vote she remembers being sent to the local polling station at Fawley School in one of the Rolls-Royces. The villagers had their own nurse, Mrs Williams, and whenever a new baby was born my mother would go round with a present of baby clothes. All the staff and their children were also given Christmas presents by my parents.

Produce from the Exbury estate made us to a great extent self-sufficient, though fish and the more exotic ingredients required by the chef were sent down from London. Milk, butter and cream were provided by a small herd of Jersey cows on the estate farm at Lower Exbury – Jerseys were thought to provide the best kind of milk for growing children – and beef was produced as well. For a time my mother took an interest in breeding prize sheep. A chicken farm, run by stout Mrs Searle, supplied our eggs, and when my father left for London on Monday mornings he always took with him two Exbury eggs to be prepared for his breakfast in the restaurant car on the early train. As a director of the Compagnie du Chemin de Fer du Nord, which ran the railway line between Paris and Calais (the construction of which had been financed by Rothschilds), my father enjoyed certain reciprocal privileges on British railways – including the right to require the London express train to stop for him at Beaulieu Road station.

All our vegetables came from the kitchen garden, which was managed by Ben Hendy; and from the hothouses we had quantities of grapes, plums, cherries and other fruit. Flowers to decorate the house were supplied by Benjamin Hill, who ran the orchid house, and by Arthur Bedford, the head gardener. Boxes of flowers, fruit and vegetables were sent up to Kensington Palace Gardens every week.

Hill had four or five men working under him; Bedford had between fifty and sixty. Bedford died in harness, just after the Chelsea Flower Show one year when Exbury's exhibits had done particularly well. He and my father were sitting together on a bench in the garden. 'Ah,' said Bedford, 'another Chelsea over,' and he sighed and passed away.

Our bread came from the village bakery, and Exbury village store, which doubled as a sub-post-office, stocked all manner of useful things – including the large bull's-eye sweets of which I used to be rather fond. The village store was run by Mr Trim, who used to claim that he could get anything at all I might want – 'even,' he would say, 'an elephant.'

There was an estate yard manned by a troop of carpenters, painters and decorators, and any work that needed to be done in the house was seen to by them. Logs for the fires were supplied by our own sawmill; a generator, tended by Bob Fields, supplied the house with electricity; and in the garages, near the East wing, we had our own fire-engine, which had its chief moment of glory when a fire once broke out in the butler's pantry. We had our own petrol pump by the garages, and during the war a German aeroplane returning from a raid on Southampton dropped a bomb just beside it, though luckily the bomb failed to explode.

Richard Miller, who had acted as the extra driver-mechanic on my parents' honeymoon, succeeded Martin Harper as head motorman and driver, as well as fireman, in the early 1920s. He had three men to help him with the maintenance of the motor cars and the driving: Page, Gamlin and Lilley. They were responsible for the maintenance of two Rolls-Royces, a 20-hp limousine and a 40/50-hp landaulette; a Daimler; the Armstrong Siddeley in which my father used to drive along the garden paths, and various other vehicles, including the estate staff bus. Page, Gamlin and Lilley were allowed to drive the 20-hp Rolls-Royce; Miller always drove the landaulette, which was kept at Exbury but driven up to London for special occasions.

During the spring and early summer flowering season my parents had regular weekend house parties. Their first guests, in May 1923, were the Earl and Countess of Bessborough, the Brazilian Ambassador and Madame Regis d'Oliviera, Mr Alexander and Lady Theodosia Cadogan, Countess Hochberg, and Edwin Montagu, the former Secretary of State for India. The Bessboroughs came down often, and were one of the few couples to bring their children, Eric and Moyra, with whom Rosemary and I made friends. A house party the next May included the Duke and Duchess of Marlborough, Mr and Mrs Winston Churchill, Lord and Lady Granard, and Sir George and Lady Holford. My mother suspected that the Churchills suffered an attack of 'rhododendronitis', and remembered them retiring to play bezique for several hours with the Granards. Mrs Ronnie Greville came to stay from time to time, and one weekend every year was reserved for entertaining a great crowd of Rothschild relations.

Many of my father's friends were prominent figures in the horticultural world of those days, and they too often came to stay. His special friends were Lord Aberconway, from Bodnant, J.C. and P.D. Williams, from Caerhays and Lanarth in Cornwall, Colonel Fred Stern and the aptly named nurseryman, Gomer Waterer. Frank Kingdon-Ward, the famous plant hunter whose expeditions my father helped to finance, used to come, and also Mr W.J. Bean, the curator of Kew Gardens and a great expert on trees. When my father used to ask Mr Bean for the name of a particular tree they had seen, he would sometimes not answer at once; but hours later, perhaps after dinner as the port was being passed round, 'Mr Lionel,' he would blurt out, '*Oplopanax horridus.*'

'Good God, Bean. What on earth are you talking about?'

'Mr Lionel, earlier today you asked me the name of a particular tree and I did not answer you. I have since looked it up and verified it.'

'Thank you, Bean. Thank you.'

After dinner my father would often entertain his guests by showing cine-films – usually Westerns or films he had taken himself – allowing the guests to drop off to sleep after the heavy meal they had just consumed.

In August 1925, during Cowes week, my parents received their first Royal visitor to Exbury. While King George V was racing his yacht *Britannia*, Queen Mary came over to tea, arriving from the Isle of Wight by motor launch at our newly constructed pier in the Beaulieu River. As the Queen was coming ashore, my father noticed that Mr Johnson, the Head Agent, had forgotten to remove his old Homburg hat. A well-aimed lunge by my father knocked the offending item into the river. In 1931 Queen Mary came again, this time with the King, after entertaining my parents to lunch on board the Royal Yacht *Victoria and Albert*.

Before the King and Queen arrived, my brother Leo, then aged four, had been told that he would have to bow to the King. Pondering this, Leo had very sensibly asked, 'What does the King look like?' – to which the answer had been, 'He has a beard.' Unluckily for Leo, all sailors in those days had beards, as became apparent when the Royal party disembarked. So as not to cause any offence, Leo bowed to every bearded figure in range, until finally the King said to him kindly, 'You've done enough bowing, my boy.'

Later in life, Leo did his National Service with the Navy, serving in the cruiser *Kenya*, on the lower deck. He also became a keen sailor in his spare time, mostly competing in Dragons, and was elected a member of the Royal Yacht Squadron. None of us quite knows to what extent his interest in nautical matters was sparked off by his boyhood encounter with the Sailor King.

When the Prince of Wales came to visit my parents in 1934, he arrived by aeroplane and, greatly to my father's annoyance, landed in the park at Exbury rather than at Eastleigh aerodrome, where it had been arranged to meet him by car. In the surviving photographs of the Prince's arrival – in which, as in John Betjeman's line about him in the 'Death of King George V', 'a young man lands hatless from the air' – everyone looks awkward and uncomfortable. Two years later, during the Abdication Crisis in 1936, my father was none the less summoned urgently to Fort Belvedere. Later he never spoke of the visit, but within forty-eight hours of the Abdication the new Duke of Windsor was driving through the gates of Schloss Enzesfeld, near Vienna, the country house belonging to Baron Eugene de Rothschild, one of our Austrian cousins.

The Duke and Duchess of York came to stay for a night in June 1936, a few months before they became King George VI and Queen Elizabeth. 'No two people,' my mother wrote afterwards, 'could have been more charming and more homely.' And the Princess Royal and her husband the Earl of Harewood spent several weekends at Exbury. The Princess was a very keen gardener, and had an excellent memory for plant varieties; every now and then she and my father would engage in a volley of Latin names.

Locally, besides the Montagus and the Forsters, my parents were on friendly terms with a number of neighbours, including Cyril Drummond – of the banking family – at Cadland, Sir Patrick Hastings, the well-known criminal barrister to whom my father leased Inchmery for a time, and Sir Fisher Dilke, who lived at Solent Cottage above Lepe Point. Another neighbour was John Howlett, the founder of Wellworthy's Engineering Company at Lymington. Mr Howlett used to claim that it was the piston rings he manufactured for Spitfires and Hurricanes which enabled them to outpace the German ME 109s in the Second World War.

Although a self-made man (quite a talking point in those days), John Howlett, who lived at Ravenscourt, near Lymington, was often invited to shoot at Exbury; and when I was old enough he used to take me fishing on the Test, at Testwood Pool. Indeed, it was with John

Howlett that I caught my first salmon in 1933, and I still have the letter he wrote to congratulate me afterwards.

'I was glad that you played it yourself all the time,' he wrote. 'I was tempted to suggest that I should take your rod over when it started to make your arm ache, but it spoils the thrill and I was glad that you kept it the whole time to yourself and not only hooked it but fought it right to the end.' Howlett used to write to me often, especially during the war, and continued to do so right up to his death in the 1960s.

As children we used always to travel to and from Exbury by train. Arriving from London, on the stopping train, at Beaulieu Road station, we would be met by the bowler-hatted figure of Bill Holland, who would drive us the few miles home in a pony-trap across the New Forest. On the northern boundary of the Exbury estate, at Otterwood on the edge of the New Forest, there was a gate to keep out the Forest ponies and deer, and beyond it the long gravel drive to the house. The gatekeeper, who lived in a cottage hard by, was named Toop, so we always knew the place as Toop's Gate – even after Toop had later been succeeded by Hunt. Both Toop and Hunt spoke with a thick Hampshire burr which was very hard indeed for us to understand.

Our nurseries were on the top floor of the house, and there we lived in the charge of a succession of nurses, nannies and governesses. One of the nicest was Nanny Hislop, who eventually left us to work for the Mosleys; and there was Mildred Varndel. When I had whooping cough I was sent to be looked after by Mildred in a small black and white cottage a hundred yards from the house.

Miss Frayling, the governess who taught us 'the three Rs', as well as history, geography and music, was an asthmatic, and Rosemary and I quickly learned that the naughtier we were, the worse her attacks became. Later on, in the school holidays, I had a tutor, Wyndham Trepte, son of the Rector of Exbury and then an assistant master at Fettes.

We did all our lessons in the schoolroom, where we also ate our meals. The food was brought upstairs by the nursery footman, Monty Wright, a friendly, fair-haired, chubby young man. We ate typical nursery fare – prunes, milk puddings and all the usual dishes that children loathe. We each had our own bedroom, and I always kept my bedroom windows open at night. This was partly so that I could lie awake and listen for the crunch of the night-watchmen's footsteps on the gravel outside. There were two watchmen, Jones and Nicholas, and when I heard one of them passing by I would call down. 'All's well, Master Eddy,' they would answer.

I had a good number of boyish toys, including tin soldiers, a clock-work train set and some Meccano. Before I learnt to ride a bicycle, I had a pedal-car, which was decked out in our smart blue and yellow livery – as were the old-fashioned perambulators in which we used to be pushed about as babies. When I was a bit older I was allowed to have my own dog, a black labrador I named Scamp.

During the week, our mornings were taken up with lessons; the afternoons we spent out of doors walking, riding or exploring the grounds. We each had a pony, and in the summer of 1923, when Rosemary had a grey called Blue Boy and I had a little roan called Kitty, Sir Alfred Munnings came down to Exbury to paint us on horseback. The finished picture shows us riding along the foreshore at Lepe, Rosemary riding side-saddle. Munnings recalled painting us 'with waves breaking in white surf on the sand'; but in actual fact Rosemary and I were required to be led round and round on leading reins by the house while Munnings photographed us and made sketches, and we only went down to the Solent for the final sitting. Sir Alfred was sufficiently pleased with the picture to include it in his list of Academy pictures in 1924, and today it hangs in our sitting-room at Exbury.

At the weekends, after breakfast in the nursery at 8 o'clock, we would be taken downstairs to see our mother at 9.30, and then again in the afternoon at 5.00. We adored our mother unreservedly, but Rosemary and I greatly resented the constant presence of her companion Alix Crofton. Mrs Crofton, or 'Aunt Alix' as we had to call her, was a Canadian whom Lord Forster had engaged during the First World War to run the farm at Lepe. Subsequently, my father thought that she would be a good person to keep my mother company. Before her marriage to Mr Crofton (who was no longer in evidence), she had been married to a Mr Westhead, and one day when Rosemary and I were eating in the dining-room with my parents my father accidentally referred to her as Mrs Westhead. 'Oh,' he then sighed, 'I always muddle up Ws for Cs.' For pealing with laughter, both Rosemary and I were at once dismissed in disgrace to our rooms – though we were soon cheered up when Witts sneaked upstairs with a tray.

My special childhood friend at Exbury was William Rattue, my father's head keeper, and I can truthfully say that in his company I spent some of the happiest hours of my life. Unfailingly kind and patient, Rattue taught me all about the flowers in the hedgerows and the wildlife on the estate, and how to fish and to shoot. On rainy days we used to sit together under a large umbrella by Gilbury Pond, hoping to catch tench and eel with a float and a worm; and later on Rattue showed me how to use a trout rod and to cast a fly. He would talk to me and tell me stories, and at the end of the afternoon would take me back with him to the lodge for a huge tea prepared by his wife – from which I nearly always arrived home late.

Sometimes I would go with Rattue and Mr Haig (from Woodside) to King's Copse, a favourite haunt of snakes and woodland butterflies. One day Rattue's little dog Teddy was bitten on the nose by an adder, and I was fascinated to see his master gently suck the venom out. In those days butterflies were plentiful, and we caught all kinds. King's Copse was a great place for the silver-washed fritillary, and once we caught a purple emperor. Spurred on by Uncle Walter's wonderful present, I began my own butterfly collection, which I kept in cases in my bedroom, and of which I was tremendously proud. Aged 13, I was with Rattue when I shot my first pheasant in a wood not far from the house; and when I was overseas during the war, he wrote to me once a week, with all the news of animal and bird life on the Exbury estate.

At the weekends my father would sometimes take me out in a boat. He had a large sailing boat called *Zeneta*, which he used to race at Cowes, and various motor boats, including *Nigella* and *Cautious Clara*. We used to go fishing off Ryde Middle for whiting and whiting-pout, with paternosters (lines with three hooks), using rag-worms for bait. Captain Embley – one of the two captains, together with Captain Rouse, of my father's yacht *Rhodora* – was in charge of the boat on these expeditions, and he always kept us well supplied with bait.

Set against my happy home life, boarding preparatory school came as an unexpectedly dreadful shock. For a term or two I had attended a London day school – Egerton House, in Somerset Street – where, so far as I can remember, I was quite happy. But Locker's Park, near Hemel Hempstead, to which I was consigned at the age of nine, was, from the beginning, a very different matter.

Each new boy was placed in the charge of an older boy for the first fortnight, and I was assigned to a boy named Illingworth. When the fortnight was up, he gave me a tremendous kick and said, 'That's it then, you dirty little Jew'; and from then on I hated Locker's Park with a passion. Once I even tried to throw myself from an upstairs window – the only time in my life that the thought of doing such a thing has crossed my mind. Fortunately, as I swung my legs over the sill, the school matron appeared and hauled me back in.

No doubt other boys, Jewish or not, shared the same feelings, but we kept these very much to ourselves. Anyone reading the letters I wrote home to my parents from Locker's Park would think I was having a perfectly splendid time playing games, collecting stamps and reading my Tarzan books.

The masters, including the headmaster Mr Holmes, were on the whole unpleasant, my Latin master Mr Fisher in particular. To forget 'ut-plus-the-subjunctive' (as in, for instance, 'Oh, that I might be a king') was the most heinous crime, earning the culprit a flurry of hard slaps about the back of the knees. One master was kind to me: Mr Malden, who taught mathematics and geography. When I was laid up in the sanatorium with an attack of conjunctivitis, and my eyes were covered in bandages, Mr Malden came and read me stories. We were all taught to be very patriotic and used to sing a song called 'Anti-Reds'. It ended with the rousing chorus, 'If the Red, White and Blue/ Is not enough for you, / If you don't like the Empire / Clear out of it.' Mr Huband, who replaced Mr Holmes as headmaster (and introduced a marginally more humane regime), taught us the facts of life.

Parents can be an embarrassment when they intrude into the world of school, and mine were no exception. My mother once came to Locker's Park for Prize Day, and I remember my heart sinking and wishing the ground would open and swallow me up as she stepped out of a gleaming Rolls-Royce wearing a huge, wide-brimmed grey hat decorated with ostrich feathers. Observing my unease, she asked me what was wrong. 'Well, Ma,' I am supposed to have said, 'it's *on the verge*.'

During the Christmas holidays, in January 1929, shortly after my thirteenth birthday, my bar mitzvah took place in London, at the Great Synagogue, in Duke Street, Aldgate. My father was a warden of the Great Synagogue, and on the Day of Atonement he used always to go there to read the Book of Jonah.

The ceremony, whereby I became a full member of the congregation, took place on Saturday 12 January. As it was the first day of the Jewish month of Shebat (the month of Trees), two Sephorim (Scrolls of the Law) were taken from the Ark instead of the one customary on an ordinary Sabbath. Each scroll was covered with a festival mantle, and one of them bore great silver bells which had been presented to the synagogue by one of my forebears. I was dressed in an Eton jacket and silk hat, and seated in the Wardens' box between my father and his co-warden Ernest Schiff.

Although I can remember only a little of the instruction I had ved in preparation for the bar mitzvah, I seem to have acquitted myself to everyone's satisfaction. Once the Scroll of the Law had been brought from the Ark to the lectern, the Reader summoned me by my Hebrew name, Solomon, and with my father at my right side and the Reader holding a silver pointer at my left, I read, or rather chanted, a portion of the Book of Exodus, nodding my head vigorously to mark the phrases. The passage appointed recounts God's injunction to Moses and Aaron to ask Pharaoh to send the children of Israel out of Egypt.

My father and my uncle Tony also read portions of the Law, and the Chief Rabbi gave an address, principally directed at me. He told the story of the life of Moses, and prayed that Moses' career might be repeated in me, and that the Law of God would sing in my heart as it sang in his. 'My dear child,' he said, 'the wonderful manner in which you have read shows that you have long been taught the Law of God. No one could read as you read unless he had studied the Law and loved it. I pray that it remains embedded in your heart until the last day.' He concluded by expressing the hope that I would follow in the footsteps of my father, live a life of honour and prosperity, and fulfil the prayers and hopes of my parents.

The last sentiment he expressed, that I should not be a disappointment to my parents, was something which always weighed heavily on me, and one of the most touching letters I ever received from my mother was one which tried to put my mind at rest on this score. Unfortunately, it is undated, but I guess it was written shortly before I went overseas in the war.

'Darling Eddy,' it begins, 'We thought your letter very nice indeed, and I just want to thank you for it. It is rare that parents and children appreciate each other, but I can honestly be bold enough to think that it is the case with your father and I and our progeny. Although we may sometimes differ slightly in our way of thinking, we fundamentally agree, and that is all that matters. I must tell you that you have never given us cause to be disappointed. May it always be so. God bless you dear boy, and may you have a son later on who will bring as much happiness into your life as you have brought to us.'

At 13, I progressed from prep school to Harrow, which I enjoyed much more than Locker's Park. 'I hope you will soon feel quite at home in your new surroundings and have a happy time at Harrow,' my father wrote to me. 'Write and tell us how you get on, and remember that one of us will always be ready to come down and see you should you be in trouble. Above all, don't be afraid of telling us your troubles. Make friends with nice boys, avoid the nasty ones. Unfortunately, there are always a few boys and men who cannot be trusted. I feel sure that you will be one of those who will always have an easy conscience.'

When I arrived at Harrow, my cousin Victor was in his last year, and much admired for his prowess on the cricket field. He played in the Eton–Harrow match at Lord's, and that summer of 1929, when he was playing for Northamptonshire against Nottinghamshire, he scored 36 off the fast bowlers Larwood and Voce. Respect for Victor, and the fact that my housemaster, Arthur Vassal, had taught my father when he was at Harrow, launched me into the school on a small but invaluable wave of goodwill.

Games, in those days, were almost on a par with religion, and a certain proficiency at games provided perhaps the surest route to the respect of one's masters and peers. Fortunately, I found that I could box quite well, and I date my real happiness at Harrow from the occasion when I won the winning point for my house, Elmfield, in an inter-house boxing competition. I also played rugby, and once, after a successful house rugby match in which I had played full-back, Arthur Vassal invited the team for a drink, after evening prayers, in his private side of the house. But I was so tired that I never heard his invitation, and instead went off to bed. Mr Vassal was very offended, and I still feel guilty about the hurt this muddle caused him.

Arthur Vassal was always good to me. Occasionally, he even allowed me to go up to London 'to see the dentist' – code for a visit to my parents, something which was strictly forbidden during term. He liked to recall how one cold day he thought he had caught my father smoking, but the smoke turned out to be nothing more than the 'smoke-rings' my father had a knack of blowing with his breath. When Mr Vassal retired from Elmfield, he was succeeded by Cyril Browne, who also ran a happy house.

My father had been the first Jewish boy to go to Harrow, and my uncle Tony was the first to become Head of School. But in my time there were quite a number of Jewish pupils, including Keith Joseph and Geoffrey Seligman. Geoffrey's family owned the house next door to ours in Kensington Palace Gardens, and used to get annoyed by the number of balls I hit over the garden wall in the holidays. Much later, I came across both Geoffrey and Keith in the City – Geoffrey when he was at Warburgs (after Siegmund Warburg had absorbed the Seligmans' bank into his), and Keith when he invited me to stand for election to replace him as an Alderman. (Pressures of work obliged me to decline Keith Joseph's invitation, but Bernard Waley-Cohen took it up and eventually became Lord Mayor.)

At Harrow, the Jewish boys were ragged a bit for not eating pork, but otherwise suffered from no special prejudice that I can remember. When, as a junior boy, I fagged for Ian (now Lord) Orr-Ewing, he was always pleasant and civil – as, I should perhaps record, was the horrible Illingworth, of Locker's Park, when I met him in later life.

Our morning chapel consisted of a visit to the 'Tin Tabernacle', an ancient temporary building which served as the classroom of the Upper Shell. There we received instruction in our religion from Rabbi Berman, though none of us, I am ashamed to say, paid him serious attention.

Once or twice my father came to Harrow to take me out for tea or to watch me play in a match and, to supplement the usual dull school diet, he gave me tick (or credit) at a local fruiterers, which was run by an old man named Ensten. It was a great treat to be able to buy a few shillings-worth of fresh fruit each week, one of the few luxuries that I particularly valued at that time.

My greatest friend at school was Griff Llewellyn, with whom I was in the same form, and whom I sat next to, at Locker's Park and at Harrow. He and I then went up to Cambridge at the same time, and afterwards, in 1938, travelled around South America together. Sadly, Griff died young, of cancer, shortly after the war.

Like all children, I looked forward to the holidays with tremendous excitement. Good doses of sea air were supposed to be beneficial to one's health, and in the summer months we spent our days swimming and playing on the beach at Inchmery, where we had a large revolving bathing hut. However, the Solent breezes were not deemed sufficiently bracing, and so for our first childhood holidays away from home we were taken by our nannies to stay at the Grand Hotel at Frinton-on-Sea, in Essex. None of us remembers much of our seaside holidays at Frinton, except for the heat of the road on our bare feet as we made our way to and fro between the hotel and the beach.

When we had grown out of bucket and spade holidays, my father used to take us cruising on his ocean-going yachts, first on the 120-ton *Rhodora*, and later on her 800-ton successor, *Rhodora II*. The name *Rhodora* was chosen by my father to commemorate a tale about an azalea (a member of the rhododendron family) which the great eighteenth-century botanist Sir Joseph Banks introduced to England from

North America. During the passage back from Newfoundland, Banks's ship ran into a terrible storm, and many of the plants that he had collected went overboard – but not the azalea *Rhodora* (now known as *R. canadense*), which made it safely back to port and cultivation.

Rhodora II had a hold which was large enough to carry a motor car – latterly an immensely powerful 50.7-hp Rolls-Royce touring saloon which my father bought in 1936 (taking his stable of Rolls-Royces to three). She was manned by a crew of twelve, and could comfortably accommodate my parents and us four children, as well as Uncle Robert and Aunt Nelly and their children, our first cousins Alain, Diane, Cécile and Elie, who would sometimes join us.

We got on very well with our cousins, and it was certainly more fun when they came. Rosemary was the same age as Cécile, Elie a year younger than me. Like us, they had been brought up mostly at home in the country – at Laversine, their lovely château above the River Oise, at Chantilly – by British nannies. They spoke English like natives – indeed, I believe they learned to speak English before they could even speak French – and consequently we found them very easy to get on with.

One incident that took place on the first *Rhodora* stands out vividly in my mind. We were moored off the Britanny coast, at Belle Ile, when there was a cry of 'Fire'. A fire had been started accidentally by one of the crew trying to light a small stove with some petrol. In his panic he had then thrown the stove overboard, between the yacht and the quay-side, setting alight *Rhodora*'s paintwork in the process, and causing clouds of billowing smoke. As we were hurried out of our cabins on to the quayside, I could hear my father's anguished shouts of 'Sauvez ma femme! Sauvez ma femme!' But he need not have worried. My mother was soon discovered quite safe, quietly helping the Chief Steward extinguish the blaze.

On our summer cruises, we sailed as far south as Spain and the Balearic Islands, and north as far as Sweden and the Baltic. One year, when we were steaming down the coast of Dalmatia, my father received an invitation to lunch with the King of Yugoslavia, to discuss the possibility of a loan, at Bled, the King's summer resort. At lunch, my father later reported to my mother, he saw the most beautiful woman he had ever set eyes on; she turned out to be Princess Marina, the future Duchess of Kent, who later came with the Duke to stay at Exbury in 1938. A few days after his lunch at Bled, my father received an invitation to lunch from the other side of the Adriatic, from Benito Mussolini; but he declined to go. When *Rhodora* dropped anchor, there would be sightseeing parties ashore, though I was always much happier dangling a fishing line over the yacht's stern or chasing butterflies.

Holidays on the yacht were not timed to coincide precisely with school holidays, so I used to have to return home early in order to get back for the start of term. When I was too young to travel alone, it was always arranged that Pawle, the senior porter at New Court, should come out to collect me, and that he and I should then return home by train. In my Locker's Park days, the thought of going back to school brought such a lump to my throat that the journey home was a much less enjoyable adventure than it might otherwise have been.

Besides the cruise, every summer my father liked to visit the French spa town of Brides-les-Bains, where he would try to shed a few pounds. This was a habit he had caught from my grandfather Leo, who used to go with my grandmother for an annual cure at the Austrian (later Italian) spa town of Levico.

As a rule, I seldom went on any outings with my parents alone. Once they took me to a performance of Noël Coward's *Cavalcade* (during which I remember they cried and held hands), and once my mother took me to the Wigmore Hall to hear Eva Tetrazzini sing. But the visit to Brides-les-Bains gave rise to one of the few regular occasions in the year when I spent a couple of days on my own, away from home, with my father. He liked me to accompany him in the car on the outward journey, while other members of the party, including the valet, the lady's maid, and my tutor-cum-companion Wyndham Trepte, went on ahead with the luggage. My mother and sisters travelled to Brides by train.

On the drive down we used to pass through a village where there was a restaurant at which my father had dined twice – on the first occasion, as a young man, with his friend Vere Bessborough. A remark made by my father to the wine waiter on the excellence of the brandy had drawn the rejoinder, 'Ah, Monsieur le Baron, il reste que deux cent quatre-vingt-dix bouteilles de ce vin – et je peux vous offrir les vendre' – an offer my father gratefully accepted. Years later, when he returned to the same restaurant with my mother on their honeymoon, the same wine waiter made exactly the same offer again.

At Brides-les-Bains, where we stayed at the Hôtel des Thermes, we used again to be joined by our French cousins, and I have a vivid recollection of Uncle Robert sitting at our table in the hotel restaurant, piling his plate high with vegetables. A surprised look he received from the waiter prompted him to remark simply, 'Il faut passer les autres' (an allusion to the need for fibre to aid one's digestion). Madame Grosclaude, my mother's remarried mother, a formidable character with a pile of hennaed hair, would come to Brides as well. As my sisters and I always spoke English to our mother, none of us was very proficient in French – and one was left in no doubt of Grand'mère's disapproval on this score.

When my father was not occupied in some therapeutic treatment at the baths, he liked to go walking in the mountains around the town. Wyndham and I used to accompany him, often on his favourite walk up to the village of La Thuile. I always took along my butterfly net, and would chase after the gorgeous swallowtails all over the mountainside. Near the top we would sit down in the grass, and my father would then light up one of the large Havana cigars he was seldom without. One of the nicest photographs I have of him captures him at that exact moment.

I left Harrow at the end of the summer term in 1934 and, once again following in my father's footsteps, went up to Trinity College, Cambridge. Two years before, Arthur Vassal had written a report recommending me to J.R.M. (Jim) Butler, the tutor in charge of admissions to Trinity. In the report, a copy of which was sent to my father, Mr Vassal describes me as 'equally zealous and keen in work and play', and makes an undeserved reference to my aptitude for the biological sciences. The report goes on to say of me, 'When he has mastered a tendency to hurry, he should do well in these or kindred subjects.' The tendency is one that I am still struggling to master.

By the time I arrived in Cambridge in October 1934, it had been arranged that I should read Natural Sciences, including chemistry, botany and zoology. At about the time of Arthur Vassal's report on me to Jim Butler, there had been an idea that I might read Agriculture, then an Ordinary rather than Honours degree. But Jim Butler wrote to my father advising against what he regarded as an unambitious plan. His advice was taken, and my father duly paid the £12 'caution money' required by Trinity once my name had been approved for admission.

To begin with at Cambridge I took things easily – in fact I did almost no work at all. The only lecture I clearly remember attending was a distinctly rowdy affair, conducted by an exasperated chemistry don. The undergraduates at the back of the lecture theatre were making such a noise that the lecturer finally said, 'Will the back bench please leave the room.' We all turned round to look – only to see the people at the back of the room pick up the bench and walk out with it.

Just as my father had done, I had comfortable lodgings in Jesus Lane, at No. 26, where I was looked after by two kindly spinsters; and as soon as I was elected to the Pitt Club – also in Jesus Lane – I spent a great deal of time there playing billiards and 'slosh' (a variant of snooker) with my friends. Generally, I lunched at the Pitt and dined in hall at Trinity. I also belonged to a Trinity dining-club called the Vatel Club, named in honour of a chef in the royal kitchens of Versailles. The club was the inspiration of a Rumanian undergraduate friend of mine, Teddy Zissu, who later died fighting with the Eighth Army in North Africa. We did not stint ourselves at club dinners, as one of the menus I kept testifies: beginning with oysters, we ate our way through *Poule au Pot Henri IV, Blanchailles au Paprika Rose, Filets Mignon à la Béarnaise* with *Fonds d'Artichauts au Beurre, Cailles à la Séville*, and dessert – the whole feast for 16 shillings a head, including four different wines.

Just off Jesus Lane I kept a horse called Rosemary (after my sister) in stables run by a man named Captain Cooper. Rosemary was looked after by Henry, an idle groom who seldom exercised her. But during the season I went out at least one day a week with the Cambridge drag hunt, and I rode Rosemary in hunter trials and went steeplechasing. On one occasion, in 1935, I even rode her at Cottenham races in the two-mile Loder Cup, wearing the family colours. We fell at the water jump, but I managed to get back up and complete the course, and I then rode in the three-mile University Challenge Whip, on a horse belonging to Captain Cooper called Fifty-Fifty. I came in last both times, cheered in by the bookies.

I also joined the University OTC and trained with the Cambridge cavalry, learning to ride and jump without reins or stirrups. I still have the receipts for some of the kit I was required to buy – £9 19s 6d for a greatcoat from Hawkes & Co., No. 1 Savile Row, £29 11s for two pairs of boots (patent mess Wellingtons and field boots), hollow trees and spurs from Henry Maxwell & Co., of Dover Street.

In 1935 there was an idea that during the long vacation, I should go on attachment to the French cavalry school at Saumur, where my cousin Guy, the son of Baron Edouard, Uncle Robert's partner at de Rothschild Frères, had been with the 11th Cuirassiers; but for various reasons this plan never came off. However, at about that time I successfully applied for a commission in the 99th (Bucks and Berks Yeomanry) Field Brigade, RA, the Territorial unit with which my family had been closely connected since before the First World War. My father and both his brothers had held commissions in the regiment as young men, in the days when it was called the Royal Bucks Hussars. It was on service with the Bucks that my uncle Evelyn was mortally wounded at El Mughar in Palestine in 1917, and my uncle Tony was serving with the regiment when he was wounded at Gallipoli.

In 1936 and 1937, I attended artillery courses at Larkhill, on Salisbury Plain, and at the Woolwich Arsenal, and I obtained my army gunnery certificates. I was at Larkhill for what was, I believe, one of the last occasions on which the Royal Horse Artillery's famous Bull's Troop (named after Captain Bull, the commanding officer at the Battle of Waterloo) was horsed. I can still feel the thrill of riding out with them at night, with the sound of the horses' harnesses jingling under a full moon as they pulled the 18-pound guns across Salisbury Plain. I also vividly remember an occasion during a gunnery exercise at Larkhill in 1937 when my battery major, Tony Clifton-Brown, received a terrific rocket from Colonel Fred Lawson for accidentally ordering me in front of the guns as they were about to fire.

With a bit of encouragement from me, and after a bit of string-pulling, my friend Peter Trehearne was also commissioned in the Bucks, in 1937, and during the war I was to serve as his battery captain in North Africa and Italy.

Back at Cambridge, with Peter and some other friends, including John Grafton (the Duke of Grafton), Hugh Massey and Michael Boardman, I belonged to a shooting syndicate near Six Mile Bottom, and one summer we all clubbed together to take some shooting arranged for us by a great friend of mine, Nicky Fitzgerald, in County Mayo – for a total cost of £45 for the whole month of September. I had got to know Nicky at Exbury, when he used to come to stay during the school holidays with two ladies who lived in the neighbourhood, Mrs Hare and Miss Whitworth, one of whom I believe was his godmother.

I have never been an especially good shot, but for a time I was a member of the Cambridge University clay-pigeon team, once winning a silver spoon for the highest score in a match against Oxford.

Although by no means a dedicated racegoer, I used sometimes to go with Paddy Bowen-Colthurst (known as 'Baldicoot') to

Newmarket races, where we would spend most of our time among the bookies. When we couldn't get to the racecourse itself we would call in at our local betting shop. In 1936, just before the Derby, Griff Llewellyn had a dream about a great race being won by a grey. Naturally, we backed the only grey in the race, the Aga Khan's horse Mahmoud – which won, at most favourable odds. When, after another, less successful speculation, I lost rather more than a whole term's allowance, my cousin Victor, by then a Cambridge don, obligingly came to the rescue with a loan of £100 – which I was able to repay soon afterwards when I had some better luck.

I had a red two-seater Alvis, which my father had bought for me from Mr George Follett, and which I kept at Marshall's Garage. Undergraduates were not allowed to drive in those days, and towards the end of my second year I was caught – not at the wheel of my own motor car, but in a magnificent Mercedes lent to me by John Grafton. I had driven up to London for the day without mishap – even switching on the supercharger going up Park Lane – but back in Cambridge the car broke down in the middle of town. I was spotted by one of the University Proctors, Mr Dykes, and the incident cast a cloud over the next few weeks. Dykes gave me a stern warning and from Trinity Jim Butler wrote to my father saying that if I was caught driving again I should have to be rusticated.

Matters were made worse by my failure to pass the Natural Sciences Part I examination at the end of my second year. Besides not having worked hard enough, I had developed an intense dislike of dissecting animals – dogfish, especially – in the laboratory, and so I came badly unstuck in the practical zoology exam. This, and the car episode, prompted a distinctly headmasterly letter to my father from cousin Victor – who had himself occasionally lent me his Bugatti – detailing my shortcomings as an undergraduate. The whole saga, particularly Victor's uncalled-for intervention, left me feeling a little bruised, but my father was very good about it all, and it was resolved that for my last year I should prepare for the Special Examination in Military Studies and the General Examination, with papers on modern British, European and American history, and French.

During university vacations I usually spent a period at Exbury, sometimes with a tutor from Cambridge whom my father would have engaged through the University Appointments Board to give me extra tuition. I would also be allowed to have friends to stay, among them Jock Colville – who memorably aggravated my father on one occasion by singing the praises of Nazi Germany, where he had recently been studying at Tübingen University. In his memoir *Footprints in Time*, Jock recounted my father's subsequent expostulation to his mother: 'Your son,' said my father, 'comes to stay in my house, shoots my pheasants, drinks my champagne, smokes my cigars and then tells me there is a lot to be said for Hitler.' None the less, Jock often came to stay again, and later on, when he was Winston Churchill's private secretary in the 1950s, he was a fairly frequent guest at New Court lunches.

In the long vacation my grandmother and Aunt Lou always invited me, along with one or two of my friends – Peter, Griff, Nicky and his sister Boodie, and sometimes Mr Howlett – to stay with them in Scotland. Each year I was at Cambridge they took a different house – Ballathie, on the Tay, then Meikleour, also on the Tay, and finally the beautiful Dochfour, on the Ness. I would get up at 7.30 to go fishing, and stay out of doors all day. During one holiday at Ballathie I landed a 34-lb salmon, the largest I have ever caught; and staying at Dochfour, Aunt Lou and Granny claimed to have seen the Loch Ness Monster. In the long evenings we would play bridge, bezique and piquet, or sometimes chess. When we were at Dochfour, in the summer of 1937, my parents arrived on *Rhodora II*, and I sailed with them down the coast to Dalmeny, where Harry and Eva Rosebery brought their guest Lady Rosse on board for dinner. After dinner, Eva and Lady Rosse played duets on the piano in the saloon.

Several times I also went fishing and shooting in Ireland, staying with Nicky Fitzgerald at his family home in County Waterford – The Island, in the River Suir. We would go snipe-shooting on the Wexford slobs, and I am ashamed to say we did a fair amount of poaching too, often in the company of an amiable old character called Captain Clark. After a day spent out in the open, Nicky would take me into some local cottage where the Fitzgeralds were known, and we would be treated to plates of delicious soda bread and eggs.

Staying at The Island one year, I had – or so I was assured afterwards – a brush with the supernatural. I was sleeping in a large four-poster bed, though not in my usual room, and in the middle of the night I was woken by the sound of a vixen calling – and then felt the sensation of an ice-cold draught blowing across my face. I got up to check the windows and to have a look outside the door, which had opened, but I could find nothing unusual. The next night, feeling a little apprehensive, I decided to have a dog in the bedroom with me, an Alsatian called Fafner, and I placed a chair against the door. Again in the middle of the night I was woken up, but this time by Fafner's growls. When I switched on the light I found that he was bristling all over, and that again the door had somehow swung open. Nicky's sister Boodie, who had a reputation in the Fitzgerald family as something of a psychic, arrived the next day, and told me that I must have been paid a visit by the Grey Lady, whom she herself had seen before. She told me that the Grey Lady was a benign spirit, and that having taken two good looks at me and decided that I was a friend, she would not be bothering me again.

Although I slept peacefully from then on, I am not sure that I should have believed Boodie's story, but for another strange incident. The Island was literally an island in the middle of the Suir, so that one reached the Fitzgeralds' castle by means of a ferry. Returning home by the ferry one evening, Boodie looked back and saw the figure of a man rise out of the water and beckon to her. She felt a strong urge to go to him, but Nicky took her by the arm and hurried her home. Next morning, at breakfast, their father announced that the Garda had telephoned to say that they were going to drag the river-bed by the ferry. They did so, and at just the spot where Boodie had seen the apparition they found the body of a drowned man.

At the beginning of my last year at Cambridge I moved into a beautiful set of panelled rooms in college, at P4 Great Court. There I was looked after by one of the college bedders (servants who made the beds and kept the rooms tidy) and my 'gyp', named Penney, who brought up my breakfast and valeted for me. In those days it was still possible to order lunch or dinner in one's rooms, and when my father once came up to visit me I introduced him to some of my friends over lunch at P4. Once only I dined with the Master of Trinity, the eminent physicist J. J. Thomson, who with Lord Rutherford had first split the atom. I am ashamed to say that my only recollection of the occasion is of the Master's badly-fitting false teeth falling into his soup plate.

Every now and again, I was invited to dine with Gilliard Lapsley, a Trinity history tutor to whom Jock Colville had introduced me. Lapsley was an affluent American bachelor and a noted snob, famous at Cambridge for his disapproval of women undergraduates. In the course of a lecture on the history of one of the more distant regions of South America, Lapsley was said to have remarked that because there were more men than women in that area, even the students of Newnham and Girton should be able to find themselves husbands. As some of the women present began to leave the lecture-theatre in a huff, Lapsley called after them, 'Don't hurry, ladies, don't hurry. The next boat doesn't leave for ten days.'

During my final year I was laid up in bed for some weeks as a result of a nose operation to correct a problem stemming from my boxing days at Harrow. While convalescing I read a number of Winston Churchill's military books, and when it came to the examinations, this stood me in good stead; I found that whole passages from them had stuck in my mind. In the last Easter vacation, I was also sent to France for a fortnight's intensive French study in preparation for the exams, as there was a particular set text which I was finding rather hard-going. I stayed with a family who lived at St Symphorien, near Tours, and studied the set text with a helpful, patient woman called Madame de Letang. On free afternoons I visited the wonderful châteaux of the Loire – Blois, Azay-le-Rideau, Villandry, Chambord and others.

On my way to Tours I passed through Paris, calling on Baron Edouard at de Rothschild Frères in rue Laffitte, and on Uncle Robert at 23 avenue de Marigny, his and Aunt Nelly's town house across from the Elysée Palace. In the evening, Elie, who was becoming a bit of a playboy, took me to a restaurant called La Coquille, where I remember eating frog's legs for the first time, and then on to a cabaret and back to his flat with two girls – an eye-opening evening by my unsophisticated standards, and one which left me nursing a thundering hangover on the boat-train the next day. However, my spell in France proved to have been worth while when, in June 1937, and to everyone's relief, I obtained a 2:1 for Military Studies and a 2:1 in the General.

There had been an idea mooted that after Cambridge I might do a stint as an honorary ADC on the staff of Lord Bessborough, who was then the Governor-General of Canada. But my father had promised that provided I got a 2:1 in my finals, he would send me on a tour round the world – and as always he was as good as his word.

2

Grand Tour, New Style

The object of my trip round the world was, as my father put it, 'to meet its peoples, to learn of its resources and to see its beauties'. Since I was destined to work at N.M. Rothschild & Sons on my return, it was arranged that *en route* I should meet various of the bank's overseas agents and contacts, principally in South America, where Rothschilds did a fair amount of business in Brazil and Chile. From these people, and from other friends of my family, I received extraordinary kindness and hospitality in the countries I visited, and also a great deal of practical help in making travel arrangements and organising expeditions along the way.

I was also provided with introductions to foreign and colonial government personnel, and to the Jewish communities of the then British territories. This was not simply because the Rothschilds were prominent in British Jewry, but more importantly because since Hitler's rise to power in Germany in 1933 my father and my uncle Tony had been active in raising funds in England to support the flood of Jewish refugees from the German Reich, and in efforts to identify possible sites around the world for refugee settlement. Consequently, I set off on my tour with a rather ill-defined brief to support wherever I could the efforts being made at New Court on the refugees' behalf, and with the thought of the threat to the Jews in Europe always at the back of my mind.

For company, I travelled with four friends, Bill How, Griff Llewellyn, Nicky Fitzgerald and Peter Trehearne, on succeeding legs of the journey. Bill came with me to Africa; Griff joined me in South America, and Nicky in New Zealand, Australia and French Indo-

China; Peter travelled with me in Indo-China, Burma, India and Afghanistan. My budget for the whole trip was £2,000, which now sounds very little, but was a considerable sum in the late 1930s.

I set out from England on Friday 29 October 1937, and arrived back at Exbury on 27 May 1939. Throughout the tour I kept a diary, and regularly wrote letters home to my parents. The extracts I quote are from those two sources. The passages I have selected relate to events which a modern-day traveller might not expect to encounter, omitting descriptions of those places, such as Machu Picchu, Bali, Bangkok and the temples of Angkor Wat, which have since become well-known tourist destinations.

My chief recreations in those days were shooting, fishing and butterfly hunting, and I set off suitably equipped with rods, shotguns, rifles and butterfly nets. But I was also keenly interested, though not expert, in the natural world in general, and so recorded my impressions of the flora and fauna I saw along the way. Much of the time I spent in Africa and French Indo-China was devoted to hunting big game, but like others who were once gripped by the thrill of stalking a buffalo or waiting for a tiger in a mirador (a makeshift hide in a tree), I have long since been more interested in game conservation – though I still enjoy fishing with a fly for salmon and trout. Remembering that my parents rather tired of my stories of going after game, I have left out most of the gorier episodes of the journey. For anyone interested in reading more, including a full account of all the shooting and fishing, there is a little book called *Window on the World*, which I published in 1949.

Although *Window on the World* was published ten years after my return to England, there was one event about which I still did not feel able to write. This was the death, as a result of a shooting accident in Indo-China, of my great friend Nicky Fitzgerald. We – Peter Trehearne, Nicky and I – were spending a few days in the jungle, near Kratie, when, on the afternoon of 2 November 1938, Nicky went off looking for gaur, a kind of ox, with a friend of ours, Francis Williams, who had come with us from Australia. As I was feeling rather tired, I had stayed behind at the camp to have a siesta. My diary entry for that day reads: 'The worst day I have yet to record. Nicky, my true and beloved friend, was accidentally shot by Francis. It was a real accident. They were going after gaur in the early afternoon, when Francis's gun, at safe and pointing forwards, somehow got caught in the bamboo and went off. At 2.45 p.m. I was woken by a boy repeating the words

"Accident terrible!" Nicky was lying unconscious on a stretcher when I got to him, and he died with me holding his hand.'

After much heart-searching and many cables to and from England, it was decided that I should continue on the tour – bearing in mind that in those days it would have taken me about a month to get home by sea. We held a service for Nicky in Saigon cathedral, rickshaws laden with flowers accompanying the coffin to church, and with the help of the British Consul made arrangements for Nicky's body to be returned to England.

My first port of call was South Africa, and Bill How and I arrived in Cape Town, on the Union Castle line ship *Arundel Castle*, on 13 November 1937.

My family's connection with Africa goes back to my grandfather's day, when N.M. Rothschild & Sons took an interest in the search for gold and diamonds. In the 1880s the bank participated in the formation of the Exploration Company, and in the purchase of the Anglo-African Diamond Mining Company, which was eventually swallowed up by De Beers. Cecil Rhodes also obtained NMR's backing for De Beers' bid for the French Diamond Company.

In 1892, in the face of stiff competition in London, the bank raised the £2.5 million 5 per cent Transvaal Loan for President Kruger's government of the South African Republic, designed to finance the construction of railways, among other things. Writing from Johannesburg on 26 March 1892, our agent Carl Meyer noted: 'President Kruger is here now and this morning I met him at breakfast in the Robinson Mine. He is a queer old Boer – ugly, badly dressed and ill-mannered, but a splendid type all the same and a very impressive speaker.'

The 1892 Loan Agreement was written in the simplest terms, and covers only half a sheet of paper. Our letter to President Kruger after the successful outcome of the loan was rather more flowery:

> As we have every confidence in the wisdom of Your Honour's Government as well as in the future prospects of the Transvaal, we did not hesitate to give our name and influence to the operation, and we sincerely hope that not only will the large sum of money raised be used with the greatest prudence and economy, but also that all expenditure will be subject to a strict and efficient control, so that in the future we may have every reason and justification to be perfectly satisfied with the action we have just taken.

In venturing to offer these suggestions to Your Honour, we beg you to believe that we are guided solely by a sincere desire to see the South African Republic not only retain but likewise increase its well-earned reputation for stability and prudence and we naturally also feel that a certain responsibility attaches to us for having introduced into the English market the securities of a country until now comparatively unknown.

With this background, and as my father was a friend of Sir Ernest Oppenheimer, my itinerary in South Africa naturally included visits to De Beers' operations – to their dynamite works, where dynamite was made for use in the mines – 'miles of concrete paths, turbulent yellow liquids in huge pans and shining black faces' – and to the mines themselves.

Rand Club, Johannesburg, Transvaal, 6 December 1937
'Kimberley was oppressively hot – 150° to 160° in the sun and up to 99° in the shade. The Diamond Mines were well worth a visit and we saw all the complicated processes of sorting. I even held £100,000 worth of diamonds in one hand! On 24 November we watched a prospector sift out two fine diamonds from the river bed at Sydney-on-Vaal and then eight of us sat down to an omelette made out of an egg from a nearby ostrich farm.

'Bill and I have been shown another dynamite works, as well as a precious metal refinery, the Klip Electric Power Station (almost as large as Battersea) and African Cables Ltd. We have visited two gold mines, Daggafontein and Robinson Deep, the latter going underground to a depth of 8,000 feet. There were ten natives and five white men in our lift, which suddenly stopped half-way down the shaft in complete darkness. The night before there had been an earth tremor and many of the pit props supporting the corridor roofs were cracked. At the 5,500 foot level, carrying acetylene lamps, we scrambled 500 feet down a shaft where no visitors had been allowed before, on hands and knees, stooping, crawling on our stomachs, lying on our backs and holding on to rocks and pit props.'

From Johannesburg we set off for Northern Rhodesia, *en route* for Kenya, in a comfortable two-engined Dragonfly aircraft belonging to Sir Ernest Oppenheimer. Flying over the 'Great Grey-Green, Greasy Limpopo River' we could see that the river was bone dry, and that on its sandy bed was gathered Kipling's 'Herd of Elephants'. Bill pointed out one old bull with enormous tusks which might well have been the one that 'got his trunk'. From Bulawayo we flew over the Victoria Falls and, dropping to a height of about ten feet, skimmed above the Zambesi. We landed and went for a walk in the forest nearby – the air heavily laden with the scent of mimosa – and we saw many great blue butterflies, toucans and hornbills. We were paddled up the Zambesi in a canoe, returning as dusk was falling and our canoe-men sang African songs. A great orange moon rose in front of us, lighting up the river as the canoe men sang.

Rhokana Guest House, N'Kana, Northern Rhodesia, 13 December
'It was strange to have the African Guard in bare feet and tarbooshes present arms to us at Lusaka where, after lunch at the Governor's residence, Lady Young showed us her two tame cheetahs, which purred like gigantic Cheshire cats. We reached N'Kana that night and stayed at the Rhokana Guest House, a long, low bungalow with flowers growing in profusion in the garden.

'Situated right at the heart of Africa, a few miles from the border of the Belgian Congo, N'Kana has a population of 2,000 whites and over 30,000 natives, nearly all of whom are employed by the Rhokana Corporation. Most of the mining engineers are either Scots or Americans. Some decent shops and a cinema have been built, and there are a golf course and recreation ground. Huge quantities of copper are extracted and refined, and the mine provides a startling contrast to the gold mines of Johannesburg. At the present time it only goes down 1,600 feet, and instead of narrow tunnels there is a fine, well-lit cavern from which shafts radiate off. Cobalt, which is found mixed with the copper, is extracted by the cyanide process. The Corporation does much to maintain a high standard of living for its employees. We were told that the Zulus, who used to be great warriors, are now the best workers.'

My father held 10,000 shares in the Rhokana Corporation, and at lunch one day at home there was an urgent telephone call for him to talk about them to his stockbroker, Otto M. Schiff. Although he hated interrupting a meal to go to the telephone, he took the call, and when he returned to the table announced: 'The Rhokana shares have gone up to £50. Mr Schiff asked whether I should like to sell them, and I said "No".' When, after my father died, I found myself liable to repay a considerable debt he had run up to NMR, and also to settle a sizeable demand for estate duty, I remember reflecting how much easier things would have been if only he had said 'Yes' to Mr Schiff. I had to sell the Rhokana shares, but by then, of course, they were not doing nearly so well.

Otto M. Schiff, my father's broker, was a nephew of the great American Jewish philanthropist Jacob Schiff, and in the 1930s he devoted much time and energy to the relief of Jewish refugees from Europe who were seeking asylum in England. He was greatly respected, and it was once said by Lord Reading, another stalwart of the Jewish refugee relief effort, that of all the letters he received there were two kinds which received his immediate attention – one was headed 'OHMS', the other was signed 'OMS'.

Muthaiga, Nairobi, Kenya Colony, 22 December
'We flew the 400 miles to Dodoma without stopping in a Wilson Airways six-seater African Rapid. At Dodoma we changed to an African Airways plane. The flight was uncomfortably rough and at Moshi we had to jettison some of our luggage. On landing at Nairobi a tyre burst and for a moment I was afraid we were going to overturn. We are now staying with Major and Mrs Freddie Ward [Major Ward was an old friend of my father's], who could not have been more kind to us. Their servants wear long, white, blue or brown shapeless frocks reaching down to the ground, allowing a big pair of brown and white feet to protrude. In order to make ourselves understood we have tried to pick up a smattering of kitchen Swahili, but the trouble is that in most of the common words the difference of one letter means a *faux pas*. I am sorry to say I have already made several mistakes, at which the servants have dissolved into laughter. Every morning my boy greets me with "M'Jambo Bwana", which sounds rather like a sneeze.

'On Saturday, Captain Gethin, a friend of Major Ward's, called to take us on a photographing expedition across the Athi Plains. Herds of antelope, zebra, gazelle and other animals inhabit the region and our car passed within twenty feet of a giraffe who craned a long neck and looked at us with great quizzical brown eyes – its eyelashes would be the envy of any film star.

'Namanga resthouse, where we spent the night, is a delightful form of open-air hotel run by Mr Meyers, close to the former German colony of Tanganyika. On Sunday we crossed the border to "Rhino Camp", motoring over the bed of a dried-up lake. Set amongst tall stately trees the camp was ideal. There were three double fly tents in which we slept, and a thatched hut, open at each end, which we used as a dining-room. In the evenings we sat round a blazing fire, listening to the bush noises, the cries of the night birds, the shrill scream of the crickets and cicadas, and an occasional grunting yawn from a hippopotamus. It seemed strange to be so far away from civilisation. Apart from Namanga there was no white man nearer than a hundred miles.

'We rose at 5.00 a.m. to look for hippopotamus, but Meyers found a rhinoceros just outside the camp so we stalked it on foot. It turned and stood looking at us. Gethin shouted to us to get up a tree. Bill tried to climb one near by but fell down each time and all I could do was laugh. At that the rhino turned and disappeared into the bush. We saw no hippo but found a herd of elephants feeding in a marsh. Suddenly a large bull, with cow and baby elephant, appeared out of the bush, followed by the rest of the herd. We were busy taking photographs when one of the elephants trumpeted. I was trembling with excitement and furious with myself for not holding the camera steady. Meyers told us to run for it, and Wainaino, our black scout, kept urging me to come back; Gethin ran to the car as quickly as he could to divert the elephants' charge or pick us up. The leading elephant, with his trunk waving and ears flapping, presented a truly wonderful sight. He turned, his family and the herd close behind. I followed up with Meyers and stood on a dead tree stump to watch the procession pass.

'In the afternoon Meyers took us to a Masai village (*manyatta*). It was encircled by a thorn hedge (*boma*) and consisted of a central square into which cattle are put at night. Surrounding the square were huts made of mud and cow-dung. Meyers and I were looking round when he noticed a young girl (*Masai inditu*) being adorned for her initiation ceremony. I wanted to take a photograph but the girl was shy and would not consent, nor would any of the women with her. They thought the camera had the evil eye. Meyers was acting as my interpreter so I told him to say I was a great Bwana sent by God to take a photograph of this *inditu* and that I came from the top of the mountain behind the *manyatta*. As there is a superstition about these mountains, which the Masai believe to be inhabited by an evil spirit – we think it must be a gorilla from their description – this called forth an "Ooh!" of amazement from the women. Meyers repeated all I had told him with embellishments, adding that I could give them special dispensation. Eventually they were convinced that the camera was harmless, but one of the older women asked: "How much has God given the great Bwana, his right-hand man, for us?" However, I took a photograph of the girl, gave the Masai salute, a touch on the forehead, and all was well, although when the chief turned up next morning we had qualms – until we found that he had come about one of Meyers's boys stealing a Masai wife!'

Meyers had lived for a time in Tanganyika, and I remember him telling us that the Germans there had to pretend to one another that they were Nazis and wanted to return to Germany, or else when word got back to the Fatherland their relations were punished and their funds were cut off. He told us how a party of Germans had come to his house to listen to Hitler's May Day speech on the wireless, and how one of them had leant nonchalantly against the mantelpiece when the Horst Wessel song was being played. No further money was remitted to him, he went bankrupt, and his parents' goods were confiscated.

For the Christmas holiday, Bill and I hired a Ford van for a trip with the Wards through central Kenya. We spent Christmas at the Outspan Hotel, at Nyeri, 6,000 feet above sea-level. The bedrooms consisted of *bandas* (grass huts), open except for two sides and the roof, and when we awoke in the crystal-clear mornings we could make out the snow-capped outline of Mount Kenya.

From Nyeri we headed off for the Rift Valley, to stay at a farmhouse. 'The birds in this region are exceptional,' I wrote home, 'lovely red and blue plantain-birds, green and orange bee-eaters, great kingfishers, a bird with a long forked tail and a bright red back – I did not see the colour on his breast as he went across the river like a ball of fire waving his tails behind him; blue Naivasha starlings – the brightest blue imaginable, all scintillating in the sun; ostriches; birds with a call like a flute in a minor key; as much variety, in fact, as any ornithologist could want. There were many red cactus plants in bloom and all sorts of flowers; also jackal, impala, antelope, eland, baboon, gazelle and other animals. I thought I heard a leopard, but was told afterwards that it was an impala grunting. There was a lack of vicious insect life, no mosquitoes and very few ants – what a wonderful relief!'

In the New Year Bill and I set off on a short safari, organised by Captain Percival, another friend of the Wards. Bill and I each had a personal boy, Mola and Wendy, and a gun bearer. My gun bearer, Congoni, was considered to be one of the finest in East Africa, and he certainly had eyes like a lynx.

On Safari, Nr Voi, Kenya, 6 January 1938

'Near Maktau, a railway halt, we saw a herd of oryx and several antelope, and a little farther on decided to pitch our tents just below the site of the camp where the ex-Prince of Wales stayed when he was out here – 3,600 feet up among pleasantly cool, grassy bushland. Bill sleeps outside which means that I have a comfortable double tent to myself. The camp is pitched under a large thorn tree with our dining-room in the open. As the grass is long there are swarms of insects – not so many mosquitoes, but ants and beetles in their thousands. Ticks seem to love me and every night I get Mola to search my back. He usually pulls off about twenty of them.

'We were up before dawn and in the scouting car, a large International, with the driver and Percival in front, Bill and myself in the middle seat and our gun bearers behind. Bill and I had agreed to take alternate shots. It was my turn and the first animal seen was an impala which I failed to stalk successfully. Going a little farther we came across some gerenuk but as they were females with no horns we left them. Then Congoni sighted a male but I could not see it. Throwing up his hands in disgust he again showed it to me. I saw what I thought was a tree trunk but in reality it was the neck of the gerenuk. I took a shot and killed the animal, an old male with good horns.'

M'Pika M'Pika, 10 January

'At Mackinnon Road Station we picked up a local called Killingozi, who is to act as our guide, and continued down a disused track to M'Pika M'Pika. By the side of the road was a huge monitor, which ran up a tree and winked at us with beady red eyes, flicking out a long forked tongue and puffing its cheeks in a great rage. The boys would not touch it as they say it bites and gives a powerful kick with its tail which is two feet long and thick.

'M'Pika M'Pika is uncomfortably hot when there is no breeze. Brightly coloured birds, rather like canaries, and toucans, whose cry resembles that of a chicken starting to cluck, make their home here. There are many yellow butterflies as well as pretty red swallowtails. We came across fresh spoor of elephant, buffalo, lion, kudu, oryx, impala, pig and eland, while on the tree under which my tent is pitched are the claw marks of a leopard.

'Just before going to dinner we heard a lion cough, the first I have heard and rather a fine sound. At midnight I awoke and pulled off ten fighting ants which had crawled under my mosquito net. Bill was awake and we roused Percival. The place was swarming with them. Mola came into the tent and just managed to light the lamp before having to run outside as the ants were attacking him in force. My tent presented an extraordinary sight; the floor was black with little specks scurrying over shoes, suitcases, boxes and clothes. We got out of bed and ran for it. On reaching the tree under which we had dined we sat down to rid ourselves of the ants, which were biting us fiercely. The boys used "Flit" and wood ash to drive them away and then moved our beds out underneath the tree.

'On Sunday morning I went off with Percival, Killingozi, Congoni and a porter. After walking for five solid hours and finding traces of buffalo that had passed the previous day, we came across some lesser kudu which grunted in an odd way like a staccato dog-bark, rather deep-throated.'

Bachuma, 18 January
'On one of our last evenings we went out and walked in line with shot-guns after spurfowl and guineafowl. Before long twenty Wakamba boys joined us. I have never shot with a stranger gang of beaters. They knew no line, they kept no line, they ran after birds, they shouted with glee, they lagged behind to collect brushwood, they bunched in groups; they thoroughly enjoyed themselves and so did we. We gave the fowl we had shot to the Wakambas and returned to camp.

'It was a sad farewell to the camp and the boys. They liked to make a fuss of it and all lined up. Percival translated into Swahili my farewell message to them. Then I shook hands (one uses both hands) and said "Kwa heri". When it came to saying goodbye to Congoni I felt very moved. I asked Percival to tell him that if ever I came out to Africa again I would have him as my gun boy. Congoni replied that he would be pleased to come if God had not called him by then – which I think was a nice way of putting things.

'In the evening we motored up to Voi, where Bill and I said goodbye as he intends to travel down the Nile before returning home. Although at times we became sick of the sight of each other, it was a real pleasure to be with him.'

After Bill had left, I spent a night in Mombasa, before setting off back to Cape Town by flying-boat, via Dar-es-Salaam, Beira, Lourenço Marques and Durban. There were only a handful of passengers, and on the last leg of the journey, because I had felt air-sick the day before, the pilot took the flying-boat above the 9,000 feet level to avoid the bumps. Coming into Durban, he spotted some pretty girls bathing, so, instead of making a smooth landing, we struck a sand bar and ricocheted off on to the water, as if we were a slate in a game of ducks and drakes. It was a relief to climb on board a South African Airways flight to Cape Town, from where I was to board a Japanese ship for Brazil.

Before leaving Cape Town, I was taken by my hostess, Mrs Caesar Schlesinger, to the Government Offices to meet General Jan Smuts, with whom my father and mother were acquainted. The General talked to me of gardens and flowers and about my African trip – and asked me if I had yet climbed Table Mountain. Shame-faced, I had to admit that I had gone up on the cable railway, and this did not impress him. His first walk up Table Mountain, he said, was one of the most memorable experiences of his life. 'He is "Africa",' I wrote in my diary, 'and I am very proud to have met him.'

Osaka Shosen Kaisha Line, MV Santos Maru, South Atlantic, 3 February

'The ten first-class passengers consist of a young South African couple, Mr Oerlichs, an employee of Cable & Wireless, with his wife and daughter, Dr Alvaro, a famous Brazilian eye specialist, Mr Zoutendyk, the South African Minister to the Argentine, and his wife, John G. Mahler, Jr, and myself. John G. Mahler comes from Chicago where he is connected with the leather and hide trade. He has had many adventures with gangsters, being once mistaken for Dillinger, the then Public Enemy No. 1. We both sit at the purser's table. The purser is a sly little man who will not speak English although he understands it perfectly well. The Japanese seem to dislike Mahler more than anyone else on the ship, but I do not think this worries him at all and he goes on talking about the China War and criticising the food quite unconcernedly. After one meal, even I had to take out the medicine chest for the ipecacuanha.

'A typical day is as follows: called 7 a.m.; bath (salt water); gongs at 8 o'clock; breakfast 8.30, followed by a game of deck golf which often lasts till 11.30. We play against members of the ship's staff, who are wily and delight in putting us in the "pond" (the baulk) which makes one miss a turn. They go out of their way to do this rather than score a point for themselves. After deck golf comes a swim and exercises, then a sun-bath; drinks 12.15; lunch 12.45; then, perhaps, a game of chess or a siesta; tea at 3.30; another game of deck golf till 5.30 or 6; drinks; dinner 7 p.m.; talk, bridge, more talking and so the time flies.'

During the whole of our passage across the South Atlantic, we did not see a single other ship; only the albatrosses kept us company, flying above the *Santos Maru*'s wake. It was dark when the ship sailed into Rio harbour about a week later, and all that I could make out of the famous bay were the lights of the city and the floodlit statue of Christ on top of the Corcovado Mountain. 'I *was* pleased to see Griff Llewellyn, who was waiting for me on the quayside,' I wrote.

In Rio, where we only spent a short time, Griff and I were looked after by a splendid old man called Sir Henry Lynch. He belonged to an old Anglo-Brazilian family and was a partner of Davidson, Pullen & Cia, an import and export firm. For many years he had also acted as Rothschilds' agent and representative in Brazil, where he knew everybody who counted in business and government circles. In those days N.M. Rothschild were financial agents to the Brazilian government, and so 'Slynch', as he was known at New Court ('Sir Lynch' to the Brazilians), was very highly valued – so much so that my father had been instrumental in the successful effort to obtain a knighthood for him.

Sir Henry invited us to go for the weekend to his *estancia* near Teresopolis, Fazenda Boa Fé, the house and stables of which were built on land which had once been a jungle swamp. Sir Henry told us that in the process of clearing the ground his men killed over eighty different kinds of snake.

'*13 February*. Yesterday Griff and I had our morning ride through the forests, where I tried, while still mounted on Tarzan, my fiery chestnut, to take films of the huge blue butterflies which flew like small birds in and out of the forest glades. Griff came across an ai – a threetoed sloth – clinging upside down to the branch of a tree, and as we drew near it hissed with rage. The three claws on its front legs looked as if they could scratch, but as this animal only moves in slow motion we were able to approach quite close and even stroke its back.

'The drive back down the winding pass to Rio in the bright moonlight was almost unreal as, far below in the valley, there were clouds pierced by the mountain tops, giving the impression of a lake dotted with islands.'

*

Griff and I set off from Rio by aeroplane to Santos, where we took the German flying-boat for Buenos Aires. We touched down at Florianopolis and at Porto Alegre. At Montevideo, in Uruguay, the aircraft refuelled, and the last leg of the journey was extremely rough, particularly over the River Plate – which was dirty brown in colour and is so wide that even at a height of 4,000 feet we lost sight of land. After a few days in Buenos Aires, where we were looked after by Gilbert Cahen d'Anvers a cousin of my uncle Tony's wife, we boarded a train for Chile.

Rothschilds had for many years been fiscal agents to the government of Chile, handling their bond issues in London. In the late nineteenth century, when a border dispute arose between Chile and Argentina, my grandfather and his brothers were able to help resolve it – after consultations with Barings, who occupied a similar position with the government of Argentina. The presidents of Chile and Argentina had sent word to London that in the event of a flare-up, there would in all likelihood be a default on their bonds; and this naturally made their bankers sit up and do some hard thinking.

Rothschilds' and Barings' solution was to suggest that the British Crown – then in the person of Queen Victoria, who had recently celebrated her Diamond Jubilee and was at the height of her prestige – might be appointed supreme arbiter to settle the dispute. All the parties agreed, the matter was amicably resolved, and in 1902 Chile and Argentina signed a treaty of perpetual friendship.

Sixty years or so later, when a dispute arose over a small, sparsely populated area in southern Chile, where the people did not know to whom they should pay their taxes, the British Crown was again called upon for assistance. Through the Privy Council, the present Queen appointed a panel of arbitrators, and I was asked by the Chilean Ambassador, Victor Santa Cruz, if Rothschilds had any documents relating to the earlier dispute. But although we searched our archives high and low, no important paperwork appeared to have survived, except for a few letters, telegrams and messages of thanks.

Hotel Burnier, Osorno, Chile, 2 March
'At Puerto Blest there was someone waiting to take us to the Customs official, Monsieur Bonnet, a polite little man who shook hands and said how pleased he was to meet me and my friend. Chattering away in French, he told us he was very musical, and that as he possessed neither a piano nor a wireless, his only consolation lay in composing

for full orchestra. Taking our passports into the Customs house, he soon came bustling out waving an armful of papers and saying, "Tout est arrangé." Then, with many smiles, he bowed us into an ancient Ford car which was waiting.

'The drive to Laguna Frias was one of surpassing beauty. The road, a narrow track, was bordered by giant ferns, behind which rose tall beech trees against a background of lofty mountains. We stopped in a forest glade which was really enchanting. It seemed to recall "some far-off long forgotten thing". The sun was shining and the contrast of light and shade amongst the huge ferns accentuated the sombre background of the trees. The road then dipped down to Laguna Frias, the most exquisite lake I have ever seen. Imagine the colour green, then the colour blue; think of emerald and azure, and mix them – that was the colour of the lake. Snow-capped mountains dipped down in an almost vertical drop to the water's edge, stately trees covered the slopes, pampas grass rustled slightly in the thin eddies of breeze coming from the heights, but the breeze never reached the lake, leaving its unruffled surface to mirror the snow in a hazy green.

'The journey across the lake lasted for half an hour. Griff and I were both spellbound; each new vista seemed even lovelier than the last. Monsieur Bonnet, his olive-brown uniform all crumpled, was reclining in the stern of the boat smiling and nodding at us, thinking, no doubt, of his music. At the farther end of the lake, and after another Customs formality, we bade him farewell.'

Santiago, Chile, *15 March*

'What a place Llifén is! Mountains sweep down to the shores of the lake, and the beautiful Calcurrupe River flows past the hotel, which is run by a nice old German called Ziegler. There are a few wooden homesteads, but no proper roads, no cars, no telephone, no telegraph, all communications being by horse and boat.

'Our first day's fishing was most enjoyable, if rather damp. Having sent the boats upstream the night before we had to ride for about an hour before reaching them. Griff and I shared one boat rowed by an Indian. Just as we were putting our tackle together the rain started in earnest, and the wind blew as it can only blow in the Roaring Forties. We had to battle our way downstream against it. I caught one fish during the morning, which we wrapped in paper smeared with butter and salt before cooking it in the ashes of a wood fire. It tasted delicious. For dessert we picked some huge wild blackberries from the banks of the river. Eventually the rain stopped, the sun came out, and I caught a small fish – and lost a large one.'

In Santiago, we were looked after by David Blair, Rothschilds' agent in Chile. By the Chileans he was known affectionately as 'Don David', and he seemed to be as highly esteemed by them as Sir Henry Lynch was in Brazil.

I was daunted to find that he had arranged a lunch in my honour at the Union Club, with no fewer than sixty-eight of the most prominent citizens of Chile, including the Secretary of State for Foreign Affairs, the Finance Minister, the Minister of Labour, and the Commander of the Chilean Navy. I was seated next to the Foreign Minister, José Ramon Gutierrez, with whom I talked in French, English and very broken Spanish. David Blair made a speech and proposed my health, to which I had to reply, and luckily everything went off quite well.

Blair also took me to the Banco Central de Chile, and to call on the Finance Minister – having first primed me to congratulate the minister on balancing his budget. And I was escorted to the Santiago Stock Exchange, a large hall with benches down each side known as the 'Bolsa de Corredores', where I listened to the calling-over of prices, though it was scarcely discernible above the din. My purchase of 1,000 government bonds (at $1 each) seemed to delight the brokers, who shouted their permission for a foreigner to buy on their Exchange.

One afternoon in Santiago I played a game of tennis with the First Secretary at the British Embassy, where, I confessed in a letter home, 'I did a dreadful thing. I had borrowed a tennis racquet belonging to the Ambassador, Sir Charles Bentinck; I did one smashing serve with it and, in attempting to repeat it, broke the Ambassadorial racquet! So would you please buy one in London and send it out to him with a card attached saying it is from me as I could not buy one out here.'

A much more worrying event cast something of a shadow over my stay in Santiago: 'What a terrible tragedy has happened in Austria!' I recorded in my diary. 'David Blair first told me the news when I arrived in Santiago, and then I read in the Chilean newspapers that Baron Louis had been thrown into prison. What will be his fate and that of the rest of the family there?'

Shortly after the German invasion of Austria in March, the Gestapo had arrested my cousin Baron Louis von Rothschild, the head of the Austrian branch of the family, and of the Rothschild bank, in Vienna. Fortunately, neither of his brothers, Eugene and Alphonse, were in Austria at the time. Louis was taken into what the Nazis termed 'protective custody', at Gestapo headquarters in Vienna, the old Hotel Metropole. Louis was a thoroughgoing old-fashioned gentleman, and later I learnt that he had refused point-blank to leave his house on Prinz Eugengasse until he had seen the chef to cancel his instructions for lunch.

Besides being one of the most prominent members of Austria's large Jewish community, Louis controlled – or so, at least, the Nazis supposed – the Witkovitzer Bergbau und Eisenhütte, a vast iron and steel works at Witkovitz (Vikovice), then in Czechoslovakia. The complex, including iron-ore and coal mines, had been acquired in 1842 by Louis's great-grandfather, Baron Salomon (one of N.M. Rothschild's two elder brothers), who was a pioneer in the construction of the Austrian railway network. To the Nazis, Witkovitz was obviously a highly desirable prize from the point of view of munitions manufacture.

The works had been owned in partnership by the Rothschilds and another Viennese family, the Guttmanns, each of the two families holding 50 per cent of the shares. However, as the likelihood of the German invasion of the Sudetenland had increased, Louis had come to an arrangement with the Guttmanns and transferred the entire ownership of Witkovitz out of Austria. A company replaced the partnership, and by 1938 the shares in the company were vested in the Alliance Assurance Company, in London, which my great-great-grandfather 'NM' had founded, with Moses Montefiore and a Baring, in 1824. Consequently, to their chagrin, the Nazis found themselves obliged to enter into negotiations with London, because at that time they had no wish to antagonise British interests or the Government. None the less, for more than a year they used Louis as a pawn in the negotiations.

Eventually, in May 1939, Louis was released, on the payment of a substantial sum put together by the French and English Rothschilds. By the time of his release, Louis's hair had turned snow white. A few weeks later an agreement was reached with the Nazi authorities to sell the Witkovitz works for approximately £3 million (about one third of its value), but then the war broke out in September, and Witkovitz simply passed into Nazi control. All the Rothschild homes, estates and art collections in Austria were frozen, and then confiscated; and it was not until 1953 that the, by then Communist, Czech authorities paid compensation for Witkovitz – somewhat on the low side at £1 million.

Griff and I left Santiago by train for Valparaiso, and from there sailed on the Grace Line ship *Santa Lucia* for Antofagasta, one of the dreariest towns on my tour – 'even the people look shrivelled up,' I noted. Next day we were driving through the countryside surrounding the nitrate fields of Pedro de Valdivia, heading for Calama, where we were to catch the international train for Bolivia.

Our *reservado* was divided into three compartments – a kitchen, bedroom with two berths and a sitting-room containing two armchairs, a stove, table and a couple of hard chairs. It was the last carriage on the train so we had a magnificent view from the veranda-type platform which led off the sitting-room. On 26 March we awoke to find the train chugging through the snow of the Condor Pass, nearly 16,000 feet above sea-level. Wrapped in ponchos we went out on to the observation platform, and just as we reached the top of the pass a huge Andean Condor glided lazily overhead. At La Paz, a motor car was waiting to take us to the home of Dr Mauricio Hochschild, a family friend who owned a copper mine at Potosí, and whose son married the daughter of one of our neighbours at Exbury, the Drummonds.

Of my brief stay in La Paz – brief because Griff and I were to set out almost immediately for Peru – what I enjoyed most of all were the long talks with Dr Hochschild. He was a cultured, intelligent man, and had much to say on the European situation. He was firmly of the opinion that there would be a major war within two years, a war which would lead to the ultimate end of Fascism. He said he thought that Russia had the greatest future, that the Germans would fight the Russians, but that, although gaining early victories, they would eventually be beaten by the inexhaustible manpower of the Soviet Union.

We left La Paz for Cuzco, in Peru, travelling with the English Railway Company. The accountant of the railway, a Mr Haig, and his wife were also going to Cuzco and they kindly invited us to share their special coach; so once again we travelled in luxury.

Hotel Ferrocarril, Cuzco, Peru, 7 April
'The Customs officials at the Bolivian end of Lake Titicaca opened every bag; they were very interested in the clothes they contained – good shoes seemed to fascinate them especially. Still, apart from

curiosity regarding my razor, strop, sponges, soap and a few other personal effects, they caused no real trouble. The *Ollanta*, in which we crossed the lake, was an English-built vessel of about 2,000 tons. It had been brought up to Puno by mule-train and assembled by Indians. We found it hard to realise that we were sailing at an altitude of 12,000 feet. We passed close to the Inca islands of the Sun and Moon. According to local tradition, Manco Capac and Mama Ocllo, the first Inca and his sister wife, came from the sun to an island in Lake Titicaca. Occasionally we caught sight of flamingos and duck, while circling overhead were white birds which resembled seagulls – actually a fresh-water species known as White Alcamarine. Moss and lichens carpet the surrounding mountains and from the reeds of the lake itself the Aymará Indians make their coracles.

'At Puno, in Peru, we boarded the train for Cuzco, where we arrived after passing through one of the most fertile valleys of the world. In places it was a mile wide, but frequently narrowed to three or four hundred yards. The hillsides were terraced and intensively cultivated. Wheat and barley were the principal crops and on the pasture lands grazed flocks of llamas, alpacas, guanacos, sheep and cattle, all tended by Indian women.'

Early on 3 April we set off by autocarril for Machu Picchu. At the village below the ruins, we were crammed into a Ford car – with thirteen other passengers, so that six of them had to stand on the running-board.

Two kilometres further on, we left the car and crossed the Urubamba River by means of a swaying, creaking wooden bridge. On the opposite bank we mounted mules and started on the long climb up the track to Machu Picchu, and there, for the first time, I saw the Andes as I had imagined them, rising steeply with sheer escarpments of rock and abundant green vegetation. The path was narrow, with a precipice on one side, and the mules had an alarming habit of picking their way along the outside edge of the path, so that suddenly one would be looking down a sheer drop of some 2,000 feet.

Flowers grew by the side of the track, and I asked one of the mule-boys to collect some for me to send home to Exbury. 'There were three varieties of ground orchids,' I wrote to my father. 'The first was small and blue with many flowers set close together, the second large red and purple with a touch of yellow in it, while the third was red with a long thin stalk. I am sending these home to you together with two varieties of yellow orchids, all packed in a box with some of the soil in which their roots were growing. The purple-yellow orchid was the hardest to obtain as it meant rock-climbing with nasty drops if one missed one's footing. There was also a vivid yellow wild sweet-pea, several vetches, cacti in profusion, dahlias (supposed to have been planted by the Incas), gladioli, and flowers that looked like red or white deadly night-shade.'

After a long slow climb the ruins of Machu Picchu came into view. We wandered round the palace and saw where the Inca king was said to have slept, and where the nobles and servants lived and kept watch. Sitting on a great slab of stone, supposed to be an ancient sacrificial altar, we ate a picnic lunch.

A day or two later we left Cuzco for Arequipa, where we stayed at the Quinta Bates, then one of South America's best-known hotels, largely on account of its characterful proprietor Tia Bates. Sadly Mrs Bates was away, and the next morning we set out for the port of Mollendo to join a boat to Callao, the port of Lima.

Boarding the Grace Line *Santa Clara* at Mollendo was a hazardous business. There were no harbour facilities and in order to embark on the steamer a passenger had to be lowered by crane to a launch, which then took one out to the boat. When my turn came to be lifted aboard, the launch below was tossing so badly in the swell that I could not be lowered straightaway, and so I was left suspended, clinging to a rope over the surging water for what seemed like an age.

At Callao we changed to another Grace Line ship, the *Santa Barbara*, bound for Guayaquil, in Ecuador. Griff and I had decided to make a short trip, following in the footsteps of the intrepid Swiss traveller A.F. Tschiffeley, from Guayaquil to Buenaventura, in Colombia – and this we managed to do, by road, rail and on horseback. The best stage of the trip was a long ride we went on, in early May, through the mountains in Colombia, from Popayán to Santander de Quilichao. I had a gutsy little roan, Griff a rather slow and nondescript animal, and our guide a small mare; we had two pack horses to carry all our luggage, a wild-eyed grey and a sturdy bay gelding.

'*2 May.* We set out on the 30-mile ride to Piendamó. The horses travelled at a Spanish trot, which means that one does not rise in the saddle at all. We took one or two short cuts up the mountains, and although it rained slightly, our rubber ponchos and bombachas kept us dry. Every five miles or so we stopped to refresh ourselves with a bottle of the local home-brew, and we plucked oranges from the trees by the side of the track as we rode along. We completed the last five miles to Piendamó in complete darkness, the fireflies flashing and sparkling in the night air. At Piendamó, we found a clean room, with bare wooden floors and, although the beds were like iron – the mattress being a board covered with straw – we were both so tired that we slept well.

'*3 May.* We left Piendamó at 8 o'clock, and by midday were riding through tropical scenery. The sun was so scorching that our faces were badly burnt. We must have looked an odd sight, each with a handkerchief made into a sort of helmet to protect the backs of our necks and wearing dark glasses. In the afternoon the road wound down very steeply and its surface was covered with loose rocks, causing the horses to slip. I was walking in front and leading my animal along what I thought was the path when suddenly I found myself looking over a precipice. I just managed to stop my horse in time. We had some difficulty turning the animals as the path was not more than three feet in width, but by cautiously backing them we managed to reach safety. I found a narrow track down which we were just able to make our way, but it was a hazardous descent.

'At dusk we reached Ovejas, where a woman came out of a dirty-looking house and said she could give us bed and breakfast. I was all for staying, but as Griff wanted to go on to Mondormo, we pressed on. It was dark by now, but the moon had risen, the stars were bright and the fireflies lit our way. Looking back on it, this was the most wonderful part of the ride: the absolute stillness, the knowledge that here were pumas, ocelots and wild animals in the jungle by the side of the road, the Andes in soft silhouette outlined by the moonlight, the chirrup of the cicadas and the sound of the horses' hoofs along the unmetalled track

'*4 May.* We left after breakfast. All the horses except mine had saddle sores, so we changed saddles and walked a great deal during the day. The road had petered out and we made our way along the only track in that part of Colombia leading to Santander de Quilichao. It wound up over a beautiful ridge, though the path was deeply rutted and covered with loose stones. We passed through tropical forest, with vividly coloured flowers and gorgeous butterflies, and at lunchtime I bought a huge pineapple from a passing negress for approximately one penny. We rode on through the fields, and saw humming-birds drinking nectar from flowers which smelt like primroses.'

We reached our destination that afternoon, and having taken leave of our guide set off by road, in a hired Chevrolet with a driver, for Calí, from where we made our way – by car, train and boat – to Panama. From there Griff was to return home to England and I was to set sail for New Zealand.

New Zealand Shipping Company's RMS Remuera, 6 June

'The days have passed uneventfully with the usual round of deck games, swimming, chess, bridge and innumerable practical jokes. Cliques were formed but no one really fought, and men have flirted with other men's wives without any heartburnings. In fact it has been a happy ship. We observed the ceremony of crossing the line amidst much amusement. I was a "bear" and threw people in the bath and ducked them. I also went through it myself, so now Neptune grants me the freedom of the Seven Seas.

'On 27 May we sighted Pitcairn Island. I went up on deck at 5 a.m. to watch the dawn come up, and I thought of the *Bounty*, and of Fletcher Christian trusting God to help him in his place of exile. It was difficult to see the landing place through binoculars, but I could just discern the cove and the surf through which the *Bounty* had been sailed to her doom. The sun had not yet broken through the clouds, so it was in a twilight that three sailing boats came out from Pitcairn to meet us as we lay pitching in the swell. I exchanged an old hat with one of the islanders, who gave me two pawpaws and a pile of oranges. The mail having been delivered, Mr Christian, a fine-looking man and leader of the community, shook hands with the captain, then climbed down the rope ladder to where the islanders were waiting in their boats. The sound of their voices singing Adventist hymns carried across the waves as they sailed back to their lonely island home, while the *Remeura*, curtseying in the swell, turned away.'

Wairakei Hotel, Wairakei, New Zealand, 13–17 June

'Since my arrival here, I have been fully occupied. I have met the Mayor of Auckland, given an interview to the *New Zealand Herald*, lunched with the manager of the Bank of Australasia, shopped, dictated letters, obtained car licences and promised the Rabbi to give a lecture to the community here. Nicky and I have also been to a State

Ball at Government House, but dancing was rather difficult because two hundred people had gatecrashed.

'Nicky and I are very happy to be together again. He talks of going back to the Embassy in Tokyo [where he had been tutor to the Ambassador's son] and feels certain that the Japanese mean to go to war. We have bought a car – "Sally", a Ford V8 of 1934 vintage – and are touring round New Zealand in her. We left Auckland on Saturday afternoon and motored to Hamilton. At first the countryside reminded me of home, but before long we were driving through woods of tall stately trees with luxuriant creepers, green foliage and, strangest of all, the tree fern whose stem is like the trunk of a coconut-tree and whose fronds are a bright yellow-green in colour. We stopped and heard the beautiful song of the Tui and Bell birds come floating through the forests. Like the rest of New Zealand, these woods are a dream of charm and unreality.'

My father was very much against my speaking to the press, and although he let pass my talking to the *New Zealand Herald*, he later wrote me a cautionary letter on the subject – after I had spoken somewhat heatedly to some journalists in Australia about Hitler and the Jews. 'Do be more careful about Press reporters,' he wrote.

It has always been a tradition of the Rothschild family never to give interviews. I always refuse. I sometimes see the City Editors of *The Times* and *Daily Telegraph* and I talk to them quite freely because they know that if they ever once quoted me, they would never see me again. The Press reporters you see going round the world will never see you again most likely, so they do not mind what they put in; nor do you know how much you can trust them. You may say that the younger generation knows more about these things than old fogeys, and that you cannot get on without Press interviews. Well, there may be something in it, but if you do see them tell them nothing but generalities – how pleased you are to see their country, what a lovely country you think it is and that you are enjoying your journey round the world. 'Toutes les vérités ne sont pas bonnes à dire.'

Ilam, Riccarton, South Island, New Zealand, 12 July
'Our introduction to South Island was one of contrasts. The first glimpse of it from SS *Wahine* revealed yet more of unsurpassed beauty. As Nicky and I stood on the deck we could see the mist rising from the limpid waters, and the first rays of sun just beginning to tint the

snow-clad mountains behind the bay. I recognised your friend Edgar Stead from the last time we met – in 1932, when I came back from Harrow OTC camp for an afternoon. He has already taken me swan shooting at Lake Ellesmere, and on a duck flight. [Edgar Stead was one of my father's gardening friends, and used to send trees and shrubs (myrtles in particular) from New Zealand for planting at Exbury.]

'On 4 July, we motored up the Eglinton Valley. After passing through Manuka scrub we came to the famous beech trees which are only to be found in this region and, driving on up the valley, we passed first the *Menziesii* beeches, their bark and branches covered with silver markings, then the *fusca* with their massive black trunks, and finally the *cliffortioides* which are stunted and covered with moss. They were a wonderful sight, and through the leaves we could see the distant, but sharply-defined, snow mountains.

'Nicky and I have been up on the Ball Glacier at Mount Cook, staying in a large wooden hut with benches, long tables and a stove at one end. We watched some extraordinary birds called Keas (a species of parrot), which in their antics were almost human. They had seen people skiing, so decided to imitate them, sliding down the tin roof of the hut on their behinds!

'We have also been on a trip with Mr Stead to the Franz Joseph Glacier, which we reached in a single-engined Percival Gull from Christchurch, flying over the Southern Alps. We flew over the glacier and landed at the bottom, in a small field near Waiho. We went for a walk in the bush which, with its giant tree ferns, mosses and palms, was quite different from anything we had seen. We flew back to Christchurch just as the clouds started piling in from the north-east.'

Huddart Parker Line, MV Wanganella, 23 July
'On 16 July I went to a meeting in Wellington, where there was a discussion about the forming of a joint Jewish Social Centre. I spoke for about twenty minutes to half an hour and my speech seemed to be well received. They have elected me a life member of the Jewish Men's Club, a great honour as there have only been seven in its thirty-year history. I accepted for the name I bore.

'In Auckland, the *Wanganella* was delayed for thirty hours because the dockers refused to load in the torrential rain which beat down unceasingly for two days. However, the time came for us to board the ship and, in sparkling sunshine which transformed the whole scene, we said goodbye to New Zealand. Gaily coloured streamers were thrown between the quay and the deck of the ship and we looked down upon a throng of people watching us leave. The streamers parted and fluttered in the breeze, the quayside faded rapidly from sight.

'Another phase in my journey is drawing to a close and, as if to ensure that our memories of New Zealand should be pleasant, it was ordained that the skies be cloudless until we passed the gaunt Van Diemen's headland and the Three Kings Islands – the last outposts of the North Island.'

Francis Williams met us off the *Wanganella* at Sydney, and took us to the Australia, which was then reputed to be the largest hotel in the Southern Hemisphere. The food there was, I recall, excellent, especially the oysters – at sixpence a dozen. Much of my stay in Sydney was taken up with interviews and dinners. I met members of the Jewish community, and made a speech at a large Jewish luncheon at which I was the guest of honour; the talk was mostly of Australia, Great Britain and the refugee problem.

Nicky and I had a great deal of discussion over what to do and see in Australia. I thought I should like to motor across Western Queensland and the Northern Territories; he was attracted by the idea of the scenery and the sport of the Queensland coastal belt. Then to confuse matters the Queensland Government Tourist Bureau started ringing us up with more suggestions for us. Eventually, a lucky chance brought us into contact with a Mr Price Conigrave, who offered to accompany us on a trip across the Northern Territory where he had been an administrator for six years. He had taken part in many semi-exploratory expeditions around Australia and had written several books about the country, so we decided to act on his advice. It was arranged that he would go on ahead to Cloncurry, where we would meet him on 4 September.

We made a plan to spend ten days motoring across the Northern Territory to Darwin. Nicky would then fly on to Java on some errand he had to do, and I was to visit Melville and Bathurst islands to see if there was anything in the suggestion that had been mooted for the formation of a Jewish refugee colony there. Apparently, we were the first party of young British people to attempt the trip from Cloncurry to Darwin since the First World War, and the whole town of Cloncurry, as well as Price Conigrave, turned out to meet our train. The next day, 5 September, having duly been photographed alongside our cars, we started off on the route which was to take us via Duchess, Mount Isa, Camooweal, Alexandria Downs, Katherine, Pine Creek and Burrundie.

It was a long, hot drive through desolate country, punctuated by mechanical breakdowns, burst tyres and uncomfortable overnight camps – not the kind of trip I should wish to make today, though at the time it seemed a great adventure. The recollection that has stuck most firmly in my mind is of a brief stop we made at a small town called Daly Waters, the only importance of which lay in its crossroads and small airport. We stopped there for tea, and met the manager of a cattle station, who, having heard my name was Rothschild, talked enthusiastically to me about the possibilities of oil in the region. To give some teeth to his story he went off to fetch two samples of sandstone, which he said he had discovered in his back yard. They looked authentic and felt oily – but then I recognised the familiar smell of three-in-one rifle oil.

From Darwin we made a trip up the Adelaide River, in a flat-bottomed, square-sterned, rickety old boat called the *Maroubra*. Just beyond the bar of the river we met the mission lugger *St Francis*, which was to take me to Bathurst and Melville islands. Nicky and Francis returned to Darwin.

'Brother Smith was in charge,' I wrote in a letter home. 'He had been a wild Australian sailor, but had one day suddenly decided to turn missionary. As there was a good breeze we set the red sails and were soon spanking through the waters of the sparkling blue Arafura Sea. By nightfall we had made the lee of Bathurst Island, but as there were no guiding lights into the Apsley Straits we anchored for the night. In the morning we rowed ashore and walked up a fine, white coral beach which stretched as far as a line of tall, stately palm trees. The Brothers and Sisters of the Mission greeted us most hospitably and gave us breakfast. Then we went to Melville Island, where I looked round Fort Dundas, long since abandoned because of the difficulty of communication. Few traces of the old houses remain, and they have been almost smothered by undergrowth. Outside the mission hut, where I slept the night, I could smell the lovely scent of the frangipani which were clustered round the window. Melville Island is one of the few places where refugees could settle, as there is plenty of water; but unfortunately it is very hot.'

Two good things had resulted from the otherwise almost completely futile conference on the plight of Jewish refugees held at

Evian-les-Bains in July 1938. America had agreed to reopen immigration to a limit of 30,000 a year, and after the conference Australia had announced that she would admit 5,000 a year – hence my diversion to Melville Island.

On 22 September I left Darwin on an Imperial Airways flying-boat, the *Capella*, which was to take me to Singapore. We flew over the Timor Sea to Koepang, on Timor, for refuelling, and then on to Bima with its lovely harbour encircled by blue hills, and long jetty teeming with gaily dressed people. From there we carried on, flying over Bali and Lombok, to Java. After stopping overnight at Soerabaya, we flew the length of Java to Batavia, and then over Sumatra and on to Singapore, where we circled down round the harbour. At almost exactly the same time as the flying-boat touched the water, Peter Trehearne's ship from England berthed alongside the quay.

Continental Palace, Saigon, French Indo-China, 29 September
'In these trying days my thoughts are for England and of you. While we were in Singapore, the European news overshadowed all our plans and we vacillated between moods of deep depression and optimism. Peter and I, as Territorial officers, left our names at HQ Singapore and were informed that should we be needed the military authorities would wire us. Of course, by the time this reaches you war may have flared up. If it does, I report to HQ Singapore and may be sent to Hongkong, Shanghai or even India.

'On 26 September we caught the SS *Gouverneur Général Pasquier*, an old boat of 1,000 tons originally belonging to the KPM Line, but now under the French flag. Her stern was high out of the water showing a single rusty propeller. As we were the only passengers, it was almost like having a private yacht to carry us across the Gulf of Siam. While on board the *Pasquier* we had interminable discussions about the international situation. Every evening I walked along to the wireless operator's room and waited for him to tune in to London. It was a most dilapidated set, however, and the atmospherics were so bad that it was easy to miss the vital part of the news.

'On the second morning out we sighted a group of islands, amongst them Poulo Condore, which is used as a penal settlement for the Indo-Chinese who have misbehaved themselves. To us it seemed a veritable paradise – great towering mountains and masses of green sweeping down to white shores or rocky cliffs. Almost hidden by the jungle were the huts of the native villages, while the red roofs of the

European houses were clustered round the harbour. A large rowing boat with a bamboo canopy came slowly out towards us followed by a little launch. French officials came aboard and we all drank aperitifs. Our "yacht" left these exotic islands a little before sundown and thrashed its way across to the mouth of the Mekong River. Next morning found us chugging slowly up the Saigon River.'

Most of our time in Saigon was spent in buying provisions for the trip we had planned into the jungle – such things as anti-mosquito Bamber oil, fishing tackle, cartridges and spanners. We had khaki suits made for us by a Chinese tailor – in twenty-four hours at a cost of £1 each, which included an extra pair of trousers per suit. In the evenings we sat outside the Hotel Continental drinking aperitifs in celebration of the Munich peace and Chamberlain's visit to Germany, though one evening we visited a high-class opium den.

'An Annamite ushered us into a dimly-lit room, along one wall of which stood a large divan with hard square cushions. In the middle of the divan was a tray on which were two small oil lamps, several pipes, some thin wire sticks, and little circular pots of opium. Along the other walls were silvery objects, plates and Buddhas, while from the centre of the ceiling hung a Chinese lantern, unlit. Various "Good Luck" writings were also hung about the place, and a bead curtain covered the entrance to another darker room, which we did not enter. The opium pipes are elaborately carved and many of them are finely lacquered. Opium itself is a dark brown syrupy liquid with a smell of burnt caramel. It is squeezed out of a small round tin box into an open bowl, a stick is put into the liquid and the drop of glutinous matter suspended over the flame to cook. It was fascinating to watch this little drop sizzling over the flame, giving off its rather pleasing aroma. The globule of opium was redipped in the liquid, reheated until it became hard, and then rolled on the wood of the bowl of the pipe.

'We had heard and read so much about this drug, yet it looked so very innocent. I was under the impression that after a couple of pipes one automatically went off into marvellous dreams, but, apparently, after about ten or twenty pipes the only effect is one of laziness and contentment, and an inability to concentrate. Peter and I tried one pipe each. I found it tasted like burnt chocolate but Peter thinks that we did not smoke enough opium to make any pronouncements on the subject.'

Sam Poutk Camp, 11 October

'After three quiet days at the bungalow, Pietri [our guide] came to tell us that he had made "un camp épatant et superbe!" He did not exaggerate. There are eight huts in a semicircle and as I write another is going up. Three of the bedrooms are canvas tents, but the rest (with the exception of Pietri's, which is a fly tent) are built out of the jungle. Posts are put in the ground and the crossbars lashed with latania palm fibres. The stalks of the palm are used for girders and benches, while the roof is made with the leaves of this remarkable tree. The sides are guarded by dried latania stalks cut short and twined together with fibre. The tables and chairs in the dining-room are the only European pieces of furniture, apart from the refrigerator which stands up in one corner. The benches are well stocked with tinned food, bottles, gun racks and cases, thermos flasks, butterfly boxes, while hanging from the ceiling are the fishing-rods and two wires on to which the acetylene lamps are hooked at night. From the kitchen hut the most wonderful French food is turned out by Bep, a one-eyed Annamite.

'One evening Gngoul and Meu [two of our men] wanted to hold a sacrifice and say some prayers, so a roasted chicken was brought all steaming to the door of the tent. On another plate there was an egg surrounded by rice into which had been stuck some joss-sticks, with an extra large one alongside the egg. They were all carefully lighted and the outer joss-sticks smoked, giving off a scent, while the larger one burnt with a flame. We were each given a handful of rice and, while the prayers were being chanted, had to throw grains on to the flame. Then there was a final prayer and we each threw on another handful. The climax came just as Nick was about to do this: there was a deafening peal of thunder, the flame went out and all the coolies gasped. Oddly, I could see no black clouds in the sky.'

Xayou Forest, 25 October

'The most important thing that happened on 18 October was the discovery of a rare orchid. We turned right off the road leading into Kratie and, as we were pushing our way through the thick neck-high grass, we came upon it quite by chance. It was a lovely flower. The petals hung down in crinkled ribbons and apparently, when in its first bloom, they slowly change from green tinted with yellow to yellow tinted with red, then red tinted with carmine, until finally the whole flower is a vivid crimson. Pietri was very excited about this discovery and we carefully collected seeds and dug up the bulbous roots which were later taken to the Botanical Gardens in Saigon for classification and planting. From its description the curator said he had never seen one of its kind before and I am going to arrange for some specimens to be sent home to you.

'We called on Lieutenant Lefèvre at Fort Pouplok. It is an amazing place and reminded me of P.C. Wren's stories of forts in the jungle. Situated, for strategic reasons, in wild country, it is the only centre of French administration in a large area of untamed Moys. Two years ago it was raided and burnt to the ground. They have a watch-tower, a moat, wooden stockades, barbed-wire entanglements and towers manned by soldiers with machine-guns. We had aperitifs and promised Lefèvre that we would pay a second visit.'

After the tragedy of Nicky's death, we left Saigon on 30 November, for Phnom Penh and Angkor Wat. We were escorted around the ruins of Angkor Wat and the imperial city of Angkor Thom, whose moat, I remember, was choked with red lotuses. We also accompanied a government archaeologist to watch the reconstruction work of the temple of Banteai Samré, and to see the Terrasse des Eléphants, an extraordinary frieze of elephants in bas-relief stretching for about 150 yards along two walls, separated by a narrow, twisting passage.

In the afternoon, Pietri arranged a Cambodian dance for us, staged against the magnificent backdrop of Angkor Wat. Three enormous elephants, with bare-chested mahouts on their backs, stood flapping their ears and swinging their trunks while in the foreground were the dancing girls, their hair powdered, their costumes covered with trinkets and their arms and legs decked with bracelets. Music was provided by flutes, xylophones and drums, and Pietri had insisted that the members of the band should have 'torses-nus'.

We were introduced to members of the local French community, and Peter and I were invited to play a game of cards with the colonel and commandant of the local garrison. After considerable formality and several aperitifs, we took our places at a green baize table, Peter partnering Monsieur le Colonel and myself Monsieur le Commandant. The game was notable chiefly for the fact that the colonel became visibly annoyed whenever Peter called a contract in a suit, and it was only after about half an hour that we suddenly realised that our partners were not playing contract bridge but plafond. This took quite a lot of explaining, as neither of us knew the French for contract bridge and the Frenchmen spoke no English.

On our last evening in French Indo-China we went to see Angkor Wat by moonlight. Reaching the top of the temple we were greeted by the chanted prayers of yellow-robed *Bonzes* (Buddhist monks). Small boys with flares led us up the stairs and through dark passages, and the moon was shining on the towers and parapets. It was extraordinarily beautiful.

British India Steam Navigation Co. Ltd, SS Karagola, 13 January 1939
'A Qantas flying-boat took us back to Singapore, and while there I spoke in aid of funds for the Jewish refugees in Shanghai, and think I have succeeded in rousing their interest in the thousands of refugees who come to Shanghai, calling in at Singapore for a brief half-hour. I went out with the pilot in his launch to meet one of these ships. It was pathetic to see the refugees crowding round the rails saying, "May we land here?", "Is there a job for us?" The Governor, Sir Shenton Thomas, has been extremely kind and has allowed as many as possible to land. But it is only a tiny percentage. A cinema show was arranged to raise money for these refugees, but unfortunately my boat sailed two days before it was to be shown. The film was George Arliss in *The House of Rothschild*.'

The House of Rothschild was a popular choice of film to show at Jewish fund-raising events. In London it had been screened by the Fund for German-Jewish Women and Children, of whose appeal committee my uncle Tony's wife, Yvonne, was the president. In a way, it seems to me to have been an odd choice of film for these events, as it does not present my ancestors in a particularly flattering light. Talleyrand and Metternich are received by the Rothschilds rather as if they were office boys, and one comes away from the cinema with the impression that Waterloo was perhaps won in the counting house rather than on the battlefield. The character of the Duke of Wellington in the film reveals state secrets from which the Rothschilds make a handsome profit; and the Barings, whose bank my family helped to save from collapse in the late nineteenth century, are presented, quite wrongly, as having been humiliated at our hands.

When I met Sir Shenton Thomas, I remember remarking on the fact that all Singapore's guns pointed out to sea, and asking him if he was worried that none of them were directed inland. It must have been a touchy subject even then; instead of replying to my enquiry, he gave me a rocket for raising the matter.

Northern Shan States, Southern Yunnan, 27–29 January

'From Rangoon we motored through the Shan States, staying for a few days in Taunggyi with Mr Fogarty, the Commissioner. While there we went on a day's expedition to see the Inle Lake, where the famous leg rowers live, and to meet the Sawbwa of Yawnghwe, the most important of the Sawbwas (local Shan chiefs) in the Southern Shan States. He gave orders for his nephew to take us to the lake in a canopied, teak longboat with an outboard motor. The boats we saw there were propelled by an oar which the natives wielded with their feet, legs and hands.

'Beyond Namtu, nearing the Chinese border, we passed mule trains driven by strange, stocky, bow-legged yellow men and filled with goods for Lashio where they pick up munitions and food for the Chinese forces [for use in the Sino-Japanese war]. There were also ox-cart caravans driven by Shans in their picturesque costume, the women with rosy cheeks and turbans on their pretty heads. The leading animals always carried a red plume and all of them wore jingling bells. These were the trains and caravans that Marco Polo saw wending their slow way down the trade routes.'

British India Steam Navigation Co. Ltd, SS Ekma, 8 February

'We drove into Namhkam on 29 January to have our government pass translated into the Shan language by the local Sawbwa's secretary, and also to obtain his seal and permission to cross the Chinese frontier. The Sawbwa himself could speak no English but we bowed and shook hands politely. Then we walked over the long bamboo bridge across the Shweli River into China. The countryside looked so peaceful and beautiful that it was hard to realise that somewhere in China a war was raging. At Bhamo we boarded the *Shwelin*, a paddle-steamer which took us down the Irrawaddy to Mandalay. Owing to the shallow draught (we only touched the bottom once) the Indian "polers" would sing out the depths of the water, which they sounded with bamboo poles every ten seconds. From Mandalay, which we reached on 1 February, we motored back to Rangoon to board the *Ekma* for Calcutta.'

Tellicherry Club, Madras, 24 February

'Our tour of India has been carefully mapped out for us by Mr Cooper of Burmah Shell. After a few days in Calcutta, Peter and I caught a train to Madras, and then on to Madura. From there we drove south to Travancore and Cochin, where I met the leaders of the Jewish Community. They told me that there are two sects in Cochin, the so-called Black Jews and White Jews, and that they have not intermarried. The first settlers, the Black Jews, landed in AD 70, the White Jews came at a later date. There are also a few "Slave Jews" who are dark-skinned but are classed with the white. The Maharajahs of Cochin have all been very tolerant and only when the Portuguese landed was there any trouble.

'"Jew Town", or the Jewish Quarter, is situated between a Hindu temple and one of the palaces and possesses three synagogues. They are well-kept and the one belonging to the White Jews contains beautiful Chinese seventeenth-century tiles. I met several of the elders, fine bearded patriarchs, many of whom could trace their ancestry back to the sixteenth century. The Dewan of Cochin, Sir Shanmukham Chetty, told me that he has offered to make over 8,000 acres of good land up in the hills to a responsible organisation for the German-Jewish refugees.

'At Mysore, Peter and I were guests of the State, and the Dewan, Sir Mirza Ismail, had arranged for us to stay at Government House, with its famous unsupported, unpillared ceiling 100 feet above the ground. We were shown the state elephants, and a household official was sent to escort us around Mysore. The splendour of the palace was quite dazzling: great rooms, marble halls, ivory-inlaid doors, solid silver doors, gold and silver thrones, glass and ivory chairs.

'On our way to Bangalore we made a detour in order to see Seringapatam, the old fort in which Tipu Sultan was killed by the Redcoats in 1799. On arrival a car was put at our disposal; a guard turned out and presented arms, and a man with a gold staff preceded us wherever we walked. Peter and I ended up the day with a dinner-party given in our honour by the Dewan which took place at Kumara Park, a palatial building in which we each have a large sitting-room, bedroom, dressing-room, tiled bathroom, a balcony and about five servants to do our least bidding.'

The Palace, Burdwan, 12 March

'We broke our stay in Calcutta by spending a couple of days in Darjeeling, which involved travelling overnight to Siliguri and then hiring a car to take us to the foothills of the Himalayas. The hill station itself was fascinating with its mixed population of Tibetans, Bhutanese, Nepalese and Indians. The porter who carried my camera had been on several of Kingdon-Ward's botanical expeditions. In the morning we were up at 4.30 and climbed Tiger Hill to see the sun rise behind the Kanchenjunga Peak. The cloud cleared in patches and the mountain stood out like an island, stained red in the early rays of the morning sun, while far away in the background we could discern the summit of Mount Everest.

'On 11 March we left Calcutta in our red box-body Ford, which was piled high with luggage as well as John and Gomes, our personal boys, and Mohamed Bakar, our driver. At Burdwan we were met by Sir Bijay Chand Mahtab, Maharadhiraja of Burdwan, whose son, Abhay, was at Harrow with us. The Maharadhiraja is No. 1 Hindu in Bengal and is the richest Zemindar [feudal landowner]. My room at the palace looked out on to a pond in a courtyard above which thousands of pigeons were circling. The Maharadhiraja told me that his grandfather, who suffered severely from rheumatism, was advised by an Indian doctor to feed the pigeons twice a day as the wind caused by the fluttering of their wings would ease his aches. "Not that he did not have other little birds which probably gave him the pains," added the Maharadhiraja with a smile and a waggle of his finger!'

Udaipur, 26 March

'After leaving Burdwan we stayed as guests of the Maharajah of Vizianagram. Unfortunately he was away, but his Dewan, a pro-Congress, high-caste Hindu, entertained us, and we also met the Maharanee and her daughter, but, as the Rajputana women observe purdah, they did not have their meals with us. Practically all the citizens of Benares are pro-Congress and, although not anti-British, desire Dominion status. One afternoon we were rowed down the Ganges in the Vizianagram state barge.

'At Shivpuri we spent a night in a hotel. A white mausoleum there commemorates the present Maharajah of Gwalior's grandmother and every day a ritual is performed as if she were still alive. An image of her is clothed, fed (the food being placed in the mouth of the image and then thrown to the crows), bathed, put in a carriage and taken to the shores of a lake where she is guarded by soldiers with flintlock guns.

'In Delhi we watched India's Legislative Assembly at work and also saw the Council of State. In the former, Sir James Grigg was introducing the financial budget for the year, while the Council of State (roughly corresponding to the House of Lords) passed nine Bills during the half-hour we were there. We also attended a garden party and lunched with the Viceroy. At the lunch there were about seventeen guests and we were all lined up in a row to be introduced. I sat next to Mr Jinnah, leader of the Moslem group in India. He said he sympathised with the Jews and knew what it was like to be one of a minority.'

After Delhi, we made for Udaipur – where we saw the Maharana being carried in an ivory chair from his palace to the Zenana quarters, escorted by his bodyguard with drawn swords – and then Bundi, the still almost medieval state nestling among the Rajputana hills. The gates of the walled city were closed at 10.00 p.m. and nothing, except a direct order from the Maharajah, could open them. Peter and I were taken up a hill in palanquins borne by eight and six bearers respectively and at the summit were given a salute of drums and fife.

We left Bundi in the afternoon of 1 April and, after tea with the Chief Minister of Tonk, an even less advanced state than Bundi, drove to Jaipur. The following morning, after a call at the palaces and the fort, we rode up the hill on a state elephant to see the Amber Palace. The Maharajah, who had served in the Household Cavalry, invited us to lunch and told us of the troubles that the Rajput States were having with civil disobedience. At Jammu we were entertained by the Huzoor Minister, Home Minister, and the Maharajah of Kashmir. The Maharajah talked to us on all kinds of subjects – food, flying, polo, racing, fishing and his bad ankle. He was surrounded by ADCs who never spoke, but laughed whenever we did. From Jammu we headed for the North-West Frontier Province, where we were to stay at Peshawar, *en route* for a visit to Kabul.

Hotel de Kabul, Afghanistan, 14 April
'The road to Kabul was magnificent. Soon after leaving Peshawar we found ourselves approaching a range of mountains, some of them covered in snow, which rose abruptly on the Indian side of the Afghan border. There looks to be only one opening in that barrier, and there is only one – the Khyber Pass.

'Fortunately, there was no difficulty over our passports, and we passed through on to the untarred road of Afghanistan. The scenery over the border was grand – fine rolling, open country, green in places, leading into the far ranges of the Hindu Kush across the Kabul River – but the road itself was shocking. From Dakka we continued to

Jalalabad and to the village of Nimla, where we spent the night at a government rest-house. Four hundred years ago the Mogul emperor Jehangir built a garden here full of white irises and cherry blossom, which were just in bloom at the time of our visit. The following morning we set off for Kabul.

'We have had a most eventful time here, sightseeing, shopping and paying calls. The bazaar was most intriguing: narrow muddy lanes over which ox or goat hides were stretched across wooden beams joining the houses; a jumble of camels, mules, horses, Afghans and purdah women who picked their way through the crowd, their white sheets covering them completely, save for stockinged ankles and high-heeled shoes; row upon row of single-roomed shops, and every now and then an alley-way leading into a courtyard caravanserai around which people lived. Every kind of article was for sale on the stalls, including jewellery, rugs, samovars, food, brass jugs and a host of strange things.

'We have lunched at the British Legation, where we met the Prime Minister and the War Minister, both of whom are relatives of ex-King Amanullah. There were two other ministers present, and one of them conversed with me most politely in French. In the evening, when I was writing up my diary, Peter asked me whether there were any Jews in Kabul. Just then there was a knock at the door and someone told me that a deputation representing the Jews of Kabul was waiting outside. They asked me if I would meet the Jewish community, so after dinner I was taken to the now deserted bazaar by Mr Schapiro, a Latvian Jew employed by a British fur company here. At the entrance to one of the alley-ways I was met by a group of men holding lanterns and, after shaking hands with them, was escorted down a narrow muddy lane to the chief synagogue – a room about the size of a large drawing-room, in which were gathered two or three hundred people.

'The men were well-dressed and the women, who stood apart, wore traditional costume with lace bonnets. I was led to a table which was groaning under the weight of foodstuffs they had prepared to show me hospitality. Although I had dined I managed to sample a little of nearly everything to please them. There were pomegranates, oranges, dried grapes, chickens, potatoes, matzos, cakes, pimentos and sweets. I made a speech in English which was translated into Persian by Schapiro and then into Hebrew, Russian and Afghan by the leaders of the different sects. They then gave me wine to drink and there were toasts.

'The community is composed of Persian Jews and Russian exiled Jews from Russian Turkestan. They asked me all sorts of questions, particularly about Palestine and whether they would be able to go there. They told me that many years ago a French Rothschild went to Bokhara, and they produced a picture of poor Louis and asked about him. Even in this remote region the family name inspires the hope that someone will help them. As the evening was drawing to a close, I asked them to sing the hymn *Adon Alom* as I was in their synagogue.'

From Kabul, we retraced our steps to Peshawar, from where we were to make our way, via Delhi, to Bombay for the ship home. At Srinagar we met the Maharajah of Cooch Behar's mother and her beautiful daughters, Princesses Ayesha and Indiridiva, who were staying in the town at the time. I was also invited to meet Dr Hjalmar Schacht, the former head of Hitler's Reichsbank, who was also there on a visit; but I produced some excuse. The Maharanee told me that, when asked what he thought of the treatment of the minorities by the Nazis, Schacht had replied in all earnestness that he had no defence for it, and that it had been one of the reasons for his resignation from the Reichsbank.

We had two wonderful days fishing on the Maharajah of Kashmir's preserved waters, and on the second day a picnic with the Maharanee and her two daughters on the banks of the Kulgam River. Although none of the ladies had ever fished before, each of them succeeded in catching some trout.

At Lahore I parted from Peter for a few days and caught a train to Sriganganagar in Bikaner State, where the Maharajah had offered a tract of land for the settlement of refugees. After seeing the Colonisation Officer about this, I was driven out along a canal bank and through the area in question. The whole site for this proposed settlement looked desolate – Sriganganagar was a green oasis in a sandy waste. But I was told that I was seeing it at the worst time of year, and that the intense heat only lasted for three months of the year.

P & O Line, Viceroy of India, 17 May
'What a terrible journey it was back to Delhi. About one hour out of Bikaner I was sitting alone in the only first-class compartment with all the fans on and the temperature at 118 degrees, when the coach had a "hot box" and had to be detached at a wayside station. A second-class carriage was prepared for me and for four hours I shared it with a Jain, his wife and two servants. The Jain's wife was in strict purdah, so the servants rigged up a sheet across one end of the compartment and I had to turn my back as she was bundled in behind it. The Jain

was extremely grateful, and offered me marzipan, and then something so hot that it made me feel ill. Water and food were passed to his wife under the partition.

'In the middle of the night the train stopped at a junction while an ancient first-class coach was put in commission. I think it must have been the first the railway ever had – no shower, hardly any water, an electric light which would not switch off and one fan which would not switch on. It was warm during the night – around 110° – but the next day the temperature went up to 130° in the shade. I poured with sweat and was so uncomfortable that an Indian passenger took pity on me and gave me some sweet herbs as smelling salts.'

I spent my last four days in India in Bombay. During the day, my time was taken up with refugee business, and in the evenings there were dinner-parties. Two were given by prominent Parsees, the only sect in India that I had not yet met. The hospitality and splendour of Maharajahs and Governors paled beside those of the Parsees. As I was ushered up the flight of steps leading to the home of Sir Cowasjee Jehangir, there was a bearer dressed in blue and silver livery on every alternate step, while attendants stood behind every alternate chair in the great marble dining-hall, which must have been a good 80 yards in length. Sir Byramjee Jeejeebhoy went one better: his bearers, dressed in gorgeous crimson and gold livery, stood on every step and behind each chair, and at his dinner-party we ate off solid gold plates.

As Mr Gandhi was to be in Bombay for a day, arrangements were made for me to visit him. He was staying in a luxurious Parsee house, but his room was quite plain, furnished only with a mattress. As he was rather weak after his Rajkot fast, he apologised for not getting up to shake my hand, but he gave me the warmest welcome and asked me to sit on a chair that had been brought in. I refused and sat on the floor, Indian fashion, to talk to him, and this seemed to please him. We spoke of South Africa, armaments, my age and India; and he expressed his profound sympathy for the refugees, and his horror at the treatment Jews were receiving. But he was adamant that non-violence and non-co-operation were the best weapons. When I asked him what use these principles were if you were being killed and murdered, he merely said, 'You will never succeed in getting anything by force without losing it.'

While we spoke, Gandhi held in his hand a mug of milk and honey flavoured with salt, and when his grandson came into the room he blew up a balloon for him.

3

From New Court to Normandy

I arrived back in England on Saturday 27 May 1939, and after a week spent sorting myself out after nineteen months abroad, I joined my father and my uncle Tony at the bank in early June.

New Court, the site which N.M. Rothschild & Sons still occupies today, is on the west side of St Swithin's Lane – a narrow, one-way thoroughfare running north–south between Cannon Street and the west end of Lombard Street in the City. The most convenient route home for my father was via Cannon Street, and for many years, until he was eventually stopped by the police – and a bold appeal to the Home Office for special privileges had met with a brush-off – he always drove his car out of the bank the wrong way down the street.

Structurally, New Court in the 1930s was unchanged since its original red brick buildings had been demolished to make way for stone in the early 1860s. The style chosen by my great-grandfather Baron Lionel for the rebuilding was reminiscent of an Italian Renaissance palazzo, and the design was produced and executed for him by the architects Nelson & Innes, whom he had also employed to build his London house, 148 Piccadilly (since demolished to make way for Park Lane), and to undertake various alterations at Gunnersbury.

A high archway set into the street-front of the bank – large enough for a carriage and horses to drive through – led off the lane into a cobbled courtyard with a well-head at the centre, around which our offices were arranged. Over the arch, which at night used to be closed by great wooden doors, hung a sign incorporating the Rothschild family's device of five arrows, a reference to the five sons of Mayer Amschel Rothschild, four of whom left Frankfurt to found sister banking houses in Vienna, Naples, Paris and London in the early nineteenth century, while the fifth remained at the house in Frankfurt. When New Court was rebuilt again in the 1960s, during my stint as senior partner, we rehung the sign of the five arrows in the new forecourt.

From the old courtyard there were three points of entry to the bank. In the north-east corner of the courtyard there was the entrance to the Front Hall, the General Office, the Partners' Room – always known as 'The Room' – and the Partners' Dining-Room; in the north-west corner was the entrance used by staff, messengers, couriers, brokers and members of the general public; and in the south-west corner there was the door to the Bullion Room, the secure vault beneath New Court which we used for the storage of gold bars.

Callers entering the bank by the north-east entrance were met by the 'Front Hall men', attendants dressed in dark blue suits with cutaway coats, whose principal duty was to screen people who wished to see one of the partners, my father or Tony. Three of the Front Hall men I remember quite well were Shipton, Piper and Ruddle. Shipton, and very possibly the others, too, had a number of relatives working amongst the New Court below-stairs staff.

The Room, which was the nerve-centre of the bank, was a long, high, oak-panelled saloon with a fireplace at each end. In the winter months, in the days before the Clean Air Act, coal-fires burned in the grates. Tony and my father sat at large leather-topped writing tables, each with a series of bell-pushes recessed into their tops, all neatly labelled with the names of the various senior clerks and servants whom the partners might wish to summon. When, passing through Paris during my Easter vacation in 1937, I called on my cousin Baron Edouard at de Rothschild Frères, I remember noticing that the desks in their partners' room – which was very similar in its arrangement to ours – also had these panels of buttons let into the tops. In the Room at New Court, my father, who was the senior partner, used to sit at the Louis XV *bureau-plat* at which, in 1875, Baron Lionel agreed to lend the British Government £4 million to buy the Khedive of Egypt's shares in the Suez Canal; and I still sit at that desk today.

Although the era had passed when there was only one partners' telephone – practically locked away in a safe – before the war there was still no internal telephone system. All our outside calls went through the bank's operator, Miss Gregory – who had quite a reputation among the staff (though not in the Room) for her barrack-room language. Each partner had a secretary; Miss Milburn worked for my father, Miss Icely for my uncle. My first secretary was Miss Livingstone, the daughter of a well-known London rabbi.

The Partners' Dining-Room, reserved for the use of the partners and their lunch-guests, was overseen by the portly figure of Reynolds, the New Court butler. Senior Clerks – as the heads of the various departments were termed in those days – had their lunch in a separate dining-room in the basement, so as to be available at all times throughout the day should a partner need to consult them. The rest of the bank's staff received a daily luncheon allowance to spend in one of the near-by restaurants and hostelries in the City. At the Throgmorton, opposite the Stock Exchange in Throgmorton Street, one could get a very decent meal and something to drink for half a crown.

The family who sat in the Room and the staff who occupied the General Office or sat in the Front Hall were two races apart, not unlike – though in the case of senior employees the division was blurred – the division between Upstairs and Downstairs in a prosperous household of the time. Ronald Palin, a long-serving employee who joined the bank as a clerk in 1925, and who was a great help to me in later years, was fond of relating a particular story about my father, which – though almost certainly apocryphal – never failed to raise a laugh among the New Court staff. Winding up a morning meeting with one of the senior clerks, Philip Hoyland, and Hugh Quennell, a partner of the bank's solicitors Slaughter & May, my father is supposed to have got up and said, 'Come and have some lunch, Quennell,' and then, turning to Philip Hoyland, 'Hoyland, you had better go and get your dinner.'

The situation was probably accentuated by the fact that a fair number of the New Court staff had actually first worked for my family in a domestic capacity; some came from families who had done so for years. Generations of New Court porters and couriers, for instance, were supplied by the Ridgway, Stephenson, Cornish and de Freyne families. 'Old Ridgway', who used to be entrusted with important errands about the City – and was consequently known as the 'Walks Man' – had at one time been my grandparents' coachman. His son, 'Young Ridgway', progressed to become the head of our Records Department, traditionally a preserve of the porters. Two porters remained on duty at New Court twenty-four hours a day, weekends included, and they were all fitted out with smart blue serge suits and black bowler hats.

One New Court staff family was descended from the crew of the cross-Channel sloop owned by Rothschilds in the nineteenth century to carry the bank's agents to and from the Continent – via which the news of Wellington's victory at Waterloo reached New Court before Downing Street. The head of the Control Department, the function of which was to keep an internal audit (and so prevent any possible internal fraud), was E.A. Mercer, who was the third of four generations of Mercers to be employed at New Court. His grandfather, Thomas Mercer, was said to have been the master mariner who brought the news of Napoleon's defeat at Waterloo to New Court. When Thomas Mercer was too old for life at sea, he came to work at New Court, later to be joined by his son, E.A.'s father, who worked at the bank for more than fifty years. E.A.'s son Ernest Mercer, who joined the firm in 1922, was the last of the family to work at New Court.

Before the war, our Foreign Exchange Department was run by Percy Wingate, with Sidney Williams as his assistant. Wingate's father had been a clerk at New Court, and Sidney Williams was the fourth generation of his family to work for the bank. Roland Williams, Sidney's son, spent his working life at Rothschilds, ending up as a partner in the 1960s.

To an extent, New Court served as a kind of family secretariat, and it was by no means unknown for bank personnel to get drawn into the family's domestic affairs. Long before my time, a proficient Italian-speaker employed in the bank's Correspondence Department was said to have used his expertise only once – when he was sent to Victoria station to meet Gina, my grandmother's Italian maid, off the boat-train. And in a room on the top floor of the bank there was an office called the Private Accounts Department, where four members of staff looked after my family's private investments, as well as other affairs – dubbed 'Whores and Jockeys' by New Court employees. The Private Accounts Department was for many years run by a man with the apt name of Wright Price.

The majority of the bank's clerical staff, all still termed 'clerks', sat in rows, at high sloping desks, in the General Office. The most senior non-Rothschild at the bank before the war was known as the Chief Clerk, a designation which was afterwards changed to General Manager. He reported directly to the partners, and could always catch their attention by standing outside the glass-panelled door at the top of some steps which led from the General Office into the Room.

The Chief Clerk when I arrived at New Court was called Samuel Stephany, a stout, clever man, who possessed an encyclopaedic knowledge of finance going back to the early years of the century. He enjoyed the complete confidence of my father and Tony, and every year or so was sent to South America – travelling by sea in the height of first-class luxury – to keep an eye on the bank's interests there. But I never got the chance to know Stephany well (he died during the war), nor indeed, before the war, to learn very much about the bank's general business at all.

The reason for this was that by the time I arrived at New Court, my father and uncle were devoting most of their time and energy to the Jewish refugee crisis on the Continent, and so when I joined them I was put to work exclusively on the refugee problem. My cousin Victor was busily at work on this too and, while not remotely interested in banking, had a room at New Court as his centre of operations. He was responsible for handling the huge correspondence of the Central British Fund for German Jewry, of which Tony was the appeal chairman, and whose fund-raising account we held at the bank.

The Fund had been set up at New Court in 1933 to deal with the first flood of refugees from Germany, in the wake of Hitler's rise to power; by the end of that year some 60,000 people, 80 per cent of them Jews, had left Germany, and an initial appeal by the Fund had raised about £250,000. The original idea was that the money should be used principally to assist settlement in Palestine, and to train young men in agriculture and the other skills they were expected to need; but it was also to provide for the maintenance of refugees allowed into Britain. My father was one of the Fund's first five joint-presidents, along with the Marquess of Reading (son of the former Viceroy of India), Dr Hertz, the Chief Rabbi, Chaim Weizmann and Nahum Sokolow, the president of the World Zionist Organisation. Although my father had been an MP, he was instinctively non-political when it came to Zionism, and he therefore assumed a conciliatory role in deliberations.

Following the notorious 'Nuremberg Decrees' of December 1935, which deprived all Jews and non-Aryans in Germany of their citizenship and political rights, the exodus of refugees accelerated, and then again after Hitler's annexation of Austria in 1938. The Jewish population of Austria numbered around 200,000, most of them in Vienna – which had an even larger Jewish community than Berlin. 'Kristallnacht', in November 1938, when the Nazis burnt down synagogues, wrecked Jewish buildings and businesses and arrested tens of thousands of Jews throughout the Reich, signalled the opening of the refugee floodgates. By the summer of 1939, 60,000 refugees were registered in England by the Jewish Refugees Committee which Otto Schiff had set up in 1933; prior to 1938, the number had been below 6,000. The Jewish population in Germany, which had numbered more than half a million in 1933, had fallen below 200,000, and the number of Jews in Austria by around two thirds.

In the light of the crisis resulting from the Nuremberg Decrees, it was felt that a bigger organisation than the CBF was needed to assist emigration. The result was the Council for German Jewry, which to begin with planned to raise £3 million, one third coming from the British and Jews resident in the Dominions, the other two thirds from America, where the Jewish population was more than ten times larger than in Britain. The Council comprised the leaders of the British, American and Continental communities, and it raised £800,000 within a short time of its inauguration in March 1936. The Council's appeal committee included three members of my family: my father, my uncle and our cousin Jimmy de Rothschild, who was at the time a Liberal MP.

Day after day the desperate plight of the Jews in Europe was brought home to us by the first-hand accounts Victor heard from those lucky enough to have got out of the Reich or escaped the concentration camps. In November 1938, he made a speech on the subject, at a meeting of the Earl Baldwin Fund for Refugees at Mansion House. 'I know that children have been shot dead,' Victor said. 'I have interviewed people who have escaped from concentration camps, and I can tell you that their experiences make the many horrors we read about nowadays seem like some nursery game. I have been the recipient of so many heart-rending letters from children, of documented reports and personal accounts from observers that it is difficult for me to believe that I shall ever become again the rather carefree and happy scientist that I was before all this began.' The matter was urgent, he explained; unless those concerned could escape within two years, an immense proportion of them would be dead. 'The slow murder of 600,000 people is an act which has rarely happened in history. It is an act that you can prevent.'

Although extracts from Victor's speech and other articles along the same lines appeared in the newspapers at the time, many people found such a state of affairs hard to comprehend. And by the time I started at New Court, the situation had become, of course, very much more acute.

When I had arrived home in May, my parents had had Lord and Lady Reading staying at Exbury for the weekend, together with my Uncle Robert and Aunt Nelly, and my Austrian cousin Baron Alphonse von Rothschild with his English wife Clarice. So all the talk at dinner on my first evening back in England had been of Palestine and the Jewish refugee situation in Europe. Palestine in particular, I remember, was a burning topic, because immigration there had been severely curtailed. As early as 1936, at the time of the Arab revolt, the Mandate administration had begun to restrict the entry of Jews; out of a group of more than 20,000 Jews who were given assistance to leave Germany in 1937, less than a fifth of them were admitted to Palestine. In 1938 the conference on the plight of refugees held at Evian-les-Bains excluded Palestine from its survey of countries for Jewish settlement; and in 1939, when the situation had become even more pressing, the British Government announced its intention to restrict immigration to Palestine systematically to 10,000 a year, and to end the Mandate after ten years.

Given this situation, alternatives to Palestine had urgently to be sought, and as well as chairing the CBF, my uncle Tony chaired the Emigration Planning Committee for Refugees, the broad aims of which were to identify sites around the world which would be suitable for refugee settlement, and to raise the money to fund it. I was given the job of helping to investigate possible locations for settlement and the likely costs. The difficulties facing us, which seemed insurmountable, were summed up by my father. 'There is no easy solution,' he wrote to me, 'very few of the refugees are fitted for outdoor life – they all have to be trained for it. Nobody wants them in the towns or professions, with very few exceptions. Madagascar has been mooted; some say it is a death trap and not a white man's country and that children are bound to deteriorate. This is being investigated, so is Australia and Paraguay. A large sum of money has been collected but most of this will go in relief. The cost of emigrating thousands of families is prohibitive unless the Government helps.'

Consequently, an ambitious plan was devised to set up a special corporation with the purpose of raising a £100-million trust fund to finance refugee settlement. The fund was to be applied to provide maintenance and training for the refugees, working capital for businesses, and investment in new industries suitable for providing them with work. Priority would be given to 'emigrants dispossessed of the means of livelihood within the territory of the German Reich'.

Separate commissions were set to work researching a mixed bag of countries for refugee settlement *en bloc*. At different stages the list included Brazil, Uruguay, Paraguay, Bolivia, Panama, San Domingo, Angola, Ethiopia, Kenya, Rhodesia, the Shan States (in Burma), Honduras, the Philippines and Melville Island, which I had visited in 1938. Territories were sought for block refugee settlement schemes because at the time it was thought that the unorganised immigration of individuals risked giving rise to anti-Semitism where it had previously not existed.

All the leading Jewish figures of the day came to New Court for lunch and talks, and Tony paid regular visits to Whitehall for discussions with the Colonial Secretary, Malcolm MacDonald, a few of whose officials were briefed to assist us. The results were very meagre: 500 refugees were admitted to Kenya, where there was already a small, well-established Jewish community; a further 100 or so were admitted to Northern Rhodesia.

By the time the war broke out, only one scheme for a settlement of any significant size in the Colonies had emerged: a proposal for the settlement of 5,000 refugees on the heights above the Rupununi Valley area in British Guiana. A pioneer party of fifty were actually ready to set sail by August 1939, but with the war looming their departure was halted. But while climatic excellence and great economic possibilities had been claimed for the Rupununi Heights, I was personally very doubtful of the scheme. For one thing, according to the independent advice I obtained from Burroughs & Wellcome, the area could only be reached through disease-ridden jungle terrain.

In the months leading up to the outbreak of war, ever worsening conditions in Germany, Austria and Czechoslovakia threatened to choke the channels of Jewish emigration by provoking a flood of refugees, and throughout this period England provided the principal haven for those fleeing the Continent. The Jewish Refugees Committee, the purpose of which was to provide for the relief and assistance of refugees in Britain, spent more than £250,000 in the pre-war months of 1939 – more than it had spent in total over the previous five years since its foundation by Otto Schiff. And early in 1939 the Council for German Jewry took over the old army camp at Richborough, on the Kent coast, as a temporary refuge for more than 3,000 young Jewish men in transit for America and other countries.

I visited Richborough with Julian Layton, a family friend and member of the camp's committee, and saw the men receiving agricultural and technical training, attending lectures and learning English. Hebrew was taught to those of them who were in transit for Palestine, Spanish to those hoping to go to South America. Few of them had any private possessions beyond their clothes, and anything they earned, for example from agricultural work in the locality, they put into the camp's common fund – from which they then received pocket money. I sensed the atmosphere in the camp to be one of genuine goodwill, and when the war broke out most of the men abandoned their plans to emigrate and volunteered to enlist in the Armed Forces – which, with the eventual formation of the non-combatant support unit the Pioneer Corps, they were able to do.

In the middle of the summer of 1939, I came down with a bad fever and broke out in a rash of painful boils. I was sufficiently ill to need a night nurse, the first being one called Nurse Duncan. Even in my delirious state I could see that she was pretty – as could my mother, who promptly had her replaced. The doctors thought I must have picked up malaria on my travels, but tests then showed that I had contracted a generalised infection of *staphylococcus aureus*, a form of blood poisoning which in those days, so I was told afterwards, was fatal in ninety-eight cases out of a hundred. Fishing the Test with Mr Howlett one weekend, I had scratched my thumb with a dirty hook, and neglected to put iodine on the wound. When the fever was at its height, I remember turning my face to the wall and hearing the most heavenly music – and wondering where I was.

The recommended cure was to stay at home in bed and take an enormous quantity of most unpleasant pills called Ularon – some days as many as twelve of them – for almost three weeks, and it was not until the end of August that I was back on my feet and well enough to travel down to Exbury for a few days before setting off for a short holiday in Scotland. I had some pigeon shooting with Rattue, took Leo out fishing on the *Nigella*, and attended the Exbury village flower show – all very normal, except that the general mood was unsettled.

On the 30th I set off for Scotland by road, arriving at Dochfour at teatime the next day. Naomi, Aunt Lou and Countess Hochberg were there (my dear grandmother had died in 1937), all very depressed about the situation in Europe and glued to the BBC news. Fishing the lower reach of the Ness after breakfast the next day was no more encouraging; the water was low and I had only one rise.

When I returned to the house for lunch there was a telegram waiting for me from the Bucks Yeomanry, ordering me to report to my battery at Taplow by noon the next day, when the regiment was to be embodied. I left Dochfour at teatime, and after an overnight stop at Stirling reached Taplow in time to report at the drill hall, before going on to my billet at the Thames Hotel. On 3 September at 11.00 a.m., the Prime Minister went on the wireless to announce the outbreak of war with Germany.

It was by then almost four years since I had received my commission, and by the summer of 1939 I had already spent a good many evenings and weekends on Territorial duties at Taplow since my return to England. I was a lieutenant in 394 Battery, one of the regiment's two gun batteries, equipped with 4.5-inch howitzers. We had worked on gun-drill and attended lectures, and there had been parades and field days. Unfortunately, though, on account of my illness, I had missed what turned out to be the last peace-time camp – near Tidworth, by Windmill Hill on Salisbury Plain – in August, and consequently I lost the opportunity of promotion to captain before the war broke out.

Until 1940, the Bucks Yeomanry was part of 48th (South Midland) Division, and in mid-September the regiment moved from the Aylesbury district to 48's divisional area around Newbury. There, with Peter Trehearne and another friend, Bill Burnyeat, I was billeted with other officers at Benham Park. Some of our men, including my batman Ernest Hicks, were at Bradford's Farm near by, and others at Bayford House. The owners of Benham very much resented the inconvenience, and were reluctant to give us proper accommodation. Benham was a large house, but all the space they would make available consisted of two bedrooms and a small sitting-room, so I shared a room with Peter and Bill.

During the months of the phoney war which followed, we trained and prepared for action, with no idea when it would come. There were inspections and lectures, sight-testing and gun-drill, map-reading and marches, and barrage exercises by day and night. I was in F troop and, assisted by Sergeant-Major 'Squitters' White, my duties included inspection of the gun stores and the men's clothes, looking after their pay and supplying the gun positions during exercises. Free afternoons were spent playing football, and in the evenings we played bridge and chess, or went into Newbury to dine at the Chequers Hotel.

Now and again I had a weekend's leave at Exbury or in London, and one Saturday in late September I went up to London to read my portion of the Law (similar to reading a lesson in church) at the Great Synagogue, and to hear the Chief Rabbi preach. In the evening I went with some friends to Quaglino's, where nearly all the men were in khaki; and the next day, dining out with my mother and Rosemary, we drank a bottle of Château-Lafite 1898. Prunier's, Quaglino's, and the Ecu de France were my favourite restaurants in those days, and after dinner I would sometimes go on to the Café de Paris.

In November, the first Regular Army units of the British Expeditionary Force left for France, and in early December, at a talk given to the officers of 48 Division by the Chief of the Imperial General Staff, General Sir Edmund Ironside, we learnt that we were to be the first Territorial division to go over to join them. Christmas and the New Year I spent at Exbury, recovering from a recurrence of my illness, and reading the memoirs of William Hickey. But by the middle of January I was fit enough to return to the regiment, only in the nick of time, as things turned out. Two days later 48 Division left for the Continent.

Early on the morning of the 17th we boarded a train for Southampton Docks, and in the afternoon set sail for France, in a convoy of four ships escorted by two destroyers. I was given a berth on SS *Prague*, which in peacetime had been operated as a Harwich–Hook steamer. We sailed out of Southampton to the boom, just off Osborne, on the Isle of Wight, where we dropped anchor until night-fall. I had an outside cabin on the *Prague*, and from my window could see *Rhodora II* at her moorings. It was to be the last time I saw her; soon afterwards *Rhodora II* sailed away, on hire to the Ministry of Shipping, and in 1940 she was accidentally rammed and sunk by a naval vessel. The authorities paid out £52,500 in compensation.

We sailed to Le Havre overnight, and disembarked in France on a clear, cold morning. After a hectic day sorting out the details of our disembarkation, and checking all the baggage and equipment, I had dinner at Frascati's Hotel. From the Assembly Area around Le Havre, most of the regiment then set off by train to the north-east, to a Concentration Area around Neufchatel and Blangy, to the west of Amiens; and there it was to remain – from February, as part of 2 Division – until the start of the shooting war in May. However, I and some other officers, together with a group of sixty men, were detailed to board an overnight train going south to Le Mans.

The winter of 1939–40 was bitterly cold, and conditions in France were severe, with snow lying in deep drifts on the ground, icy roads and heavy frosts at night. It was so cold on the train that there was ice a quarter of an inch thick on my compartment window.

After settling the men into Chaunzy barracks, at Le Mans, we spent the night at the Continental Hotel – where three Guards officers made disparaging remarks about our battledress – and two days later we all set off for Base Reinforcements Camp at Pornichet, near La Baule, on the coast not far from Nantes. It was an area I had got to know a little during a summer cruise on *Rhodora*. Twice *en route* we changed trains, at Rennes and Redon, and after a short rest at Nantes continued to Pornichet. My fellow officers and I were billeted at the Hôtel de Plage; the men were under canvas, a mile and a half away, where it was freezing cold and there were no proper facilities or sanitary arrangements. My own situation was greatly improved when I found that my parents had some friends called Sulzbach who lived near La Baule, and who kept more or less open house for me and my friends.

In early February I again fell ill, this time with measles. Hicks looked after me as best he could until I was taken off to No. 4 General Hospital BEF, set up in Hôtel L'Hermitage at La Baule. When the doctor came to see me he said, 'Well, I would have diagnosed you as scarlet fever, but measles you've been brought in with, and it's with measles you'll remain.'

I shared a room with two other measles victims, Ronnie Morrison and a north-countryman called Harding Stourton. Morrison, who was in the bed next to me, kept me in fits of laughter, but at the same time noticed that I was getting steadily more ill, and experiencing terrible pains in my side – and so one evening he called the nurse in to see me. The nurse duly summoned the doctor, who turned up in full mess kit and in the process of examining me asked, 'What's that scar?' When I had answered, he turned to his assistant and said, 'You bloody fool. Why didn't you tell me he'd had his appendix out?' It turned out that measles had been compounded by a kidney and lung infection called pyelonephritis, and two nurses were allotted to look after me round the clock. The day nurse, Sister Mary Dorrington, was exceptionally kind to me, and I have kept in touch with her ever since. Many years later my wife and I visited her and her husband in Northern Nigeria.

Towards the end of March I wrote to my father to say that I was well on the way to recovery, and that at last I could go out for walks and enjoy the sea breeze; and not long afterwards I was discharged from hospital for duty at the Pornichet camp. At that stage it was by no means certain that I would rejoin the Bucks; regulations laid down that after twenty-one days in hospital one joined a pool from which a posting to any unit in the division might follow, and so for the time being I stayed at Pornichet, in limbo.

Although I was still only a first-lieutenant, I found myself second-in-command at the camp to a Major Wilson, whose overriding concern was to secure his own promotion; and we did not hit it off. Because he had no one but me to assist him, he not only withheld my request to rejoin my regiment, by then at Forges-les-Eaux, between Rouen and Amiens, but – so I later found out – even declined to tell me on the two occasions subsequently when the Bucks called for me.

There were between two and three thousand men in reserve at Pornichet, all of them demoralised by the conditions there. When I returned to the camp from hospital, they had received no pay for several weeks, the quartermaster-sergeant had issued no equipment, and they were poorly clothed and fed. So my pressing task was to arrange for them all to be paid, to get them clean clothes and generally to make life more decent for them all round. That done, it came as no surprise that the whole mood at the camp changed.

In early April we received sixty second-lieutenants from England, recently commissioned into various regiments. Gradually they were called out of reserve to join the BEF, and eventually I myself succeeded in setting out on a troop-train for Forges-les-Eaux base camp, towards the end of the month.

Having reached Forges-les-Eaux, I and a handful of other officers had to supervise the unloading of the train, to see that around 2,000 men were moved into the correct tents and marquees, and to provide all of them with rations and equipment. Hicks fitted up our tent, and we took all our meals under canvas.

There was no running water at the camp, only a small stream for washing, though torrential rain soon turned the whole place into a quagmire. I had to go into Rouen repeatedly to make arrangements for gravel and stones, and on one visit I called in at the cathedral, just as a service was ending, and the peaceful atmosphere gave my spirits a great lift. I had also heard that Jules de Koenigswarter, who was married to my cousin Nica (Victor's younger sister) and serving in the

French army, was stationed at Rouen, and he and I had tea together before I returned to camp.

On the night of 6 May, I left Rouen by train for Cherbourg, for ten days' leave in England (leave continued to be granted right up until the start of the shooting war on 10 May). From Southampton I took a train up to London and telephoned my father at New Court as soon as I got to Kensington Palace Gardens. We dined together at the St James's Club, after which I went on to Prunier's with my girlfriend Eve Sheehan, and I made the most of the next couple of days in London. On the second evening, I dined with my father and Eve at Claridge's, after which Eve and I went to the Café de Paris, where there was a gala night in aid of *Blighty*, the BEF newspaper.

I had got to know Eve through a Mrs Featherstonehaugh, who ran a kind of high-class escort agency. Consequently, my parents did not really approve of Eve, and were fearful that she and I might become too attached. Although their fears were unjustified, Eve and I grew very fond of each other, and I used often to call at her flat in Carlton House Terrace. She was quiet and charming, and had a beautiful voice with the hint of a Welsh accent. She also had a young son called Tony, and once or twice I took her to visit him at his prep school, near Farnham. In 1940 Eve's flat suffered a direct hit. Her maid Johanna was killed instantly; Eve herself was away from home at the time.

I returned to France on 17 May, once more to Forges-les-Eaux. Two Division, including the Bucks, had by this time moved up to the River Dyle, east of Brussels, from where they were soon to be forced back to Dunkirk. All the news was of the advancing German troops, and of the retreat of the Belgian and French armies; and on 28 May we heard the news of Belgium's capitulation.

Within a few days I was again setting out for Cherbourg, this time on a rather more tortuous journey. From Forges-les-Eaux, I got as far as the railway station at Serqueux, but there found that the railway lines had been cut. All the roads were jammed with streams of retreating French soldiers and officers, a good number of the officers with their womenfolk in the staff cars. I made my way to the nearest command post, where I was shown a map marked up with the latest German positions, only a short distance away, and I was put in command of 500 men, with orders to lead them south-eastwards for evacuation.

On foot and by train we made our way down to Cherbourg. The journey took several days and nights and was on the whole uneventful – luckily, in view of the fact that we had only thirty-five rifles between 500. We left Forges-les-Eaux in the dark, and out of the darkness called the familiar voice of Major Wilson – to tell me that I was marching my men in the wrong direction, and insisting that we turn about. Fortunately, I knew he was wrong, and as soon as he had disappeared back into the gloom I gave the order 'About turn' and we marched to safety.

We sailed for England from Cherbourg on board the SS *Bruges*, and at Southampton I was ordered to join a train for Northwich, in Cheshire, to temporary billets at Marbury Hall, there to await further orders.

During late May and early June the regiment assembled in Yorkshire, at Halifax, where I joined them – together with my little terrier Pip. The Bucks had suffered what were to be its worst casualties of the whole war at St Venant, shortly before the evacuation from Dunkirk. My own battery (now B battery) had, I learned, acquitted itself especially well, and I only wished I had been there. They, on the other hand, all seemed to think that I had gone missing, and greeted me quite effusively. Once re-formed, the regiment moved from Halifax to take up positions along the stretch of Yorkshire coast from Hornsea to Filey, supposedly to make ready for a possible German invasion – with which we should have been hopelessly under-equipped to deal. I was billeted at Hunmanby, a short distance inland from Scarborough.

June 1940, with the fall of France and the Germans' march into Paris, was a profoundly worrying time for everyone, and my family had its own reasons for being especially apprehensive. Twice that month I managed to get down to London, where I found everyone at home and at New Court in a state of high anxiety. Family pictures at the bank were being crated up to be sent to Exbury for safe storage, and, on my first visit, I learnt that cousins Elie and Alain, both cavalry officers, had gone missing. It turned out that they had been captured by the Germans at the Belgium end of the Maginot Line, and sent to a military prison camp in Germany. With so few male Rothschilds left, it was imperative that the family should take precautions, and so arrangements were made to send my brother Leo and Tony's son Evelyn to America, on separate ships.

On my second visit, I went with my father – who was in a state of great gloom and foreboding – to New Court to sign all the papers that would be needed to settle Exbury in the event of my death. We then heard the news on the wireless that a ship, unnamed and possibly the one carrying Leo to America, had been torpedoed in mid-Atlantic. To our relief, an hour or two later, it turned out to have been another vessel.

The summer in Yorkshire was otherwise one of routine – kit inspections, route marches, lectures, gun-drill, digging gun-pits and making bombs (which I was not very good at) – briefly enlivened by a mock battle. In mid-July, a mood of despondency was added to the general tedium when we learnt of a new army scheme to transfer ex-BEF personnel to non-BEF units, which meant that the Bucks would soon be exchanging some officers and men with another division. Shortly afterwards it was announced that Peter Trehearne was to be one of the first officers the regiment would lose in the exchange, news which I personally found very dispiriting. But as Peter was my best friend, I decided to apply for a transfer with him – feeling very disloyal to the Bucks, but having decided I would rather stick with my friend. My application was granted, and a few days later Peter and I – he was by then the junior captain in the Bucks, I was the senior subaltern – were exchanged for two officers in the 110th Field Regiment RA, Manchester unit. 'Damned sporting of you to come, Eddy,' were Peter's exact words to me at the time – it seems we really did speak like that in those days. The 110th was scattered all over Yorkshire and the north-east; I was posted to B troop, at Duncombe Park, between Helmsley and Scarborough.

Relief from the routine in Yorkshire came in the form of an occasional expedition, memorably to see Eve when she arrived for a few days at Scarborough. I was also invited by Major Ross, the only officer I came across in the 110th who was consistently nice to me, for the odd day's grouse shooting up on the moors. And one evening in early September I remember going into Scarborough for a dance. Half-way through the proceedings, when I was actually on the dancefloor, I received a tap on the shoulder and someone whispered into my ear the word 'Cromwell', the codeword for the invasion of England. For a split second it was as I imagined it must have been for the British officers at the Duchess of Richmond's ball on the eve of Waterloo – though this time it was only a scare. At the Jewish New Year in early October, I got leave to drive over to Harrogate to meet my parents and Naomi for the New Year's service at the local synagogue. On the major festivals, I nearly always went to synagogue with my father, and before Yom Kippur we always ate grouse together for dinner. The rabbi in Harrogate preached on the rabbinic tale of the tree being gnawed away by black and white mice, and the drops of honey. My father, I remember thinking, was looking in very poor health.

Straight after returning from Harrogate, I learnt that the regiment was to spend the winter on the north side of the North Yorkshire moors, in the area to the south of Middlesbrough, and that it was to be my job to find billets for the officers. After inspecting a number of properties, I eventually settled on two houses, one called Undercliffe, the other Ayton Firs. Both were a short distance from the then largely Quaker village of Great Ayton (one local resident was Mr Fry), where we established our battery office. Ayton Firs, set in a curve of the Cleveland Hills about 14 miles south-west of Middlesbrough, belonged to Colonel Harold Kitching who, though himself a Quaker, had served with the Durham Light Infantry at Salonika during the First World War.

Colonel Kitching was not keen to have us at Ayton Firs, but he put up with us stoically once the decision to requisition half the house had been made. For one thing he was concerned for his daughter Anne, who was living at home working as a VAD at a local hospital, and whom I first met on 17 October 1940. Anne and I became friends and subsequently corresponded, from time to time, throughout the rest of the war. I even sent her some scent called 'Shocking', by Schiaparelli.

In 1946, at a party I gave after the Eton–Harrow match at Lord's, I introduced Anne to my great friend from Cambridge days Malcolm 'Mac' Harrison – and the following spring they were married. After I myself married, my wife Elizabeth and I kept in touch with Mac and Anne, and they used often to come to stay with us at Exbury. Many years later, after Elizabeth and Mac had both died – within six months of each other – Anne agreed to marry me. Anne spent Christmas Day 1940 working at the local PIA – the Public Institute of Assistance – and is now proud to say that she is probably the only Rothschild ever to have spent Christmas Day in the workhouse. Her first sight of me was from behind – walking naked down a corridor on my way to her father's bathroom at Ayton Firs.

Towards the end of November I got a few days' leave, and took Peter to Exbury with me to shoot. I used to find that a day in the out-doors with a gun was the best way of forgetting one's worries for a few hours. My childhood friend Eric Bessborough put into words precisely my sentiments in his memoir, *Return to the Forest*. It is not simply the shooting you remember, he wrote, but the old-man's beard in the hedgerows; the berries on the shrubs around the clumps in the garden; the crisp drag of the shooting shoe over the stubble; the elegance of the trees and the variety of the weather. The warmth of early October afternoons, the mists of November, the south-westerly gales of All Hallowe'en, the snow at Christmas or the limpid light and longer days of late January, when the branches of the beeches are etched grey against a sky which is clearer than at any other time of the year. Those were the days which made you forget the dull tedium – sometimes the anguish and fear – of the return to school, to the war or merely to humdrum work. Only this kind of outdoor sport made you forget, almost all the day through, what was soon to come.

At Exbury, I learnt that the Germans had been night-raiding Southampton, and on their way home had been dumping bombs all over the area, one of which had destroyed some of the greenhouses. Returning to the house after showing Peter and me the bomb damage, my father pointed to a small cabbage patch which had recently been created just outside the drawing-room windows. 'My war effort,' he solemnly announced, and we all burst out laughing. About a week later, I received a letter from my father about another air raid.

'We had two disturbing nights at Exbury,' he wrote, 'a stick of bombs fell in the Home Wood starting in the river and finishing by the Cross Paths. One fell on a fir tree in the Winter Garden, blew the whole top off and decapitated a pigeon; another fell just above the Middle Pond and blew a lot of my shrubs to pieces, and another just above the Cross Paths also blew some rhododendrons to smithereens. Hundreds of incendiaries were dropped at the same time and lit up the whole wood so that the village thought the house was on fire. Luckily the ground was wet and they did no damage, but six of the villagers came up within five minutes to see if they could help.'

At dinner with my parents in November I had met Colonel Robbie Burns, whom I had come across before in France, at the Pornichet camp. He was now commanding the 77th (Highland) Field Regiment, RA, at Sway, near Lymington. He told me that he had been impressed by the way I had taken care of the demoralised men at Pornichet, and he invited me, and Peter, to join the 77th, originally a Territorial unit from the Glasgow and Galashiels area, now in 4 Division. It already had two batteries, but was being re-formed with a third, which Colonel Burns asked us to join as battery captains. Neither Peter nor I had ever settled down with the 110th, so we both decided to transfer. An extra incentive was that Mac Harrison was already serving with the 77th.

Our transfers eventually came through, and by the end of January 1941, we were stationed with the 77th, just along the road from my friend John Howlett at Lymington. I ended up sharing a room with Mac, in a comfortable house called White Gables. Four Division was manning a 50-mile stretch of coastline, roughly from Portsmouth to Lymington, and there was every expectation that a German assault on England would be launched at any time, possibly along the south coast. One of the many advantages of being near home was that I was able to arrange a supply of Exbury eggs for us to have in the officers' mess. The only really burdensome aspect of my new situation was that as battery captain I had to deal with disciplinary matters at courts martial, which I found difficult.

In February, I was one of a small group of artillery officers to be sent on a Forward Observation Officers' course at the naval gunnery training school at Portsmouth, HMS *Excellent* on Whale Island. We learnt to use a new kind of wireless and were introduced to Oerlikon and Bofors guns, and we practised gun-aiming at ships from an electronically operated machine (which rolled) and on the miniature range. A day or two after completing the course I succumbed to yet another bout of illness and had to spend a week in Lymington hospital.

Throughout the spring and summer of 1941 we remained on the Hampshire coast. New drafts of troops came and went and the days were filled with maintenance, training, lectures on gun calibration, ammunition, fuses and all related subjects, as well as Tewts (tactical exercises without troops) and full-scale exercises with code-names such as Locust and Stampede. I was also sent on another two courses, this time to Larkhill, to learn about smokescreens, barrages and aerodrome defence – and where I also ran across Major Adams, who in 1938 had looked after me during my visit to Siam. One day we all went to Winchester to hear General Montgomery speak on the current situation, and at each break in his talk he announced in his odd voice, 'Gentlemen, you may now cough, shuffle and spit if you want to, but then you are to be silent.'

One of my regular duties as battery captain of 455 Battery was to inspect the equipment. If any small item was missing, I would have to send for the sergeant to account for it, and then, if he could not produce it, fine him. That done, I used at once to refund him the fine myself. To keep the men properly dressed I got clothes for my battery by signing a chit at the quartermaster's stores, when technically I should have gone through regimental HQ. For that I got a dressing-down from Colonel Burns – delivered with a broad smile on his face.

I used regularly to go home to Exbury for dinner, and more than once Colonel Burns came with me. Night-time German bombing raids on Southampton were at that time routine, and the park at Exbury would be lit with flares to distract the enemy planes (my father's idea of using Exbury as a home for evacuees had been rejected on account of the house's proximity to Southampton). Towards the end of the evening, I remember Witts pulling back the curtains to reveal the whole park apparently ablaze. Burns, thinking that the park really had caught fire, said, 'Dammit, I can't sit drinking a man's port and watch his park burn.' However, instead we set off back to Sway, and on the return journey our car narrowly escaped being hit by a bomb from a German aircraft shedding its load on the way home. We jumped out of the car and lay in a ditch, and seven bombs landed in a field by the road, but not one of them exploded – the first of a number of lucky escapes I was to have over the next four years.

As summer turned to autumn our training intensified, and finally we received an order to mobilise to go overseas. All kinds of rumours were circulating, one of which, that we were about to leave for Russia, seemed to be confirmed when we were issued with winter clothes and a special type of oil for use at temperatures well below zero. But the mobilisation was cancelled, and we learnt that we were to be sent in groups up to Scotland for combined operations training, near Inverary.

Towards the end of January 1942, when I had not yet left Sway for Scotland, I received the news that my father, who had been ill with cancer for some months, had only a few days to live. Mercifully, I was granted leave, and I managed to get up to London in time to be with him when he died peacefully in his bed at Kensington Palace Gardens on the 28th. We buried him in the family plot at Willesden cemetery, and held a memorial service for him a few days later at the Spanish and Portuguese Synagogue, which attracted a huge congregation.

During a visit to New Court when I was trying to sort out my father's affairs, I saw his old friend Jack Churchill, Winston's brother. He had a message for me from Winston: since I had already been in action in France, ought I not now to stay at the bank to help Tony? Now my father, who was already a major in the Bucks when the First World War broke out, had not gone overseas on active service; NMR was then a bank with fewer close rivals in London than it has today, and my father gave in to pressure for him to remain behind to support the other partners, his two ageing uncles and my grandfather. From one point of view this was perhaps as well, for by the end of 1918 all three of them had died; but the memory that he had remained in England during the war, while most of his friends and both his brothers had gone to the Front, was to haunt my poor father for the rest of his life. So in the course of the inevitable discussion with Tony, I recalled how much my father had always regretted being shackled to the bank in the 1914–18 war, and asked Tony if he felt able to carry on alone. He said he could, and that I must return to my regiment if I wished. The decision I made to do so is one I have never regretted.

Owing to the complicated nature of my father's estate, I did not rejoin the 77th until mid-April, by which time my battery had moved up to Greenock. Colonel Burns had left the 77th and gone to the artillery school at Larkhill; his place had been taken by Colonel William 'Willie' Pike, who was to remain our colonel until 1944, and who was the finest commanding officer I encountered during my time in the Army. Before the war he had served in India – where, he used to reflect, 'soldiering was so much more fun on a full establishment of men and horses' – and after the war he went on to become Vice-Chief of the Imperial General Staff. He was a brilliant, charming man, and one who, to a junior officer such as myself, possessed the outstanding characteristic of a consistently even temper.

One day, towards the end of April 1942, Colonel Pike sent for me. The Admiralty, he said, had requested my presence down at Exbury as a matter of urgency. He had obtained a travel pass for me to catch a special train leaving Glasgow that evening, and I was to make my way home in double-quick time. Exbury was in turmoil when I arrived: the house was to be requisitioned by the Admiralty, who required the building to be cleared within forty-eight hours. Fortunately, the pictures and porcelain had previously been packed up and sent away, some to Tring and some to Swyncombe House, near Henley-on-Thames. Witts had got permission for us to retain the two panelled rooms in the house as store-rooms for the largest pieces of furniture, and we kept the use of the large strong-room in the cellar for silver and smaller valuables. Other items from the house were distributed among the houses in the village.

I made two requests to the Admiralty: one, that my mother should be allowed to live at the laundry for the rest of the war; and secondly, that any estate workers or pensioners remaining at Exbury should be allowed to stay in their own cottages. Both my requests were granted, and we hastily set about adapting the laundry for occupation. Exbury House, meanwhile, became the stone frigate HMS *Mastodon*.

All through the rest of the war it was reassuring to know that Witts remained at Exbury as my caretaker, and kept an eagle-eye on everything that went on. One signal service he did me was to save the wine cellar from the predations of a Captain Swinley, the commanding officer of *Mastodon*, who in 1944 had the idea of cheering up his officers before D-Day. When Swinley threatened to break into the wine cellar himself if Witts continued to refuse him access, Witts had the presence of mind to telephone a number he had been given for use in an emergency. Within the hour a man from the Admiralty had arrived to take charge of the situation, and Swinley, I believe, was later moved on.

Back up on the west coast of Scotland, we experienced some reorganisation: tanks joined 4 Division, and combined-ops became a new feature of our training. We spent a lot of time practising sea-borne assault landings, in which, as battery captain, I always had to be one of the first ashore; it was my job to ensure that the battery was supplied with ammunition and food without a hitch. But it was not until February 1943 that we once again received orders to prepare for action – this time in a hot climate – for which, by then, we all felt well prepared.

4

Assaults and Batteries

In mid-March 1943, we joined a convoy at Glasgow. I had a berth in the *Johann van Oldenbarnefeld*, the flagship of the Dutch East Indies Line and one of more than twenty troopships, transports and warships in the convoy. Among them was the *Windsor Castle* – sister ship of the *Arundel Castle* on which I had sailed out to South Africa in 1937 – which was now carrying nurses. We set sail on the morning of 16 March for an unknown destination, though once we were at sea, this was revealed to be North Africa.

During the voyage, officers gave talks and briefings on the general situation awaiting us. American forces had landed at Casablanca, Oran and Algiers the previous November, and the (British) First Army – soon to be swollen by the ranks of 4 Division – had landed in eastern Algeria, near to the Tunisian border. The Germans, since their rout by the Eighth Army at El Alamein in November, had retreated to Tunisia, where they were maintaining a firm grip on the ports of Tunis and Bizerta. I gave a talk about the local people we were likely to encounter, including the small, ancient Jewish communities of the region.

After nearly a week at sea, and a rough passage through the Bay of Biscay, we slipped through the Straits of Gibraltar at night; in the darkness one could make out the towering, blacked-out mass of the Rock, and on either side of the straits the lights of the neutral Spanish ports twinkled across the water.

The *Johann van Oldenbarnefeld* had a small anti-aircraft unit, consisting of a single Oerlikon gun, on which each artillery captain on board took a turn of duty. My turn came the night before we landed at

Algiers, and that night the convoy was attacked by enemy aircraft; but to my great disappointment, the ship's captain refused my request to open fire. And so as I lay back idly on a hatchway, gazing at the other ships in the convoy, I saw the *Windsor Castle* struck by an aerial torpedo. She sank, but with the loss of only six lives.

Next morning we berthed in Algiers harbour and marched to a transit camp; other ships in the convoy continued on to ports as far east as Bône. This was because, with 4 Division's arrival, First Army's objective was to launch a final assault on Bizerta and Tunis, the hub of enemy operations in North Africa, and in doing so finally clear the continent of German and Italian forces. In December, First Army had fought its way to within 15 miles of Tunis, but had then been forced to pull back to the area west of a small, muddy town called Medjez el Bab (the Ford of the Pass), where the River Medjerda flows out of the mountains on to the plain of Tunis. Thirty-five miles south-west of Tunis, and on the main route from the west, Medjez was a strategically vital point – and our first destination.

The journey from Algiers to Medjez was about 500 miles. The roads were reasonably good, and the combination of a warm Mediterranean climate and an attractive countryside – wheat fields and vineyards near the coast, mountains thick with vegetation inland – made the trek quite agreeable. Towns were few and far between, but wherever our long column of vehicles came to a halt, the local inhabitants appeared to sell – or exchange for cigarettes – chickens, eggs, fruit or whatever other provisions they had. Communication at that level was easy, as most Arabs spoke or understood a bit of French.

At the beginning of April, we reached Béja, a small town at an important road junction 20 miles west of Medjez; to the north-east ran the road to Bizerta, via Hunt's Gap; to the east the main road to Medjez and Tunis, via Peter's Corner. The divisional history of 4 Division records that the Germans 'held the commanding heights among the mountains from Hunt's Gap to Longstop Hill [about six miles north-east of Medjez], which rises from and commands the valley of the River Medjerda. From Longstop Hill, the front crossed the Medjerda to the Djebel Bou Aoukaz [another hill], and then ran eight miles southwards to Peter's Corner, eight miles east of Medjez on the Tunis road.' Tenth Brigade (4 Division comprised 10th and 12th brigades) moved north from Béja towards Hunt's Gap; 12th Brigade, to which my battalion belonged, set off in the direction of Medjez – and a few miles beyond Béja, at Oued Zarga, we came under attack for the first time. Enemy fighter-bombers attacked the road with machine-gun fire. Only a few men were injured, and it is gratifying to record that our divisional anti-aircraft gunners shot down seven German aeroplanes. About half-way between Béja and Medjez, we turned north into the hills and mountains.

My regiment was assigned to support the Black Watch in driving the Germans from their positions in the area around a hill called Djebel Remel, principally, in the case of my battery, by providing artillery cover for the attack. My own specific task during the battle was to keep our troop positions supplied with ammunition, fuel and rations, and to see that our vehicles were positioned under the best cover available. We were subjected to regular bursts of enemy bombing and shelling, and the day before the Black Watch forced the Germans out of their positions, my regiment lost two officers – Robin Fullarton and Neil Rankin – and quite a few men.

Four Division's next objective in the push for Tunis was to plough its way along the road through Medjez and Peter's Corner to the hills overlooking the plain of Tunis and the city itself. We had been warned to expect a fierce enemy counter-attack, likely to be waged with infantry and tanks, and this commenced one night at Banana Ridge, just south of the road out of Medjez. My recollections of that night are confused, but I do remember that at one point I got lost in my truck, and two soldiers lying in a ditch by the road told me that if I went any further I should be driving through German lines – and as at that moment the Germans began to mortar us, we turned round as fast as we could. An hour or two later, having recovered my bearings and gone back to the wagon lines for supplies, I found that the Germans had cut the line between me and the guns, and occupied our brigade dressing-station in the process.

This enemy counter-attack was known to the British as Operation Lilac Blossom, after the German soldiers' supposed fondness for wearing scent. It lasted for several days and nights, but was beaten off and failed to prevent the division's advance to Peter's Corner. When it was over, Colonel Pike called all the officers together and said, 'Gentlemen, you've already been through a pretty rough experience. But I want you to remember this: that things are never as bad as they seem and, conversely, they are never as good.'

Our last full-scale battle in Tunisia came in the last week of April 1943, on the ridges beyond Peter's Corner, where my battery was again involved in supporting the Black Watch. The fighting, by day and night, was intense, and the 77th lost two captains and two majors, one of whom Peter Trehearne replaced. My most vivid memory is of a fearless Black Watch pipe major distracting the enemy by playing his pipes; the Germans turned their guns on him, but he survived and won the Military Medal. One personal disappointment was that when, at one stage during the battle, I was heading off on some supply errand on a motor cycle and drove past two Germans lying in a ditch talking and smoking, brigade headquarters refused permission for me to mount an attack. 'We've got to keep absolutely quiet,' I was told. 'They haven't spotted us yet.' Also, I missed the end of the action – asleep in a slit trench dug for me by Hicks. I must have been truly worn out, because immediately behind the trench there was a battery of heavy guns, and it was only after they had stopped firing that I awoke.

Tunis was taken in early May, but strong German forces were still holding out in the Cap Bon peninsula. In order to isolate them and force them into surrender it was essential to break through Hammam Lif, a coastal town about 15 miles east of Tunis, in a defile at the northern end of the mountain range cutting off the peninsula. Although the Germans had made this vital bottle-neck impregnable, as they thought, with artillery, mines and snipers, the town was taken. Major-General von Brioch, of the 10th Panzer Division, who was later captured, said that he simply had not thought that a breakthrough at Hammam Lif was possible. However, it was accomplished, and the 77th then passed through to the plain which extends across the base of Cap Bon, and at night proceeded to sweep in a pincer movement around the peninsula. Fifty-two thousand Germans and Italians surrendered to my division – of a total bag of more than 250,000 – and there was no disguising the defeated troops' delight that for them the war was over: many of them (notably the Italians) came in singing and cheering.

For three days I was responsible for feeding 10,000 prisoners in a compound which we had made them put up themselves. Because the RASC had most of the supplies, we gave up a fair quantity of our own rations to feed the prisoners. Fortunately, I managed to blow open a German paymaster's safe which was full of French francs, and so was then able to scour the Arab villages in the vicinity for chickens and goats and suchlike. Not all the prisoners appreciated my efforts.

One German captain came up to me saluting and demanding to know when he was going to get his food, which prompted the reflection that the situation might have been rather different had the boot been on the other foot. Another German officer persistently shouted 'Heil Hitler!' So Peter Trehearne had a gun brought up and – probably in breach of army regulations – meted out 'No. 1 Field Punishment'. The German was strapped to the wheel of the gun and left out in the sun until he eventually quietened down.

The weather was glorious, and the cornfields around Tunis were full of wild flowers. One day I lay down in the grass and counted twenty-three different varieties within reach. The troops let their hair down in Tunis, drinking and brawling, rather to the bewilderment of the locals: 'Pourquoi les Anglais se combattent?' I was asked. In early June, First Army was summoned to the magnificent Roman amphitheatre at Carthage, a few miles outside Tunis, to hear an address by Churchill. He gave an inspiring performance – cigar waving, V signs and a rousing speech – and got a tremendous reception. When the King came out to inspect us not long afterwards, Colonel Pike presented me to him, and the King said some kind words to me about my late father. At Carthage we were also entertained to a wonderful, light-hearted concert given by Beatrice Lillie and Fred Emney in the amphitheatre.

At the end of June, we left Tunisia for the region around Bougie, on the Algerian coast, where 4 Division remained throughout the summer and autumn in a state of limbo. Regular letters from William Rattue, with all the news of Exbury, helped to dispel the many longueurs.

Exbury, 11 July 1943

Dear Sir,

A bomb has been dug out at Exbury House and a fine big fat fellow he was. What a good thing it never went off. I am afraid if it had it would have lifted the garages over the house, and the house would have had a pretty bad shaking-up.

They are busy digging up the other one in front of the house now, but they don't think it's as big as the first – which was a 2,500 lb bomb. I don't think many of us would have been very comfortable that night had we known.

I have been round with the officer in charge who said that there are lots more not gone off, but he doesn't think they'll get them out. They may get the two out by the Alderbed, but it all depends on whether Jerry drops any more duds.

We have been having some very bad weather the last few days. Last Tuesday we had the worst thunderstorm I have ever seen, then a terrific hailstorm with hailstones as large as marbles, and large marbles at that. Any young partridges or pheasants that were caught out in it without any protection will have perished. I feel sure that a good many that were in the open fields must have been killed, though those in the corn will have stood a chance. I haven't seen a covey since, but that's nothing to go by, for everything has been so wet, and the grass and the undergrowth too thick to see anything.

Today it has been raining all day, and yesterday the same. It's keeping the harvesting back. The corn is all getting ripe; a few fine days and it would be in full swing. I am afraid if we don't get it fine soon, the potatoes will be going bad, as they don't like a lot of rain. I see yours are looking very well in Redlands. With some fine weather, there should be a good crop, and not so much charlock in the potatoes this year as there was last year. Do you remember what a job we had to get through it partridge shooting? I don't know if we are going to get any kale this year. I haven't seen any yet, but I hope there will be some roots or cover of some sort to get the partridge into – especially if I have to kill a few birds for Mrs Lionel. But I hope you will be home for that.

14 July. I wrote the above on Sunday night, and had hoped to finish, but just as I had got that far, Mrs Searle came for me to come and kill a fox that had taken one of her hens; it came in daylight and took it close to her door. Well, dear Sir, I have been looking for it ever since and haven't got it yet. I am having a hunt through East Wood with a few guns tomorrow night, so with a bit of luck we may get it. I should think it very likely there are some cubs. East Wood is very thick, with bracken higher than my head, so it will be very difficult to get through; nothing but the dogs will move the cubs.

I should think by the look of the tracks there is a deer in there, but I shall not kill it now because if the weather clears and it gets hot, it wouldn't keep a couple of days. It may come in useful later on, for we are not too well off for a bit of meat – though I have got a nice few chickens coming on, so we can have a good dinner sometimes.

We had a good meeting at the church last evening, to fix up the flower show. It looks as if we are going to have a good one. One of the officers at the House and a sergeant from Inchmery are getting out the sports programme, and we are going to have a boxing event in the evening. They would have liked to have a rifle range and some shooting at targets, but I think that would have been too dangerous – too many people about on a bank holiday.

I came past Exbury House this morning and they were just getting the bomb out in front of the house – nothing like so large as the one by the petrol pump. They are going to get the others out in the park and the one in the bottom of the home wood.

I am pleased to say that Pip is keeping very well. She is beginning to grow a new coat, the old one is all come out. The other dogs are all well.

I shall be pleased now when the harvest starts so that I can see what birds there are about. I have seen several hares about lately, but I don't think there will be many rabbits in the corn this year. Watson is finishing up the thresh-ing of last year's corn this week. I don't think they've got many rats in the ricks; I think they cleared them out pretty well last year.

There will be lots of wildfowl round the shore when this war is over. They tell me there are lots of young duck all round on the mud this year.

I have seen some very nice fish rising in the Beaulieu River lately. I think I shall have to have a try off the end of the pier some evening.

Well, dear Sir, I think that's about all I can get in this week, so I will con-clude hoping you are keeping in the best of health.

Yours faithfully,
W. Rattue

In December, we were finally ordered to prepare for a move at short notice, and by Christmas, having been ordered to abandon – most reluctantly – nearly all our equipment, we were assembled in staging camps near Algiers. Shortly afterwards we were steaming east-wards out of Algiers, and on down the Suez Canal to Ataqa, where, by New Year's Day 1944, we were camped out under canvas in the desert. We then began training for an assault landing planned for Rhodes, where, again, I was to have the hair-raising honour of being one of the first officers ashore from the landing-craft. The new equipment we were provided with was not up to an acceptable standard, and so at the first opportunity I went to the local DAQMS, who to begin with was extremely offhand. However, as soon as I gave him my name his whole demeanour was transformed. 'Good Lord, sir,' he spluttered. 'Don't you remember me? I'm "Chunks" Gunner. I worked for your father at New Court.' And from then on I got everything we needed.

The Rhodes plan was soon cancelled, and instead I got leave to visit Cairo with Peter Trehearne. We had planned to stay at Shepheard's Hotel, but as Cairo was at that time crawling with Allied troops, when we arrived at the hotel we found that there was not a room to be had; it was already full up with senior officers. However, my uncle Tony had given me the name of one of Rothschilds' contacts in Cairo, Felix Mosseri, of our correspondents Banque Mosseri, and I telephoned Felix to explain our problem. He came round at once and arranged with the manager for Peter and me to be given a huge suite of rooms, where we were soon luxuriating in the first decent bath we had had for a year – and enjoying a bottle of well-iced champagne.

Almost as soon as we got back to camp, 4 Division's next move was revealed: we were to go to Italy. British troops had entered Naples at the beginning of October 1943, and in the ensuing period the Allied Armies – the British Eighth Army, commanded by General Sir Oliver Leese, and the American Fifth Army, under General Mark Clark – had advanced northwards. They had reached an area rather less than half-way from Naples to Rome, where the route was blocked by the German Gustav Line, at the Liri Valley – the southern entrance to which, where the Liri River flows into the Garigliano, is dominated by Monte Cassino. In January the Germans had repulsed a strong Allied offensive on Cassino, and on 15 February, a few days before I landed at Naples, the ancient abbey of Cassino was all but wiped out by Allied bombing, though the Germans were still not dislodged.

The night before we landed in Italy I had one of only two dreams I have ever had in which my father has appeared to me. I dreamt he was standing at the foot of my bed, looking at me, quite silently. On the day the war in Europe ended I had precisely the same dream again.

From Naples, where Vesuvius was in eruption as we entered the harbour, we moved up to the Garigliano. The third Allied offensive on Cassino had not yet commenced, and the Garigliano sector was therefore relatively peaceful – much to our relief, since many of the troop reinforcements recently arrived from England and elsewhere were still fairly raw. My battery, for instance, was camped next to a brigade of Brazilians who, although they were the best-paid soldiers by far (better even than the Americans), could certainly not have been described as experienced. But there was time for training, and also for the occasional foray down to Naples for dinner or a visit to the San Carlo opera house. My introduction to Verdi's *Force of Destiny* took place at Naples, with Beniamino Gigli singing the lead. In view of his advancing years, Gigli fought only one stage duel instead of two, but the Italians stood on their seats to applaud him. Because Gigli had sung for the Germans, British officers had been instructed not to clap – but we did, as hard as we could.

On 15 March, the third battle of Cassino commenced with the obliteration by bombing of the town of Cassino, at the foot of the mountain below the monastery. But 4 Division's part in pushing back the Gustav Line did not come until May. In the meantime, between training and overhauling all our equipment, at the end of April I managed to get four days' leave to go to a rest camp at Forli, on the Adriatic, where I met up with my sister Rosemary's husband, Tony Seys, who was serving in an anti-aircraft regiment. Rosemary had parted from her first husband Denis Berry, Lord Kemsley's younger son, and had made a very happy second marriage to Tony.

On my return, in early May, we were ordered to set about siting and camouflaging our guns in the country around Cassino, and transporting thousands of rounds of ammunition to the battery positions. We had to bring the guns into position at night, and I well remember the tension when one of my battery's guns slid off the track and we had to winch it back on as quietly as we could – fearful of being seen by a German observation post on the mountain. Shortly before battle was joined on the night of 11 May, Field Marshal Alexander announced that every person of the Jewish faith who so wished should attend a special Passover ceremony. It was a moving and beautifully arranged service, attended by many of my co-religionists from different regiments in the area.

Every night at 10.00 p.m., for several weeks, our guns had commenced firing a great smoke-screen – Operation Cigarette. (Keith Joseph, who, unbeknown to me at the time, was also an artillery officer at Cassino, and whom I used later to see in the City, earned the nickname 'Smoky Joe', as a consequence.) At 10.45 p.m. on the night of 11 May we fired our last round in Cigarette, and for the next fifteen minutes the only sounds to be heard from my battery position were the song of nightingales and the faint hum of the fireflies which hovered in clouds over the countryside. There was not even the sound of a truck or a human voice. Then on the stroke of 11.00 came a great roar of artillery, and across the horizon the air blazed with flashes. It was one of the most dramatic nights of the war.

The ensuing battle lasted until 18 May, when a detachment of Polish troops occupied the monastery of Monte Cassino. Throughout the battle, I was responsible for handling the ammunition for my battery's eight 25-pounder guns, and they fired so many rounds that we had to change the gun barrels three times. I had two close brushes with death, one when I had to go down to the bridge across the Liri River to deliver a bren-gun carrier to my major. A shell exploded close by and I was wounded by flying splinters – only slightly, but I was bleeding quite badly. I climbed back into my jeep and my driver insisted on taking me to the nearest first aid post. However, as the post was already full of men who were much more seriously wounded, I decided to return to the gun lines. I had not gone more than 50 yards when the first aid post was wiped out by mortar fire. My second close shave came towards the end of the battle, when I and some others were taking a breather in a ruined farmhouse. Seven shells landed outside, which by rights should have knocked us to pieces, but every one of them was a dud.

At the end of the battle it was my duty, as battery captain, to blow up all the gun charges (bags full of cordite). For 25 pounders there were three charges of varying strength, to be used according to the distance over which one wished to propel the shell. As there were thousands of charges left, I had to dig a huge pit and lay a fuse about 30 yards long. Having lit the fuse and retired to a safe distance, with my tin hat on and my hands over my ears, I was still almost deafened by the blast.

From Cassino we pressed on northwards to Rome, and *en route* I was detailed to bring up the rear of the column. Although slow-moving, we were none the less among the first British troops to enter Rome, which we reached as dusk was falling. Our divisional signs were already on all the major buildings, but as there was a curfew there was no one about in the streets. After North Africa and the stench of death at Cassino, the smell of a civilised city is something I can never forget. We paused in Rome long enough for me and others of my faith to attend a service of thanksgiving for the victory at Cassino at the Lungotevere Cenci synagogue, after which we pressed on with the division to a concentration area beyond Viterbo, 50 miles to the north-west.

Field Marshal Kesselring, having regrouped his troops, was preparing the next main German line of defence in Italy – the Gothic Line, far away to the north, beyond Florence. But in the meantime the line on which the Germans had resolved to make their stand ran through Lake Trasimene – taking its name from the lake – and so it was in the direction of Trasimene that 4 Division began to move off on 22 June. By 1 July, after ten days' hard fighting, the Allied push had pierced the Trasimene Line, forcing the Germans back, and we continued to advance north-west to Arezzo and Florence.

The Germans had blown up all the bridges over the Arno leading into Florence, except for the ancient Ponte Vecchio, and had blocked the southern approaches. Their main line of defence lay in the hills to the south and east: they were holding fast on the south-eastern spurs of the Incontro range, high ground which was certain to be resolutely defended. It was a naturally strong position, once more with a German-occupied monastery – the Incontro Monastery – at its centre.

Fierce fighting began towards the end of the first week in August and on the 8th Incontro fell. During the final assault one of our guns was knocked out by a German shell; it looked as if there was a German observation post in the monastery's bell tower. I put my tin hat on and rushed forward to tend a man who had been badly wounded in the explosion and thought to myself, 'This is where it all ends for you, Eddy' – but the next round fell on the spot I had just left, and once more I survived. The South Africans had the privilege of being the first Allied troops to enter Florence itself, which was a disappointment – if only a minor one – to 4 Division. We all felt that since we had taken the main brunt of the battle, we should have been accorded the honour ourselves.

A period of general rest and relaxation followed, though equipment had to be cleaned and maintained and we had to undergo a certain amount of training based on our recent battle experiences. But for a few weeks we remained safe from any threat of enemy fire. There were concert parties, and visits to the neighbouring towns of Pisa, Lucca and Perugia, where we had our mess.

Colonel Pike had reluctantly left us in Egypt, to return to England to take command of a gunnery OCTU at Catterick. In Italy, we were also deprived of the company of Major Douglas Kennedy, an unconventional officer who had added considerable colour to our lives. When the war broke out, Kennedy was a retired regular gunner running a large farm in Shropshire, and had recently set up a company exporting British livestock abroad. Once back in the Army, he continued to spend a great deal of time on the affairs of the livestock company, using the breast pockets of his battledress for filing. Eventually, he was transferred from the regiment to AMGOT, the military organisation tasked with helping to restore civilian government in Italy. At one point, put in temporary charge of a jam factory in Naples, he arrived at regimental HQ with a crate of marmalade for the officers' mess.

Willie Pike's place was taken by Colonel Gordon Freeth, whose appointment did not work out well. On his arrival, Freeth called us all together, and opened his address with the words, 'I model my life on Jesus Christ.' He then proceeded to inform the men that they would do one hour's maintenance on their vehicles every morning, willy-nilly. In consequence, he never became very popular. But at Monte Cassino Freeth left us – on a posting to an American unit, I believe – and, after Peter Trehearne had again temporarily held the post, he was replaced by Colonel Wainright, a regular soldier who gave the impression of disliking the Territorial officers under his command.

Wainright moved me on, as a temporary measure, by sending me on an artillery course, and then, on a more permanent basis, by arranging for me to go to the School of Artillery at Eboli – where, however, to my great delight, I found that the Commandant was my old friend Colonel Robbie Burns, who immediately invited me to be his adjutant.

Life at Eboli was not arduous; my job was chiefly administrative and involved looking after some sixty officers. My efficient assistant was a young officer called Peter Barber, who had been acting adjutant before my arrival. He and I shared a Nissen hut together and became good friends, and after the war, when he had married his Italian wife, Marina, he came to Exbury to stay with me and my mother, and subsequently became our estate manager.

Shortly after I arrived at Eboli I was sent for by Colonel Burns and told that I was to undertake a mission to Rome – to accompany the Archbishop of Campagna to the Vatican for an audience with Pope Pius XII. The Archbishop's cathedral, as I remember, had been damaged by an Allied shell, and it had been agreed that we should make good the repairs. The Archbishop was anxious to give the Pope this news in person and, owing to the then chaotic conditions for travel in Italy, had requested transport and an escort.

When we arrived at the Vatican, the Archbishop asked if I, too, would like to have an audience with His Holiness. Except for Field Marshal Alexander and his staff, few, if any, British officers had been accorded this honour since the liberation of Rome, and as a Jew I felt doubly proud to be asked. It was the first time I had visited the Vatican and, I suppose like any tourist, I was awed by the size and grandeur of the interiors, above all by the Sistine Chapel and the great flight of steps we ascended to the ante-room outside the Pope's apartments. At the top of the stairway we sat on a bench, where a steady flow of cardinals and papal attendants bustled past, and two Swiss Guards with their huge halberds stood sentry at the entrance to the audience chamber, into which we were presently admitted.

The Pope was seated, very imposingly, on a dais at the far end of the room, with a monk kneeling in prayer by his side; the Archbishop kissed his ring and the Pope motioned us to sit by him on two gilt *fauteuils*. We spoke in a mixture of French and English, and he asked after my family. When, as Cardinal Pacelli, he had been responsible for looking after the Vatican's finances, he had maintained a small Vatican account with de Rothschild Frères in Paris. He appeared intensely distressed when I referred to the terrible things that had been happening to Jews in Germany, and twice said, 'We must see that this never happens again.'

The audience lasted about fifteen minutes, and when it came to an end both the monk and the archbishop kissed the Pope's ring, and each of them received a small gift. As I was wondering what I ought to do, he turned to me and said, 'I hope you, too, will accept a small souvenir from an old man,' and he presented me with a rosary, which ever since has been one of my prized possessions.

I returned to Eboli to find Peter Barber in a great stew over an important-looking letter that had arrived for me from England. The envelope bore the seal and initials of the Secretary of State for War, and was marked 'Most Immediate, Air All the Way'. Inside it I found another envelope marked 'Prime Minister', within which was a note from Winston Churchill – thanking me for a present of three hundred of my father's cigars, which I had asked my uncle Tony to send him!

In November 1944, while I was still at Eboli, I decided to apply to join a new field regiment which had been launched as part of a War Office initiative to create a Jewish Infantry Brigade Group, under the command of Brigadier Ernst Benjamin. In September, the Prime Minister had announced in the Commons that the Government had decided to accede to the request of the Jewish Agency for Palestine that a Jewish Brigade Group should be formed to take part in active operations. 'I know,' Churchill went on to say, 'that there are vast numbers of Jews serving with our forces and the American forces throughout all armies. But it seems to me indeed appropriate that a special Jewish unit, a special unit of that race which has suffered indescribable torments from the Nazis, should be represented as a distinct formation amongst the forces gathered for their final overthrow.'

With Colonel Burns's consent I applied to join. He had agreed at once, and in his report on me to the Commander of the Royal Artillery Training Depot to which I was soon afterwards sent, he was kind enough to describe me as 'enthusiastic, patriotic, and full of energy' – a description which I have since tried my best to live up to. No sooner had the arrangements for my move been made than I received a letter from the Chief Rabbi in London.

8 November 1944

Office of the Chief Rabbi

Dear Captain de Rothschild,

I gather that you are considering the question of taking over the command of a Jewish Palestinian Unit that is to form part of the Jewish Brigade.

I earnestly hope that my information is correct. It would mean a great deal, not only to the men under you, but to all members of the Jewish Brigade, and indeed to Jews everywhere.

From your own point of view, it should prove an excellent experience in organising and leading Jews – never an easy task. And in view of the tradition of your noble House, it is, I think, of paramount importance that you should have just this experience.

There may be individuals in the Jewish units whose disappointment over British policy in Palestine has turned them against Britain, and there will no doubt be people who will use the Jewish Brigade as an argument to support their demands for further concessions in regard to Palestine. But all this should only strengthen you in your determination to stress the closest association of the Jewish Brigade created by HM Government and not by the Allied Nations with the British Cause.

I hope that you are keeping well, and I pray for your safe return to your dear ones at home.

Very sincerely yours
J.N. Hertz
Chief Rabbi

After attending a battery commander's course at Eboli, I went to the depot at Tivoli, where I was promoted major and joined 604, or 'P', Battery, one of the three batteries of the 200 (Jewish) Field Regiment, RA, which formed a component of the Jewish Infantry Brigade Group. Behind the idea for the formation of a Jewish brigade was the thought that, together, Jews might fight better than ever, and certainly, in P Battery, we quickly became a close-knit force, even designing our own flag. Officially, the only flag we could fly was the Union Jack, but we also flew a blue and white one with a golden Magen David at the centre, in the middle of which my battery put a blue 'P'. When, during an inspection one day, the inspecting general asked, 'What's that flag?' I got away with, 'Sir, it is P Battery standard.'

The Brigade – *Chativah Yehudith Lochemeth* (Jewish Fighting Force) in Hebrew – was made up of men from all over Europe. There were refugees from Germany, Austria, Czechoslovakia, Hungary, Romania, Russia and Poland, but also black Falashas from Ethiopia, Jews from the Yemen and a host of others. Altogether, I believe, more than fifty countries were represented. The men under my command were mostly refugees from Europe, though some already had homes in Palestine.

In late February 1945 we moved up the line to the Senio River, the last outpost of the Allied advance that winter, where we took up positions on the ridge of hills sloping down to the river's southern bank. The north bank of the Senio was held entirely by the Germans, and our task was to clear them away, as a part of Allied Command's preparation for the final push in Italy. Our brigade entered the sector shortly before the Passover Festival, and throughout the whole week of the festival we were supplied with matzos instead of bread, as well as, on the first night, wine from Baron Edmond de Rothschild's vineyard at Rishon Le-Zion in Palestine, and haggadahs from which to recite the story of the Exodus, as is customary at Passover.

To begin with, there was very little military action, though every day I went up to the forward observation post to see my young captain, and to have a look at the German lines across the river. But eventually the day came when we put down a smoke-screen, crossed the Senio and drove the Germans back. I crossed the river with Colonel Ben Artze, who was commanding the 1st Battalion of the brigade group, and later went on to become a general in the Israeli army. On the far bank we were held up by machine-gun fire, and visibility was greatly hampered on account of the smoke. But I had a map reference and my wireless set (strapped on to a mule), and so was able to direct my battery's fire. Miraculously, I had been given the correct reference of the enemy post we were aiming for, and our first shells knocked it out completely.

With the Germans in retreat, we pressed on from the Senio for Bologna, 'P' Battery in support of an Italian Free Brigade unit which was mopping up Axis troops of Croats and Uzbeks. Shortly before we reached Bologna, an Italian general led me to a place where he had laid out the bodies of his fallen men, many of whom were disfigured with the most horrible mutilations. When we arrived at Bologna itself, the main square was teeming with Free Poles and other troops shouting and waving flags, and the whole city was already *en fête*. I seemed to be about the only British officer in the place, and so it must have appeared. A civilian came up to me and said, 'Inglese?', and when I replied 'Si', a bottle was thrust into my hand – a wonderful bottle of old brandy.

Nearing Udine, on the last day of the war in Europe, an aeroplane circled overhead and I had a strong sense that I was going to be killed. I dived for cover, the first time I had done so in Italy, but the plane flew off – and that night I again dreamt that my father was standing by my bed.

Udine, which the New Zealanders had liberated, was teeming with unruly Serb irregulars, all armed, and the problem arose of how to get them to surrender their weapons. I do not know who came up with the solution, but it was arranged that Field Marshal Alexander should take the salute at a march-past on a dais in one of the town squares – for which I turned out part of the guard of honour, with a 25 pounder on each side of the dais. This square, it so happened, led into another square, with a narrow exit. As the Serbs went singing and cheering past they found that they were unable to get out of the second square without handing over their weapons.

For two days my trucks were then used to return Uzbek soldiers to the Russian zone. The frontier was a humped-back bridge with a Union Jack flying on one side, the Hammer and Sickle on the other. All day long, as the Uzbeks crossed over, tearing off their medals, one could hear the sound of gunfire; later we learnt that the Uzbeks had all been shot as they reached the other side. When a train arrived from Yugoslavia carrying Russians who had fought on the Tito front, it was my duty to provide them with food. I met the Russian colonel who was in charge of the train, and, seeing a desperately sick woman, suggested she should be taken off the train and sent to hospital. Twice I asked him, and twice he refused.

The mood in 'P' Battery at the end of the war was muted; so many of my men's relatives and friends had disappeared into concentration camps or been killed. And so rather than organise a celebration I asked the rabbi attached to the brigade to conduct a short service of thanksgiving for our deliverance, which was attended by many non-Jews as well.

On 20 June 1945, I circulated the following note to my battery.

What I Expect of All My Battery

I was immensely proud and pleased with my Battery. You are the ambassadors of us Jews. You are the men of Eretz-Israel, who are showing what Eretz-Israel is and will be. I, therefore, expect more of you than I would do of other troops.

I expect:

1. Instant discipline in obedience to all orders whatever they may be from any NCO or Officer superior to you.
2. The highest standard of smartness in turn-out of yourself.
3. Proper dress at all times when on duty, and when off duty out of billets.
4. The highest standard of cleanliness and hygiene.
5. Kit laid out in the morning properly and your billets scrupulously clean.
6. The highest standard of saluting to ALL Allied Officers.
7. Decent behaviour in public and courtesy to women.
8. Personal pride in yourself, your Battery, your Regiment and your Brigade.
9. Alertness when you are on guard duty.
10. Hard work when you are told to get down to a job to get it done.
11. Self-sacrifice to your comrades.
12. Honesty in all dealings with your own pals and with civilians.

I am not a great believer in tremendous 'Bullshit'. I do believe, however, in a standard of which 'P' Battery can be justly proud. Bear yourselves like soldiers, like the men of Eretz-Israel and Jews you are. Onward together we march for a cause no less sacred than that for which we have just fought.

Edmund de Rothschild
Major RA Commanding 'P' Fd. Bty, RA

Towards the end of July 1945 we moved up to Tarvisio, on the borders of Austria, Italy and Yugoslavia. Until a few weeks before we arrived, the town had been used by the Germans as a convalescent depot for their sick and wounded, and they had obligingly left a lot of supplies behind them. Owing to the geographical location, Tarvisio and the land around it presented a tempting opportunity to the Yugoslavians for a little surreptitious expansion, and one day I had to go and see the local Yugoslav commander whose troops were in occupation of an extra six mile-wide band of land. He was not pleased to be asked to withdraw, but fortunately, in view of our considerably stronger fire-power, he had little choice. But so as to keep things amicable, I organised a friendly football match.

While at Tarvisio, I managed to pay a visit to Berchtesgaden, and to go up in the lift to Hitler's eyrie, the 'Eagle's Nest'. It had already been looted, and there were smashed gramophone records lying all over the place, and the ivory had been torn from the keys of the Führer's piano. Seeing a mass of broken Sèvres porcelain, I wondered if it had been stolen from one of my cousins' homes.

Soon the brigade received orders to proceed on a carefully mapped-out six-day journey to Leuze, in Belgium. We proceeded via Lienz, the Brenner Pass, Innsbruck, Garmisch-Partenkirchen, Augsburg and Ulm. The fourth day was spent driving up what was then known as the Reichs-Autobahn, passing Württemberg, Baden, Heidelberg and finally arriving at Mannheim, where we crossed the Rhine. As far as I know, we were the only unit of field artillery to cross the Alps, and all along the way in Germany people were surprised to see the Magen David painted on my truck at the head of the column.

When we entered Mannheim – through an archway which still bore the repulsive legend *Judenrein* (Clear of Jews) – the word went out, 'Mishmerdach! Die Juden kommen! Die Juden kommen!' and people flocked towards us. All our guns had been cleaned up and I ordered my men to march at attention, so as to look as smart as possible. When several hundred people gathered around us in the main square, there was a scuffle; and from out of the crowd emerged a sad, gaunt little group in concentration camp garb who came up to my truck to kiss the Magen David; it was an emotional moment. Afterwards, we visited more than one concentration camp, where we saw some terrible sights; and since the war I have never been able to feel at ease in Germany.

From Belgium, where we arrived on 2 August, we received further orders to press on to Holland, principally to supervise the lifting of thousands of German land-mines at Venlo. There I was placed in charge of a German engineering regiment, and each day I went out on to the minefield with four Germans, two walking in front of me and two alongside. They worked well, and once they had lifted a set number of mines they were repatriated to Germany.

That done, we returned to Belgium where we were put in charge of guarding a huge dump of stores, and from where I sent off my men in turns on what was nominally 'forty-eight hours' leave to Paris'. In fact, almost every one of them went off to search the concentration camps for surviving relatives, or to try to organise their passage to Palestine – and thus in many cases they were away for a period nearer to two weeks than two days. To disguise the number of men absent during inspections, I used to tell those remaining to wear their forage caps first on one side and then the other, moving down the line as discreetly as they could. When one inspecting general said to our cook, Sergeant Heller, 'I've seen you before, haven't I?' Heller had the good sense to reply, 'Oh yes, sir. You've seen my twin brother.'

Many returned from leave despondent, with bad news or no news at all.

When one man, Gunner Gasco, had not returned after a fortnight, I felt obliged to report him absent without leave. But he turned up a few days later, with a remarkable story to tell. In the Russian zone he had been taken acutely ill with appendicitis and, on producing his AB64 (his paybook), had been taken to a near-by hospital for a successful operation. Released from hospital, he had met his sister, purely by chance, wandering past the hospital gates. Naturally, I was anxious that any punishment Gasco received should be as lenient as possible, and therefore obtained the colonel's permission to punish him myself. I then had him up in front of me and told him as sternly as I could that he had let the whole side down, and asked him if he would be prepared to accept my punishment. He agreed – and his face lit up when I told him he was to be confined to barracks for twenty-eight days, and afterwards repatriated to Palestine.

In May 1946 I was demobilised and returned from Cherbourg to England on the *Prague*. The purser I knew was still on duty, so we had a little whisky together.

5

Junior Partner

Except for a few doors and windows blown in by near-by blasts, New Court escaped the worst of the wartime bombing. Its survival was all the more remarkable since the Salters' Hall, which was at the back of the building, had been almost completely flattened by a direct hit. After the war, the Corporation of the City of London offered us the freehold of the Salters' site for £2 million, and my uncle and I were tempted to accept. But at the time the price seemed too much for us, and so – regrettably, with hindsight – we turned the offer down.

A team of the bank's older employees had remained on fire-watch duty at the bank throughout the war, and my father had seen to it that the whole of the top floor was evacuated and filled with sandbags. The fire-watch team was led by Harry Brooks, who had been recruited to New Court by my father after the First World War. The two men had met when my father was for a time in charge of recruitment in the City, and Brooks, then a sergeant, had been assigned to assist him at his small office on St Swithin's Lane, just across the road from New Court. Henry Southgate, who had been my parents' under-butler at Kensington Palace Gardens, spent many nights on ARP-warden duty at New Court, putting out any incendiaries which landed on the roof. After his house in Mayfair, No. 42 Hill Street, was destroyed by a bomb, my uncle Tony had virtually lived at New Court, too.

Before the bombing began, most of the bank's remaining clerical staff and our files had been moved down to Tring for the war's duration. But by the time I returned in 1946, they had all moved back to London, and the New Court organisation was once more up and running. The bank's business continued to be divided up among its well-established departments, the most important of which were the Bills Department, the Dividend Office, the Credit and Foreign Exchange departments, and the Bullion Department, which took care of all our dealings in gold.

The business of the Bills Department, processing bills of exchange, was fundamental to traditional merchant banking. Put at its most simple, a bill of exchange guarantees payment for goods by the purchaser's bank to the vendor's bank (most often in a different country), once all the agreed conditions of the sale have been met. The older London merchant banks – many of them, like Rothschilds, established by merchants turned bankers in the nineteenth century – built up their business by accepting bills on behalf of buyers known to them, and by undertaking to pay the bills at the maturity date. The benefit to the seller was twofold: payment was assured, and the seller could elect to sell or 'discount' the bank's 'acceptance' at the finest – that is to say the lowest – rate in the Discount Market, prior to the bill's maturity (the contractual date for payment). This system came to be known as the London Acceptance Credit, and the Accepting Houses Committee, of which Rothschilds was one of the first members, was, and remains (though now under a different name), the group of merchant banks that undertake financing of this kind, and whose bills are ultimately re-discountable at the Bank of England at a 'fine rate'.

The Dividend Office's function was to issue and service the loans Rothschilds made, which constituted the second main plank of the bank's business. These loans, mainly to foreign governments and overseas corporations up until the late 1920s, were, and still can be, raised by the issue of bonds – mostly bearer bonds in the pre-war days. Once issued, the loans had to be serviced, often for many years. That is to say, the coupons – pieces of paper attached to the bonds which the bondholder had to cut off and produce in order to obtain payment of a dividend – had to be processed and paid at certain stated intervals. If, for example, a bond was issued with a life of twenty years and the dividend was to be paid twice yearly, the bond would have forty coupons attached, and the bondholders would present these to us for payment, one at a time, as they fell due. In practice the bondholders' banks would present the coupons to us – the 'paying agents' – for payment of the interest.

It was my great-great-grandfather, N.M. Rothschild, who introduced the payment of interest on foreign loans by means of sterling-denominated coupons. In 1818 he masterminded a sterling (rather than a thaler) loan to Prussia, which was issued in London and Berlin; interest was payable in London, in sterling. Previously, foreign bonds in London had always been issued in foreign currencies, which meant that, owing to fluctuating exchange rates, British investors could never be sure how much interest they would receive. As agent for the foreign government, 'NM' issued the bonds himself, and paid the interest in pounds.

As servicing the loans continued for many years after the original issue, the Dividend Office was one of the busiest departments at New Court, even when new business dried up, as it did in the 1930s. The office provided a good training ground for staff, and both Peter Hobbs, who went on to become our Investment Manager and general New Court *homme d'affaires*, and Michael Bucks, whom in the 1960s I appointed the bank's first partner from among the staff, both began their careers there. When I rejoined the bank after the war, we were still dealing with a number of pre-war government issues, in particular with Chile and Brazil.

Foreign exchange dealing is another traditional merchant banking activity – Samuel Montagu actually began his career as a foreign exchange dealer in Liverpool – and after the First World War foreign exchange dealing had become an extremely active and profitable branch of Rothschilds' activities. Constantly fluctuating exchange rates had presented good opportunities for arbitrage, and the foreign exchange department had generated consistently high returns for the bank. Most of the world's recognised currencies were dealt in, though by the time I entered New Court in 1939 exchange rates worldwide had settled down, and the department's activities had correspondingly been much reduced.

In the early inter-war period, Rothschilds and the other London banks had lent a great deal of money, short term, to Germany, Austria and Hungary. In 1924, for instance, Rothschilds, with Schroders and Barings, arranged a 7.5 per cent loan for the Hungarian government, of which £8 million was issued in London; and in 1926 we arranged a 7 per cent bond issue for £1.25 million for the Counties of Hungary. Many of the banks in these countries asked for acceptance credits, whereby their individual clients could draw bills on London accepting houses; and although the Bank of England insisted that there be an underlying commercial purpose to these transactions, the money was generally used as capital to bolster the countries' industries. Using the system in this way was known as 'kite-flying'. Consequently, after the Wall Street Crash, the foreign banks found themselves unable to repay the interest, let alone the principal, on their debts – because they had borrowed short-term to lend to their industries long-term – and so standstill agreements were reached between the three countries' banks and London. Rothschilds was owed in the region of £1.5 million – perhaps equivalent to £40–50 million in today's money.

Faced with the prospect of widespread defaults, the Credit Department at New Court became an increasingly busy place. Up until the outbreak of war, Philip Hoyland, the head of the Credit Department, spent most of his time trying to find ways of freeing payments made to us in the blocked, or non-convertible, currencies in which the borrowers wished to pay. After the war, in 1948, the Hungarian banks proposed shipping the surplus of the country's wine crop to London for sale, hoping that the sterling proceeds could be used to defray their pre-war debts. Rothschilds was to handle the London end of the transaction, but I remember that the plan – which involved around 1.5 million litres of wine – had to be abandoned when we received a report from the wine merchants we had commissioned to undertake an assessment. 'This wine,' their report concluded, 'is on the point of collapse.' Eventually we were obliged to write off all these debts – though some of the wine, called Leanyika Maid, was quite drinkable.

The Bullion Department was responsible for all the bank's dealings in gold, and for the gold bars belonging to the bank or its clients which were stored in the Bullion Room beneath New Court. Government or other borrowers could provide collateral for loans in the form of gold bars, valued at a given price at the time of the transaction and then held by us in our vault. Before the war, the Bullion Department was looked after by Clem Cooper, afterwards by Norman Raven.

The room at New Court best known to the outside world has always been the Gold Fixing Room. It was, and the room which replaced it in the 1960s reconstruction of the bank still is, the setting for the twice-daily fixing of the gold price by the bullion dealers who make up the London gold market. In my day there were five brokers: Mocatta & Goldsmid, Johnson Matthey, Sharps Pixley (formed from the amalgamation of Sharps & Wilkins and Pixley & Abell), Samuel Montagu and ourselves. Mocatta & Goldsmid, founded towards the end of the seventeenth century, was the firm with the longest record of dealing in gold bullion, but Rothschilds have been active in the business since the Napoleonic era. My ancestor NM succeeded in becoming an agent of the Government for the purpose of arranging finance for the British armies overseas. Wellington was having difficulties paying his troops in the Peninsular War, and NM, with the help of his four brothers and the family's agents on the Continent, came to the rescue by smuggling gold bullion and coin through the French lines in ox-carts. There used to be a trunk at New Court containing a wonderful collection of women's clothes of the period – shawls, petticoats, bonnets and so on – reputed to have been used as disguises by my ancestors and their agents.

Among the documents in the bank's archives is a collection of papers which belonged to John Herries, who became Commissary-in-Chief of the British Army in 1811. In a letter to Herries from the Chancellor of the Exchequer, written with the concurrence of the Prime Minister, Lord Liverpool, Herries was authorised to employ Mr N.M. Rothschild, 'it being of the utmost importance to the public service at the present moment that the Commander of HM Forces in the South of France should speedily be supplied with a larger sum in specie [coins] applicable to this expenditure in that country than it has been found practicable to procure through the Bank of England or any other channel'. The letter goes on: 'Upon consideration of the magnitude of the objects in view, of the despatch and secrecy it requires, and of the risk which may be incurred, it is not thought unreasonable to allow Mr Rothschild a commission of 2 per cent.' One of the bank's relics which I used to show to visitors to New Court was an old chart listing the gold coins and ingots which NM smuggled across France to pay Wellington's armies.

The walls of the Gold Fixing Room were hung with the portraits of the European monarchs to whose governments NM also paid out millions in subsidies on behalf of the British Government at that period. The Commissary-in-Chief's account for 1815 records payments totalling £9,789,778 15s 10d, on which NM was paid his commission in gold ingots, doubloons, Portuguese gold coin, Bombay mohurs, Fredericks d'or and French gold coin. (After Napoleon's deposition in 1815, James de Rothschild, in Paris, was empowered to receive £120 million in war expenses and indemnity claimed by the Allied powers, and most of the moneys passed through his brother NM's hands in London.)

The monarchs depicted in the Fixing Room are the Emperor of Austria, the Kings of Prussia, Portugal and Holland, and the Empress

– rather than the Emperor – of all the Russias. One story has it that the Tsar would not tolerate the idea of his portrait hanging in a Jewish bank, and so instead he sent a portrait of his wife; but in any case it is the best of the pictures we received.

The gold price has always been fixed at a kind of auction conducted by Rothschilds' representative. The participants sit around an oval table, each of them equipped with a miniature Union Jack flag on a stand. Rothschilds' man begins by announcing a starting price – originally in sterling, later in US dollars – and then moves it up or down in response to the demand and supply indicated by the brokers, who nowadays keep in touch by telephone with their offices and clients around the world. The 'fixing price' is reached when all the participants signify their agreement to a price-level by laying down the flags on their desks. After fifteen years' suspension, the gold market was resuscitated with the same procedures in 1954.

The usual method of dealing in gold was in bars weighing 400 ounces, though to meet special demands in various parts of the world British refiners manufactured smaller bars as well. Rothschilds, besides dealing in gold, were licensed assayers and melters of precious metals, and for more than a century the bank owned its own refinery, at 19 Royal Mint Street, near the old Royal Mint by the Tower of London. Confusingly called the Royal Mint Refinery (RMR), the Royal Mint had actually relinquished control of it in 1852, when Sir Anthony de Rothschild – my great-grandfather Baron Lionel's younger brother – acquired it on a lease. Until then we had been permitted to use the facilities to refine precious metals for ourselves, and afterwards we continued to receive gold and silver for refining on the Royal Mint's account, as well as on our own.

Originally the refinery was located within the Royal Mint's buildings, and Sir Anthony's lease contained a clause binding us to refine up to 100 lbs of precious metal sent by the Master of the Mint at any one time, and to return the correct quantity of refined metal within fourteen days. When the lease on the building expired, the bank transferred the operation to a property near by.

The principal business of RMR was to melt down and refine the quantities of raw gold which were shipped to us from all over the world, much of it latterly from the gold-mines of South and West Africa (the lease was originally taken in the wakes of the Californian and Australian gold rushes). We refined to a standard .995 bullion purity, known as 'good delivery', and all the resulting new bars were branded with our stamp – properly called a 'chop' – bearing the letters *NMR*. English refiners' chops have traditionally been accepted all over the world as evidence of good, accurate refining and assaying. Until we sold the refinery to Engelhard Industries in the 1960s, we acted as suppliers of gold bars to foreign governments, banks and bullion brokers all over the world, as well as meeting the requirements of the Treasury and the Bank of England.

When, during a visit to New York in the 1950s, I was on my way out of a meeting at the Chase Manhattan Bank, one of their clerks came up to me to shake me by the hand. 'I am,' he said, 'one of the seven clerks working on your bullion account.' He then asked me how I was proposing to get back to my hotel. I explained I should be going by subway – and he insisted on accompanying me to the subway station to buy me a complimentary ticket.

During the war, part of RMR was converted for the production of precision armament parts, out of which grew the Tring-based Royal Mint Refinery Engineering, a light engineering plant. Wartime production included fuses for 25-pound shells, and post-war all kinds of things, from lipstick casings for Coty and Elizabeth Arden cosmetics to ticket machines for the London buses, as well as small aircraft parts. After the war, in London, we installed a new rolling-mill at the refinery which could produce copper foil of a micro-thickness – one eighth of one thousandth part of an inch – for use in the printing industry.

Positions at New Court had been kept open for staff who had gone off to fight or work for the war effort, and many of them came back. Samuel Stephany, our old Chief Clerk, had died during the war, and his job was taken over by Hugh Davies. Davies had previously been head of the Bullion Department, and so was not very experienced in the banking side of things, but he had an outstandingly able young assistant in the person of Michael Bucks. Philip Hoyland had also died, and his place was taken by Roland Williams; Harry Brooks continued in charge of the Dividend Office. Henry Southgate's wife was in charge of the kitchen.

The bank partnership deed still only allowed members of my family to be admitted as partners. In order to preserve the partnership from possible extinction during the war, my father and uncle had put their heads together with the accountants Peat, Marwick & Mitchell, and as a result had established a corporate partner, which they called

Rothschilds Continuation. The deaths by the same bomb of Lord Stamp (formerly Sir Josiah Stamp) and his eldest son had impressed on them powerfully the necessity of making some such provision.

Even so, since my father's death in 1942, Tony had had no one with whom to discuss the bank's affairs or to share the burden of directing its business. Making me a partner was clearly not going to solve this problem: my pre-war secondment to work on refugee matters meant that my knowledge of banking remained virtually non-existent. In the absence of a suitable Rothschild to turn to (Victor continued to show no sign of interest in banking), Tony decided to take on David Colville, the brother of my friend Jock, who before the war, when he was still only in his thirties, had been treasurer of Lloyd's Bank. David also spoke fluent French and German, which had been put to good use during the war when he served as a British liaison officer on board French destroyers.

Although we were distantly connected to the Colvilles (Jock and David's step-grandmother, the Marchioness of Crewe, was a daughter of the 5th Earl of Rosebery and Hannah de Rothschild), the relationship did not qualify David for a partnership. But he was given a desk in the Room, and was in every way treated as an equal.

As treasurer of Lloyd's, David had got to know all about the London money and discount markets, though he was not so well-informed about other aspects of banking. Consequently, in David's early days at New Court, Michael Bucks was occasionally heard to sigh with resignation, 'Poor old David. As usual, he's got a firm grasp of the wrong end of the stick.' However, David was an immensely valuable addition to New Court and, as my uncle was beginning to run out of steam, the burden of day-to-day business came increasingly to be shouldered by him and by Michael Bucks, when the latter succeeded Hugh Davies as General Manager. David and Michael were two men whose advice and encouragement I was to value for more than twenty years, and when Tony departed from New Court after suffering a crippling stroke in 1955, they became the mainstays of the bank. In 1960 David became the first non-Rothschild to be made a partner.

With David in harness, Tony decided that it was time for me to do a short *stage* – what would nowadays be called 'work experience' – at two banks in New York, and afterwards to go on a whistle-stop tour of the United States. Tony foresaw a developing role for Rothschilds in America, and as a first step, during the war, had assisted our French cousins Edouard and Robert in setting up a joint-venture company with a Dutchman called Peter Fleck, of the Dutch firm Pierson, Heldring & Pierson. The company, Amsterdam Overseas, later became, with NMR's involvement, New Court Securities, and later still Rothschild Inc., an investment bank whose share capital was taken up by New Court and rue Laffitte. It was arranged that I should do stints at two New York houses with which Rothschilds had long-standing associations: Kuhn, Loeb – a venerable institution which in those days shared pre-eminence with Morgan Stanley – and the Guaranty Trust Company.

I sailed for New York on a February afternoon in 1947 on the *Queen Elizabeth*, in the company of my sister Naomi and her little daughter Jocelyne. Early on in the war, Naomi and a dashing young French officer, Jean-Pierre Reinach, had fallen in love, but my father had told them that they were too young to marry. However, after Jean-Pierre had been captured in occupied France, and had then escaped, via Algeria and Portugal, to America, and finally returned to England, my father relented. But six months after their marriage at the Great Synagogue in London – the last great occasion my father attended there – Jean-Pierre, who had joined the Free French, was killed on a parachute drop into France in 1942. Jocelyne was born after her father died.

At the end of the war, Naomi went to France to help look after Jewish refugee orphans, and she was coming with me to New York to marry Bertrand Goldschmidt, the pioneering French atomic scientist. As a young man, Bertrand had worked with Marie Curie, and at the time of his marriage to Naomi he was working on the separation of plutonium at Chalk River, in Canada.

Neither Naomi nor I could believe our eyes at the quantity and variety of food on board the *Queen Elizabeth* – mountains of white bread, butter, bananas, roast beef and all manner of things rarely seen since before the war. The passenger list included several friends and acquaintances, among them Olaf Hambro, the chairman of Hambros Bank (whose son Jocelyn, like me, was sent to America to do a *stage*, though in his case at Brown Brothers Harriman), and one of the Seligmans who had lived next door to us in Kensington Palace Gardens. One very beautiful passenger whom we did not know turned out to be Elizabeth Taylor.

During the voyage, when we were not eating and the ship was not rolling too much, I played squash and luxuriated in the Turkish baths; and in the evenings we danced and looked at films in the ship's cinema.

Terence Rattigan was on board, and one of the best films showing was an adaptation of his play *While the Sun Shines*.

On arrival in New York we were met on the quayside by Bertrand and our cousin by marriage Clarice, Baroness Alphonse von Rothschild. Coming out of the customs house I remember there was a great scramble for porters, and Clarice – who was English, a member of the Montefiore family – had got their measure exactly. 'Friend,' she said, collaring the nearest man, 'you'll get a big tip if you hurry. And here is something now.'

Clarice was a formidable character. She had been widowed in 1942, but after the war had returned to Austria to reclaim Alphonse's beautiful estate of Langau, to the south of Vienna. *En route* by train she had found herself sharing a compartment with a Russian colonel, who gave her what she took to be a lecherous look. Knowing that the train was about to enter a long, dark tunnel, she leant across and offered him a cigarette – and then kept her cigarette lighter burning until the train emerged from the other end of the tunnel.

There was quite a collection of Rothschilds living in New York at that time, almost entirely as a result of the war. Alphonse had taken his family to settle there in 1940, and Clarice, together with her daughters Gwen and Betty, was still living in the apartment at 1040 Park Avenue where Leo had lived with them during the war (until 1943, when he returned to England).

My French cousin Alain and his wife Mary, with their two children Eric and Beatrice, were also living in Manhattan, where Alain was working at Amsterdam Overseas. Mary had left France for America in 1940 after Alain, who had been taken prisoner by the Germans, had managed to get a message to her telling her to flee. The next year Marshal Pétain signed a decree confiscating all the Rothschilds' property in France. Alain's parents, my Uncle Robert and Aunt Nelly, had also left France for New York in 1940, but had then died within a year of each other, Nelly in 1945, Robert in 1946. Robert's niece Renée de Becker was living in their old apartment. Outside New York, my cousin Eugene was living at Still House, in Locust Valley, on Long Island; his brother Louis was living in Vermont.

It was my first visit to America, and I remember being staggered by New York's towering buildings and extraordinary skyline – and also by the heat of my rooms at the Stanhope Hotel, and the contrasting cold outside. I was greatly struck by the fact that all the stores were full to capacity with goods, and that among New Yorkers there was, even then, an all-pervading sense of urgency. As on board ship, in restaurants one ate enormously, if not always quite as planned. Dining alone in a restaurant soon after my arrival I ordered what I expected to be a plain piece of veal with a green salad. Instead, the waiter proudly presented me with a thick piece of brown meat with a fried egg on top, together with a piece of toast piled high with smoked salmon, fish paste, Brussels sprouts and sweet potato. The salad consisted of lettuce, two slices of grapefruit and half a pear, all in a vinaigrette dressing. But there was only one genuinely tiresome thing about New York at that time: wherever I went, people seemed to be talking with pleasure about the impending collapse of the British Empire, and of Britain's new second-division status in the world.

My spell at Kuhn, Loeb was not a particularly agreeable experience either; I was made to feel very much the poor relation. In addition to my obvious ignorance and to the low estimation generally expressed of Britain's prospects, this was also, I suppose, in part a consequence of the steep – almost vertical – decline in Kuhn, Loeb's business with New Court. Between the wars, Rothschilds had been making large bullion shipments to Kuhn, Loeb, both for their own and our joint accounts, and we had participated with them in a lot of American security transactions. Kuhn, Loeb had also acted as the principal clearing centre for our dollar receipts and payments in New York. But under the Glass-Steagall Act of 1933 (part of Roosevelt's New Deal), American banks had had to choose between investment and commercial banking, and Kuhn, Loeb had opted to become purely an investment house. Thereafter, though by arranging an account nominally in overdraft Rothschilds had been able to go on clearing payments, our banking business with them naturally declined. Furthermore, while we continued to pass them the bulk of our American security business, as a result of the loss of American securities to the British Treasury, and of exchange controls, our security transactions had dwindled to vanishing point.

So I was put to drudgery in the bank's book-keeping, cashier's, stock transfer and credit departments. Even worse, for several weeks I was consigned to Kuhn, Loeb's statistical department, where I had to compare breakdown figures of tobacco and chemical companies, and to help compile a series of statistical reports on a collection of ball-bearing companies – the Swedish Ball Bearing Company, the Actua Roller Bearing Company, and Fafnir Bearings. During a spell in the syndicate department, I attended a syndicate underwriting meeting, where the officers of an oil company whose shares were being put on the market answered questions from the underwriting firms. It soon dawned on me that the nuts and bolts of banking were never going to be my greatest strength.

Three members of the Kuhn, Loeb management took the trouble to be friendly – Sir William Wiseman, who was then the senior partner, John Schiff, a kinsman of the great Jacob H. Schiff who put Kuhn, Loeb on the map by financing American railroads and steel-mills, and Johnny Meyer, whose wife Odile was the sister of my cousin Nica's husband, Jules de Koenigswarter. At lunchtime, Johnny and I used to go and feast off oysters and strawberries and cream at André's restaurant by Brooklyn Bridge, sometimes with my cousin Alain's old friend Eric Warburg, who also worked at Kuhn, Loeb (the Warburgs were connected to the Loebs by marriage). Before Alain went off to fight in the war, Eric had given him a pair of binoculars which probably saved his life: hanging around Alain's neck, they deflected a German bullet which would otherwise have entered his chest.

In March 1947, it was Johnny Meyer who opened a telegram for me from London which read: 'Pleased to inform you have been admitted to partnership with effect from 1 January 1947.' When I spoke to Tony on the telephone afterwards, he said he did not know whether to offer me his congratulations, or to commiserate – a dilemma with which I rather sympathised.

At the Guaranty Trust Company, I had a marginally more interesting time, though New Court's business with them was also much reduced. During the early part of the war, before Pearl Harbor, Rothschilds had held large dollar balances and certain securities with their London office, who then deposited them for us in New York. After the war they still held certain securities for us, but our account had become inactive. Dan Grant, who was a vice-president in the Guaranty Trust's New York office when I arrived there in 1947, had previously been the manager of their London office and a frequent visitor to New Court. He took me under his wing and I worked in the trusts, and imports departments, which I certainly found more interesting than compiling statistics about ball-bearings.

In my free time I used to go to the Harmony Club to play squash or to take a steam bath, and also to the Harvard Club. In the evenings I would go with cousins and friends to dine at Longchamps restaurant, Giovanni's, the Persian Room at the Plaza, and sometimes to El Morocco – then a favourite haunt of Margaret Sweeney, later the

Duchess of Argyll – where there was a good dance band. One evening, at the Metropolitan Opera, I heard Melchior sing Parsifal.

I also regularly attended fund-raising dinners for Jewish refugees. Since returning from the Army, I had become a member of the council of the CBF, renamed the Central British Fund for Jewish Relief and Rehabilitation, and the dinners I attended in America were organised by the American equivalent, the Joint Distribution Board's United Jewish Appeal, which aimed to feed, clothe and give support to some 250,000 displaced Jews. Usually, I would be called upon to make a speech, after which the hat would be passed round. Hundreds of thousands of dollars might be raised in a single evening.

Once or twice, at the weekend, I went out to Long Island to stay with Eugene, who was becoming very hard of hearing. Eugene's deafness was to enter legend at New Court, as a result of an incident at lunch when Victor was present. 'Well my boy,' said Eugene, turning to Victor, 'and what are you doing with yourself at Cambridge these days?' 'Research into the sex life of plants,' replied Victor. 'The sex life of France, you say? Now that is certainly a very interesting subject.'

The main family event of 1947 was Naomi's marriage to Bertrand on 26 February. In contrast to pre-war family weddings, it was a quiet occasion. At the simple ceremony, performed by a liberal rabbi, Naomi wore a pretty mauve dress with a veil and a flower in her hair; and I was honoured to be allowed to give her away – prompting many sad thoughts of our poor father, who had performed the same role at the Great Synagogue not long before he died.

Then, shortly after the wedding, Naomi fell seriously ill. With Eugene's help, we whisked her off to hospital, where she had to have a tubercular kidney removed. Naomi has had extraordinarily bad luck with her health: aged 42 she contracted polio, as a result of which she has now for many years been confined to a wheelchair. It was in the early days of the polio vaccination, and before a trip to Portugal she had seen to it that her children were vaccinated – but thought that she was old enough not to require vaccination herself. In the course of the trip she contracted the disease – and since then has been more brave about her condition than one would have thought humanly possible.

I left New York in mid-April, travelling by train to St Louis, Kansas, and then New Orleans. The pattern of my visits to each place was more or less the same: I paid courtesy calls at the local banks, made speeches at Jewish refugee fund-raising dinners held at hotels or Jewish clubs, and in between tried to do a little sightseeing. At St Louis

I spoke at the Meadowbrook Club, at Kansas at the Muehlback, and at New Orleans to about 1,000 people at the Mount Sinai. In all I attended twelve fund-raising dinners in the United States, and one in Vancouver.

From New Orleans I went on to Houston and Galveston, and after a two-day break at the Phantom ranch – a wonderful bungalow hotel at the bottom of the Grand Canyon – I took the train through the Arizona desert to California, ending up at the Beverly Wilshire Hotel, Los Angeles. After my speech at a fund-raising dinner held at the Hillcrest Country Club, pledges were received of nearly $2 million – at the time, I was informed, the largest sum ever raised for a charitable cause in one evening. Another evening I was also taken to the Mocambo night-club, where in a short space of time I was introduced to Merle Oberon, Myrna Loy, Greer Garson, Gary Cooper, Rosalind Russell and Cole Porter. The next day, at lunch, my eyes opened even wider when I met an elderly woman called Mrs Newhouse who was rumoured to have been Uncle Alfred's mistress at Halton. I thought this rather improbable, though Mrs Newhouse did tell me how very much I resembled my cousin Harry Rosebery.

From Los Angeles I set out for San Francisco, where I attended a great flower show and visited the arboretum, and from there, in the company of the nurseryman John Henny, I set off northwards along the Redwood Highway. All along the roadside I remember seeing *R. macrophyllum*, the rhododendron indigenous to the West Coast, as well as the lovely, sweet-scented azalea *R. occidentale* and masses of ceanothus. Motoring along the shores of the Pacific, there were magnificent redwoods, cedars and Ponderosa pines; and as we turned inland to the mountains, heading for Oregon, we drove through a majestic forest of *Sequoia sempervirens* (the Californian redwood).

Our route took us up through the Cascade Mountains to the Rogue River Valley, and then on to Medford, with its famous pear orchards, where we stayed. After a day's fishing with General Eisenhower's brother (who had got in touch with me after reading *Window on the World*), we continued on up the Rogue River Valley, climbing up the Cascades through pine forests to Crater Lake, where, at 7,000 feet, there was snow lying close by the road. From there we continued on to Salem to stay with Henny's business partner Jock Brydon, to discuss the possibility of sales of Exbury plants in America. After another flower show at Portland, Oregon, I set off on my own for a short fishing holiday in Canada, finally returning to New York, via

Chicago, and boarding the *Mauretania* for home towards the end of June.

Staying in Chicago, where I again attended Jewish fund-raising events, I was taken out to a restaurant one evening by a prominent Chicago attorney named Lew Silverman, to whom Dan Grant had given me a letter of introduction. At one stage in his career, Silverman had acted for Al Capone, and rather than ask for the bill when we had finished our magnificent dinner, he simply placed a one-dollar note on the table. He explained to me that his dinners at this restaurant were always 'on the house'.

Once back in England I took up my place at New Court as the new junior partner. Work in the Room, in those leisurely days, began at between 10.00 and 10.30 a.m. My uncle sat at a desk in the middle of the Room, with David Colville in one corner by a window, and with me in the other. The business of the day began when Hugh Davies or Michael Bucks brought in the morning's post, all in a book which was passed around for us to see if there was anything likely to result in some business. Davies or Bucks would have opened and read most of the letters beforehand, so as to be ready to answer any queries my uncle might have, and to take his instructions.

It was our practice in those days for all letters, cheques, bonds, bills of exchange and other such papers to be signed by a partner; per procuration signatures were virtually unknown. In consequence, there was always a mass of documents waiting to be signed. One of our senior stockbrokers, Denzil Sebag-Montefiore, of Joseph Sebag & Co., remembered that whenever he came to see my uncle in the Room at New Court, Tony would carry on signing without looking up, and seemed hardly to have time to talk. Once I became a partner, I was able to share the burden of the interminable signing; but if ever, before putting my signature to a document, I ventured to say to Tony (as, to begin with, I frequently did), 'I'm afraid I don't quite understand this,' his reply was invariably the same: 'No. You wouldn't.' My arm was kept busy signing none the less, and to assist me in coping with the deluge of paperwork I had an excellent, helpful and loyal secretary in the person of Miss Elaine Coles.

Day to day, Barings might telephone my uncle to ask if Rothschilds would be interested in taking a small piece of underwriting, for example, some shares in the Commonwealth Development

Corporation; then Evelyn Baring would call round in person with the papers for my uncle to see. Every morning, a crowd of brokers – from Cazenove's, Sebags and Panmure Gordon – also came to give us the news of share prices and movements on the Stock Exchange, and nearly all of them went away with at least a small order to buy or sell. Sebags were one of the stockbroking firms with whom we dealt most often, and before the war I remember being introduced to one of their elderly partners, Alfred Waley, who as a young man had been brought to New Court to meet my great-grandfather Baron Lionel, who died in 1879.

One of our regular callers was a bill broker named Toby Jessel, who wore a monocle and had the knack of reading upside down. One day I left among the papers on my desk a note with the words 'Mr Toby Jessel is an Old Ass' – and when he read it his monocle fell out, bouncing on the end of its cord.

As the new partner of Rothschilds, I was conducted around the City by my uncle to be introduced to the partners of the other merchant banks. For instance, at Barings, then at 8 Bishopsgate, I was introduced to Sir Edward Peacock and his fellow partners in the bank's old oak-panelled partners' room – very much like our own at New Court. The partners were all lined up to meet me, standing with their backs to the fireplace, as if posed for a group portrait. At the Bank of England, an even more formal call, I was introduced to the Governor, Lord Catto, who had succeeded the celebrated Montagu Norman.

The pace of life in the City at that time was still slow, and business was difficult. While routine banking had continued throughout the war – coupons had continued to be processed and dividends paid by the bank's skeleton staff at Tring – other merchant banking activities had ceased. There had been no new issues or loans, and stringent government restrictions on overseas security transactions, tight controls on imports and exports, and draconian foreign exchange regulations limited to a great extent our traditional fields of action. Moreover, the continuing weakness of sterling meant that the prospect of issues for overseas borrowers was likely to remain bleak.

Rothschilds, like other merchant banks, was therefore obliged to pay much closer attention to business possibilities on the domestic front. As a result, we floated a public share issue for Town Tailors Ltd (of Leeds) in 1946, and the next year one for Cussons & Sons, the old-established soap and toiletries manufacturer. Also in 1947, with

Barings, Hambros, Helbert Wagg, Lazards, Morgans and Schroders, we were involved in a £15 million 3 per cent debenture stock issue for the Steel Company of Wales; and we made a £9.6 million offer to shareholders of Shell Transport & Trading Ltd. In 1951, we co-sponsored, with five other London merchant banks, the first public issue of World Bank stock in the forty-eight member countries outside the United States – an issue to the public of £5 million of 3¼ per cent stock of the International Bank for Reconstruction and Development.

One of the responsibilities I was given was to keep an eye on the Royal Mint Refinery, monitoring its weekly output and seeing to the welfare of the 300 men and women we employed there; every week I toured the refinery with our manager, Ken Belcher. The continued closure of the London gold market and restrictions on international movements and transactions in bullion had greatly reduced the refinery's activities in processing precious metals. Nevertheless, we resumed the production of 10-tola bars – small bars of gold, each weighing 3.75 troy ounces, a size which traditionally was preferred by the Indian and Arab markets. (An Indian measurement, 1 tola is the weight of 100 tola seeds.) Moreover, two new processes had also begun to be developed and expanded: one for supplying a range of semi-processed non-ferrous metals for industrial use; the other for the refining of silver coinage minted from a quaternary alloy of silver, copper, nickel and zinc. By the early 1950s, we were also producing as much as 500 lbs a week of the micro-thin copper foil, mostly for De la Rue. And a man at the refinery named Steele devised a new method for producing extremely thin copper wire, coated with silver or gold, which was in great demand for use in printed electrical circuits.

There was one notable area in which the bank very quickly became more active after the war than we had ever been before – the documentary credit business. The reason for this was that in the aftermath of the war no international buyer or seller knew, or had any systematic means of checking up on, another firm's commercial standing, and so the safest and most convenient means of conducting any business was by opening a letter of credit. If, say, a buyer wants to import a shipment of iron ore, the exporter agrees to enter a contract to ship the required quantity of ore at a given price – and asks the buyer to instruct his bank to open a documentary credit in the seller's favour. Once this has been done, the buyer's bank instructs its agent in the town of residence of the iron ore supplier to inform the exporter that on submission of specified documents – including the bill of lading, insurance certificates, certificates of quantity and quality of the iron ore countersigned by a specified assayer, and an invoice – the agent will pay the invoice amount.

In essence, the documentary credit is therefore an undertaking by the issuing bank that on submission of documents to its agent, the agent will pay. If the agent adds his own guarantee of payment, it becomes known as a confirmed credit; otherwise it is an unconfirmed credit. In the late 1940s the documentary credit rapidly became the principal means of settling payment for exports and imports. At New Court, Roland Williams was put in charge of a new documentary credit department, and in no time at all had half a dozen staff working under him. Furthermore, besides dealing with our own documentary credit business, we were also able to give a hand to Siegmund Warburg in conducting his.

From the mid-1930s, a lot of German Jewish refugees had begun to arrive in London, most of them more or less penniless, but all keen to start up in business as soon as they could. Many of them passed through New Court, and we did our best to provide the short-term financing necessary to enable them to establish their small businesses, in scrap metal, textiles and so forth. One of the people we financed, a man named Shamah, became involved in the timber business, and during the war invented a method of reconstituting wood shavings with resin to produce a substitute for timber called plimber (chipboard), which was used for temporary housing. After the war we helped Shamah open a factory, and among those at the opening ceremony I attended was Harold Wilson, then President of the Board of Trade. When Mr Wilson came up to ask me who I was, I replied, 'The overdraft' – which seemed to amuse him greatly – and for many years afterwards we always had friendly dealings.

By far the most notable among the refugees was Siegmund Warburg, whose family's private bank, M.M. Warburg, were Rothschilds' correspondent bankers in Germany. My father and Tony had, I believe, both done *stages* at Warburgs during their early years at New Court, and Siegmund had spent a short time at New Court in the 1920s.

After Hitler had swept to power in 1933, Siegmund left Germany to settle in London for good. After discussions with Rothschilds and Barings, the Warburgs had set up a London entity, the New Trading Company, of which Siegmund now took charge – and subsequently, after the war, renamed S.G. Warburg. However, although after the war Siegmund already had a good number of clients – mostly companies

established by Jewish *émigrés* with capital provided by New Trading –
S.G. Warburg was not yet a member of the Accepting Houses
Committee, and so was limited in the scope of its activities. We there-
fore agreed to set up acceptance credits in our own name for
Warburgs' account, in doing so taking the risk that Warburgs would
meet their liabilities. This continued until Siegmund's acquisition in
1957 of Seligman Brothers, who were members of the Accepting
Houses Committee, enabled Warburgs to accept in their own right.

Abroad, even though exchange control restrictions made new
banking business difficult to transact, there was plenty for us to do in
sorting out old problems, notably in South America. In 1949, we were
able to reorganise the long-term sterling debts of Chile – largely
thanks to Harry Brooks, who had been out to Chile the previous year.
A Chilean government delegation came to London and signed an
agreement with us authorising an offer to bond-holders of all the
interest on amounts outstanding since before the war; and a similar
agreement was reached with Brazil.

Harry Brooks, Michael Bucks, Roland Williams and Norman Raven
all began travelling abroad, renewing the bank's pre-war relationships
with correspondent banks and old clients. Michael first went to Paris
to visit the French banks, and to see if anything could be done to help
my cousin Guy to get de Rothschild Frères back on its feet. Guy had
succeeded his father Baron Edouard at the bank, and one of the
things on which he, like us, was concentrating his efforts at that time
was the burgeoning documentary credits business. So Michael Bucks
was able to give his staff some help and advice in that area. From Paris,
Michael went on to visit our contacts and correspondent banks in
Holland, Scandinavia and South America.

While Norman Raven visited bankers and gold bullion dealers in
the Middle East, at Cairo, Beirut and Baghdad, Roland Williams went
to Italy and Portugal, and then on to South Africa, Kenya, the Gold
Coast (now Ghana), Nigeria and Egypt.

In Italy, Roland visited banks in Milan, Rome and Siena (including
the Monte dei Paschi di Siena, reputed to be the oldest bank in the
world), as a result of which a number of them opened new sterling
accounts with us in London. They also advised their clients to open
up letters of credit in favour of their customers with Rothschilds –
thus providing us with some large sterling balances earning interest.
During the wartime German occupation, the Italians had hidden away
all kinds of goods – ceramics, textiles and other merchandise – all of

which, after the war, were in extremely short supply, and great demand, elsewhere in Europe.

In Portugal, where Rothschilds' connections stretched back to the 1820s, Roland called on all the major banks, and also on the recently founded Banco do Continente e Ihlas (later renamed the Banco Português do Atlantico). The latter promptly opened its main sterling account with us at New Court. Roland attributed this success in part to the fact that he had spoken to the bank's directors in French, rather than English – something which no other visitor from London had ever attempted to do before.

As a consequence of Roland's visit to West Africa, the Nigerian government placed the enormous Cocoa Marketing Board sterling account with us in London, and we also became involved in financing shipments of Volkswagen and Jaguar motor cars to Lagos, a venture run by a charming, go-ahead Greek called John Mandilas. In Accra, Roland had talks with Barclay's bank officials; Barclay's were advancing money to goldminers against semi-refined gold, which was then being shipped to us in London for refining. Renewed contact with South Africa led to Rothschilds' later participation, in 1957, in the consortium which gained control of the Central Mining and Investment Corporation – an echo of the days when my grandfather and his brothers had supported De Beers and Cecil Rhodes.

I made my first post-war foreign trip at the end of 1946, before going to America, though it was on a strictly family matter. Just after Christmas we received the news that my uncle Baron Robert had died in Lausanne, and I was deputed to go out to Switzerland to take the family's messages of sympathy to his children Alain, Elie, Diane and Cécile, all of whom had gathered there. Travel by air at that time was difficult to arrange, but I none the less managed to get a seat on a flight at short notice – in an unheated Lancaster bomber specially chartered by the Government, from Skyways Airlines, to carry bullion for the Bank of England to Basle.

During my brief stay in Lausanne I met, for the first and only time, Baron Henri de Rothschild, the man who, in the Edwardian era, had challenged my father to the motor race from Paris to Monte Carlo. I was taken to see Henri by his daughter Nadine Thierry, in a hot, airless room where Henri was sitting in a large armchair and wearing a quaint, turban-like arrangement on his head – much as I imagined a Turkish pasha to look. On a table by his side he had a box of huge matches, considerably longer than the cigarettes he continually smoked, and the matchbox was surrounded by boxes of pills and medicines for his various ailments. He was not in very good health, and kept muddling me up with my father. In later years, I used to see a good deal of Henri's son Philippe, who made such a success of his wine-making enterprise at Mouton Rothschild.

My first overseas business trip was to Austria, with Michael Bucks in 1949, to visit the Voslau Woollen Mills and several Viennese banks. The Voslau mills, which were situated in the Russian zone outside Vienna, had recently opened a large sterling letter of credit with us in London, and three Austrian banks – the Creditanstalt, the Austrian National Bank and the Oesterreichische Länderbank – had all indicated a willingness to direct a share of their documentary credit business to us at New Court. S.M. von Rothschild und Sohne, the family bank, was still notionally in existence, though none of my elderly Austrian relatives had had the will to return there to take up the reins.

We were taken to Voslau in a kind of military personnel carrier, the Russians at the border post directing the beam of their hurricane lanterns through the windows at our faces (we had been told to look straight ahead), and checking the underside of the vehicle. The director of the mills was a Dr Franz Mayer-Gunthof, and I shall always remember an incident on the guided tour he gave us. At one place in the factory he informed me that a local Communist sympathiser was present, who must on no account learn that a Rothschild was paying them a visit. Dr Mayer-Gunthof then went up to the man and engaged him in earnest conversation until I had been shepherded past unseen.

I was particularly interested to visit the Creditanstalt bank, because I had so often heard it spoken of at home, and at New Court, in the past. In 1931, two years after the Wall Street Crash, the collapse of the Creditanstalt, then the largest bank in Austria, had precipitated a severe international financial crisis – and the bank's chairman at the time of its collapse was my cousin Baron Louis. The Austrian Rothschilds were major shareholders in the Creditanstalt, and Louis, who was also senior partner of S.M. von Rothschild, had been the Creditanstalt's chairman for ten years.

The rescue of the Creditanstalt therefore became a matter of honour. Initially, Louis injected huge cash sums of his own and the Austrian family's, and then his English and French cousins stepped in, too. Although entirely independent of the family bank in Vienna since before the First World War, both de Rothschild Frères and N.M. Rothschild helped out with their resources. For several years, my father also undertook the gruelling task of acting as chairman of the Austrian Creditanstalt International Committee, the body set up to negotiate a settlement satisfactory to all the international parties involved, as well as to the Austrian government.

On my visit to Vienna in 1949, the Creditanstalt's officials not only talked to me about documentary credits, but also about their interest, and Rothschilds' possible participation, in the Tauernwerke, a hydro-electric plant under construction near the Gross Glockner Pass. At the time, however, that did not appear to be a particularly attractive business prospect for us. Before the failure of the Creditanstalt in 1931, we had issued a £2 million loan to the huge hydroelectric company Vorarlberger Ilwerke, at Bregenz, which eventually supplied power to all the Ruhr. The borrowers had long since defaulted on the loan, and we were more concerned to clear up the payments outstanding on that. This objective we eventually achieved, after numerous visits to Austria by Harry Brooks and Ronald Palin.

However, from 1952 hydroelectric power, though not in Austria, was to become something of a preoccupation of mine – for more than the next twenty years.

During my uncle's time as senior partner, luncheon at New Court ran to a strict timetable. At 1.00 p.m. precisely, a blind would be drawn down over the glass panel in the door between the Partners' Room and the General Office, signalling that Tony and I had gone to the Partners' Dining-Room. Lunch itself, invariably preceded by a glass of dry sherry, lasted for one hour exactly, no matter whom we were entertaining. My uncle's guests were a mix of people (usually between two and six of them) from the worlds of finance, politics and Jewry, with a sprinkling of his personal friends, and sometimes one of my own. One man who came to lunch with us from time to time was Tony's friend Sir Eric Bowater, a swashbuckling personality in the City of those days. Sir Eric had inherited a small family business, founded by his grandfather, which by the time he died in the 1960s he had built up into the world's largest manufacturer of newsprint. Another fairly frequent guest was my old friend from Cambridge days, Jock Colville, who was Winston Churchill's Private Secretary. Whoever the guests were, and however much they might have liked to linger, after the customary one hour Tony would get up from his chair and announce that it was time to return to work.

On a hot August day in 1952, an hour or two after Jock had returned to Downing Street from lunch at New Court, he telephoned to pass on a message to my uncle from the Prime Minister. The message was in fact more of a request: could Tony spare the time to see Mr Joseph Smallwood, the Premier of Newfoundland, who was on a visit to London in search of British know-how and investment for a great commercial enterprise? Naturally, my uncle agreed to see Smallwood, but before he had the chance to make any arrangements he received another telephone call, this time from Eric Bowater – who wanted to know if he might bring Mr Smallwood to lunch.

At that time, Smallwood was quite unknown to us, although he had recently given a press conference in London which had received a certain amount of coverage in the newspapers. However, it was Smallwood who had led the Dominion of Newfoundland, which included both the island of Newfoundland and the mainland territory of Labrador, into the Canadian Federation in 1949 – seventy-three years after the invitation to join the federation had first been extended. Smallwood's background was in journalism, pig-breeding and trade-unionism. As a boy, he had masterminded a strike at his school under the slogan 'More Molasses, Less Pudding', and I doubt very much that Tony would have agreed to see him had he not come with such an impressive brace of introductions. Churchill, we later learned, had himself only agreed to grant Smallwood an interview because the request had come via his old Canadian friend Lord Beaverbrook, with whom he had shared a memorable experience in Newfoundland during the war.

In 1941, before Pearl Harbor and America's entry into the war, Churchill had crossed the Atlantic in the battleship *Prince of Wales*, for a shipboard meeting with President Roosevelt in Placentia Bay, on the south-east coast of Newfoundland. One of the subjects for discussion was Britain's need for war materials, and so Churchill requested Lord Beaverbrook, his Minister of Supply, to join them. Travelling under the code-name 'Newspaperman', Beaverbrook flew over the Atlantic in an unheated bomber, but on landing at Gander had no clear idea as to how he should travel the 200 miles from there to Placentia Bay.

'Get him here by air,' Churchill is said to have instructed the Governor of Newfoundland, Sir Humphrey Walwyn; but Sir Humphrey pointed to the low, heavy cloud cover pressing down on the ship's masts and said that it was obviously not flying weather. 'How long does it take by train?' Churchill asked. Sir Leonard Outerbridge, the Governor's private secretary, explained that if there were a train available it would take Lord Beaverbrook at least eight hours to reach them. 'Then get him here by road,' Churchill demanded. 'There is no road,' said Outerbridge. 'Good God,' exclaimed Churchill, 'what a country!' Beaverbrook improvised and got there, by an imaginative cross-country and sea route involving most known methods of transport.

'Lord Beaverbrook,' Jock Colville later recalled, 'rang me up one day to say that the Prime Minister really ought to see Mr Smallwood because it was scandalous how little British investment was going on in Canada, and Mr Smallwood had a most interesting proposal. At that particular period [1952], the Prime Minister and Lord Beaverbrook were not seeing very much of each other – not because friendship was flagging, but merely because Lord Beaverbrook had very largely retired from public affairs. Therefore, interventions by him were rare, and for this reason all the more to be respected.' And so it came about that Smallwood was invited to call on Churchill at Downing Street.

The proposal which Joseph Smallwood outlined at the meeting was for the exploration and development of the untapped natural resources of an area of Newfoundland roughly the size of England – 'an empire in itself', as he described it. Because of Newfoundland's ancient ties with Britain (Newfoundland was England's oldest colony), and because, as Smallwood explained, the people of Newfoundland took great pride in their English roots, he wanted to offer to British interests 'the biggest real estate deal of the present century'. He was careful to emphasise that American capital was already beginning to exploit Labrador's rich iron ore deposits, and that he and his fellow countrymen did not want their province to be cornered solely by US investment.

In an appeal to Churchill's sense of history and adventure, Smallwood used to relate how he went on to cite the East India Company and the Hudson's Bay Company as models for the consortium of British companies he had in mind to tackle the venture. Altogether, according to Jock, he put his case over 'extremely well, very straightforwardly – it was a masterly exposition of a grand design.' Churchill's response was most encouraging. 'I like the feel of it,' he said. 'It is a grand imperial concept, but not imperialistic.' And Churchill asked to be kept informed.

That same day Jock had been lunching with us at New Court, while

Churchill was attending the wedding of his niece, Clarissa Churchill, to Sir Anthony Eden, then the Foreign Secretary. Consequently, the Prime Minister had been in a relaxed mood when Smallwood arrived for the Downing Street meeting, enjoying a drink and a cigar. Returning to the Savoy Hotel afterwards, Newfoundland's Attorney-General, Leslie Curtis, who had accompanied Smallwood to No. 10 and sensed his premier's satisfaction with the meeting, remarked darkly, 'You know, he's been to that wedding. He's not going to remember a bloody word of what we've said.'

But as soon as Smallwood had left, Churchill turned to Jock to ask, 'Whom do we know in the City?' When Jock replied, 'Rothschilds,' Churchill at once said, 'Good. I know Tony well; and the family. They shall do it. Ring up Tony and tell him from me that I would like him to see Mr Smallwood.' And the story goes that Churchill then began to sing to himself some lines from the Lord Chancellor's nightmare song from Gilbert & Sullivan's *Iolanthe*: 'The shares are a penny, and ever so many / are taken by Rothschild and Baring, / And just as a few are allotted to you, / you awake with a shudder despairing.'

At the time, Smallwood obviously knew nothing of this sequel and so, after Curtis's remark, returned to his hotel somewhat deflated. But a short while later, out of the blue he received a call from Eric Bowater, asking him if he would like to lunch at Rothschilds the next day. Bowater and Smallwood had become acquainted because of Bowater's pulp and paper mill at Corner Brook, on Newfoundland Island, and at around the time of Newfoundland's entry into the Canadian Federation the two men had had talks about the necessity for attracting foreign investment to develop the new province's potential.

Of his first lunch with us at New Court, Smallwood remembered finding my uncle a rather formidable man – he confessed that Tony was 'the only man in the room I feared at all' – and he felt uneasy on being placed at the head of the table. The occasion was later fictionalised in the opening pages of the satirical novel *Clapp's Rock*, by the Newfoundlander politician and writer William Rowe, who for a time served in Smallwood's cabinet. The Hon. Percy D. Clapp, the Prime Minister of Newfoundland and Labrador, goes to lunch in the City with Lord Smythe, the head of 'one of London's well-known merchant banks'. During lunch, Percy Clapp spends twenty minutes telling a French de Rothschild all about wine, and then explains how Newfoundland won both World Wars.

In fact, Joseph Smallwood did not reveal his unease, and it was with great interest that we listened to what he had to say. He began by describing Newfoundland as 'probably the greatest storehouse of undeveloped natural wealth left in the world'. 'My idea is this,' he went on. 'We want you to come and develop it. We don't want you to come and sit on it. We want you to come and develop it, and we are prepared to be generous. What we would do is begin by giving you twenty, thirty, sixty thousand square miles; seventy or eighty thousand – there's lots of it.' Over all this vast tract of territory, Smallwood explained, the company accepting his offer would have the rights to explore for minerals, and to establish mines to develop any commercial deposits found; to cut timber; and to harness rivers. That day, Tony for once relaxed his rule, and we remained at lunch until 3.00 p.m.

By a stroke of good fortune, it so happened that the next day the heads of two of Britain's leading mining companies, my father's old friend Vere Bessborough, chairman of the Rio Tinto Company (and former Governor-General of Canada), and Sir Ernest Oppenheimer, chairman of the Anglo-American Corporation of South Africa, were coming to lunch at the bank; and Smallwood was delighted at my uncle's suggestion that we should tell them about the proposal. As soon as the premier had left New Court, Tony and I returned to the Room and got down a large *Times Atlas*. I remember Tony looking at the map of Labrador and remarking on the word 'Unexplored' which was written in great letters across the whole territory.

The interest shown by Lord Bessborough and Sir Ernest Oppenheimer when they visited us the next day encouraged Tony to get in touch with others of his acquaintance whom he guessed might have an interest in the scheme. If Bowaters were to be in the consortium, he reasoned that Lord Rothermere's Anglo-Newfoundland Development Company, the operators of Newfoundland's other pulp and paper mill, would also want to join. Since the 1920s, Anglo-Newfoundland had profited from the development on its land of the Buchans mine, one of the richest base-metal mines in the world, and so might be expected to take an interest in the possibilities for further minerals exploration.

Lord Leathers, the shipping magnate and industrialist who was Churchill's Minister for Co-ordination of Transport, Fuel and Power, was given the job of assisting Joseph Smallwood in London, and he proposed the additional involvement in the consortium of English Electric, a suggestion with which we readily fell in. Their role was to

My grandfather Leopold de Rothschild

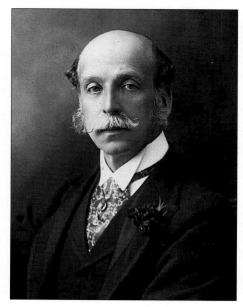

Uncle Alfred, Leopold's elder brother

My grandmother Marie de Rothschild,
photographed by my father at Gunnersbury, *c.* 1910

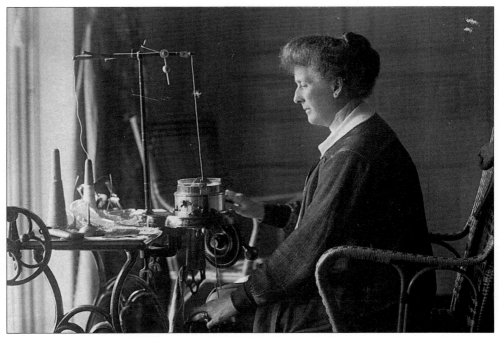

Marie's elder sister, Louise Sassoon – my Aunt Lou

Gunnersbury, the Large Mansion, my grandparents' residence
during the summer and autumn months

Ascott, my grandparents' house in Buckinghamshire,
one of a network of Rothschild houses in the county

My father Lionel, taken at the time of his
engagement to my mother, 1912

My mother Marie-Louise with the Prince of
Wales during his visit to Exbury in 1934

With my sisters Rosemary (*left*) and Naomi in 1923

Rosemary on Blue Boy and EdeR on Kitty, riding along the
Solent foreshore at Lepe, painted by Sir Alfred Munnings in 1923

A three-legged race on the deck of *Rhodora*:
EdeR with Moyra Ponsonby
Rosemary (*far right*) with a friend

The 800-ton *Rhodora II*, the second of my father's two ocean-going yachts

My first salmon, caught on the Test, 1933

Taking a nap in the car near Melbourne, Australia, September 1938

With M. Lefèvre (*left*) and Peter Trehearne in French Indo-China, October 1938

Lieutenant de Rothschild, of the Royal Bucks: EdeR (*seated, second from the right*)
with members of 394 Battery, 1935

Soon to join the British Expeditionary Force in France: with my batman,
Ernest Hicks, who before the war was one of my parents' footmen

Just married to Elizabeth, 22 June 1948

With (*from left to right*) Elizabeth,
Charlotte, Nicholas, Lionel and 'Jip'

Sharing a joke with Kate

Tony, my father's youngest brother

The entrance front of the old New Court, St Swithin's Lane

The Partners' Room at New Court, painted by Norman Hepple, with (*from left to right*) Michael Bucks, my brother Leo, Evelyn de Rothschild, EdeR, Philip Shelbourne, Jacob Rothschild and David Colville

With John Tweedsmuir at the Hamilton Falls, Labrador, in 1957

Annapolis Royal, in the Bay of Fundy: installing the turbines of the
world's largest tidal power unit

'I don't call you Rothschild-san; I call you Spoilt-child-san,
because you have so many geisha parties'

In conversation with David Ben-Gurion in the front hall
of the new New Court, *c.* 1965

Filming at Kate's marriage to Marcus Agius in 1971. The cine-camera
was given to me by my father as a twenty-first birthday present

Exbury House, completed for my father in 1923: the last substantial old-style
country residence to be built by the Rothschilds in England

With Anne, on an expedition organised by Ian Player in the South African bush

With Anne, on our way to a state banquet at Guildhall, EdeR wearing the star and sash of the Japanese Imperial Order of the Sacred Treasure, 1st class

assess the potential hydroelectric power which Smallwood assured us could be harnessed from the waters of Labrador's great Hamilton River. Sir George Nelson, the chairman of English Electric, appointed his colleague Sir John Woods to take charge of liaison with the project.

In the weeks which followed, Smallwood paid several more visits to New Court, accompanied by his Director-General of Economic Development, Dr Alfred Valdmanis, who had a rather dubious background. He had been Minister of Finance in pre-war Latvia, and later a special assistant to Hjalmar Schacht in Germany. Smallwood always had hopes of engineering an economic miracle in Newfoundland, and had turned to Valdmanis and other advisers, including the British wartime spymaster Sir William Stephenson, for assistance. One result had been the formation, under William Stephenson, of Nalco, the Newfoundland and Labrador Corporation, a government utility set up to exploit timber and mineral resources. Another, rather more hare-brained idea, and one which did not come to fruition, was a scheme to build a replica of the southern German town of Rothenburg ob der Tauber, where it was planned to manufacture toys.

A few words exchanged between Alfred Valdmanis and my uncle at one meeting at New Court almost aborted the whole Newfoundland venture. Valdmanis came to see Tony privately, to tell him that for a $1 million under-the-counter payment the iron-ore concession in Labrador could be Rothschilds' alone. Tony showed Valdmanis the door, and the suggestion so appalled him that for some time afterwards, though without choosing to publicise the reason, he refused even to see Smallwood.

But in the meantime we sent Peter Hobbs, our investment manager at New Court, to Newfoundland at the head of a small, informal delegation to find out more about Smallwood's proposition. By the end of Hobbs's visit it had become clear that no deal would be worth while which did not include full rights to the development of the Hamilton River. The hydroelectric potential of the Hamilton (or Great) Falls – which were higher than Niagara – presented by far the most obvious possibilities, even though the team from English Electric were concerned that there were no major power-consuming industries located in the area.

Eventually, when the Valdmanis episode had blown over, and under pressure from Lord Leathers ('You did Suez,' he said, 'so why can't you do Newfoundland?'), Smallwood was again asked to come to New

Court. On that occasion, my uncle outlined his ideas, based on Hobbs's reports and the discussions he had had with the various consortium members, as to how the venture might proceed. Tony then left, to attend a governors' meeting at St Mary's Hospital in Paddington. But as the time had come to sit down and set out on paper an outline of the way in which the concession would work, before my uncle left he announced, 'My nephew Eddy will now take over.'

So Joseph Smallwood and I returned to the Room, where there were large maps of Newfoundland and Labrador on two easels, and we sat down to thrash out an agreement in principle, which we called a 'basis of contract to be made between the Newfoundland government and the London group'. It consisted of eleven clauses, covering two sheets of paper, and under its provisions the consortium was to be granted exploration rights over 50,000 square miles of mainland Labrador and 10,000 square miles on the island of Newfoundland. The precise area was to be chosen within a year of the agreement being signed. In return, the consortium undertook to spend at least $1,250,000 on exploration and development every five years from the signing of a final agreement and periodically to return a certain portion of the concession area to the Newfoundland government.

As the afternoon wore on, I wondered whether the premier might enjoy a little light relief in the evening. The whole project we were discussing seemed to me at the time so gigantic, remote and improbable that I invited him to accompany me to see a light-hearted show at the Victoria Palace – a performance by Bud Flanagan's *Crazy Gang*, a collection of slapstick comedians. Once there, I laughed solidly from beginning to end. Indeed, years later, Smallwood recalled his embarrassment as, he said, I had thrown myself around in my chair and roared with laughter, so that anyone watching me would have thought I had gone off my head.

A few days later Peter Hobbs flew back out to Newfoundland, this time with Hilary Scott of our solicitors Slaughter & May. Proceeding from the two-page outline which Smallwood and I had produced in London, Hobbs and Scott hammered out an agreement with Leslie Curtis and his lawyers in Newfoundland's Justice Department. A formal fifteen-page document resulted, which served as the Principal Agreement between the Newfoundland government, N.M. Rothschild, and the consortium, which, it had by then been decided, would be called the British Newfoundland Corporation. The agreement was initialled by Smallwood and Hobbs on 11 March 1953, and passed by the Newfoundland legislature at the end of the month.

Under Rothschilds' leadership, the consortium making up the British Newfoundland Corporation consisted of the seven original companies we had approached – the seventh was the Canadian company, Frobisher Mining – while seventeen other companies, representing banking, insurance, mining and industrial interests, had also agreed to participate. The other banks involved were Morgan Grenfell, Kleinworts, Hambros, M. Samuel, Schroders and Robert Benson Lonsdale, a group which was later to be joined by the Bank of Montreal and the Royal Bank of Canada. Among the other participants in the consortium was the Suez Canal Company, whose name gave an added 'imperial' flavour to the whole venture.

In May 1953, the Newfoundland government passed a special Act formally granting the Corporation the 60,000 square-mile concession for twenty years. At the end of that period, provided various financial obligations had been met, the Corporation would still retain 20,000 square miles for development. The signature of assent to the Act was that of Sir Leonard Outerbridge, who had met Churchill in Newfoundland during the war when he was secretary to Sir Humphrey Walwyn, and who had gone on to become Governor of the province.

Because huge tracts of the concession area on mainland Labrador were inaccessible, it was to take some time to carry out a thorough mineral exploration, though preliminary examinations undertaken by field parties on the ground, and by two Beaver aircraft, indicated that the concession held quantities of iron ore and other minerals, including silver, copper and titanium. Moreover, our area contained some 1,500 square miles of virgin black spruce forest, one of the last such important stands of timber in North America east of the Rocky Mountains, with a potential value, in those days, of between $1 and $2 million.

But still the most promising of all was the Hamilton River and Falls, which together constituted the greatest remaining untapped source of hydroelectric power in North America. The Hamilton River, which flows into Lake Melville, is one of the largest rivers in eastern Canada, second only, perhaps, to the St Lawrence; the falls, at 246 feet, were 60 feet higher than Niagara, and within 16 miles of them the river fell by a further 1,000 feet. Smallwood used to give a graphic illustration of the volume of water involved. Enough water flowed over the Hamilton Falls every five minutes, he used to say, to fill all the bath-tubs in Newfoundland in six seconds, or twenty-eight football pitches to a depth of ten feet. Initial estimates indicated that the development of all the water-power at our disposal could generate as much as 7 million horsepower, roughly 75 per cent of all the electric power then produced in Britain.

From the outset it was envisaged that the Corporation should be run from Canada, with as many Canadian personnel as possible. Sir Mark Turner, Rio Tinto's finance director, suggested that the first general-manager of the venture should be A.W. 'Bill' Southam. He came from an Anglo-Russian family, and had seen action in the First World War with Dunster's Force, one of the few British units to fight against the Bolsheviks in Russia. Though not himself a Canadian, Southam was an expert on Canada and the Canadian economy, and was convinced that economic co-operation between Canada and Britain would be of mutual benefit. The idea of contributing to this enterprise appealed to him strongly, and he accepted our invitation at once.

He went to Labrador straight away, and soon discovered that, with the ice still in the lakes in June and the first snow returning in September, the prospecting season would be short – perhaps ninety days at most in the south, even less in the north. This did not leave us long to select our 50,000 square miles from the 70,000 available, and it was clearly imperative that preparations be made to get geologists and prospectors into the field as soon as possible to produce a detailed survey. So Southam lost no time in hiring the services of an experienced Canadian geologist, Dr Paul Beavan.

Beavan's geological surveys were disappointing. Only two major ore deposits were discovered, one of copper, at Whales Back in Newfoundland, the other of uranium (for which there was at that time no great demand), in the Monkey Hill region of Labrador. Furthermore, despite the quality and abundance of timber, the fact that ice blocked access to the Labrador coast for six months of the year made the establishment of a timber or paper export business impractical. Consequently, the development of the Hamilton Falls became an even more attractive proposition than before, and one which, if it were going to be profitable, clearly required the most thorough examination. The resolution of three issues in particular was going to be fundamental to the Hamilton project: how to harness the huge volume of water; how to convert the power into electrical energy at a price which would make it competitive with other power sources available in eastern Canada; and where to find the market to consume the vast energy – which estimates suggested would be enough to meet all the energy needs of three cities the size of Montreal.

While these matters were being looked into, I was involved in the search for a prominent Canadian to head the Corporation. On the advice of Sir Edward Peacock, the senior partner of Barings, it was decided that we should approach Mr B.C. 'Bertie' Gardner, the chairman of the Bank of Montreal, and I was deputed to go to Montreal to extend the invitation. Accompanied by my wife Elizabeth, I sailed on the *Queen Elizabeth* to New York for a meeting with Bertie Gardner in Montreal. During the voyage I came down with mumps, but after a period of recuperation in New York, I was well enough to take the train up to Montreal, and to lunch with Gardner at the Mount Royal Club. Having listened in silence to my story, he finally said, 'I am interested; I am definitely interested. I will think it over.' And a short while later he accepted.

I made my first visit to Newfoundland in September 1954, and it got off to a memorable start. Before meeting Eric Bowater at Corner Brook, I travelled on the bullet train from St John's, the capital on Newfoundland Island, to Grand Falls, where there was to be a great Labour Day celebration. On the train I shared a compartment with the jovial High Sheriff, Mr Cahill, and as the train swayed and rocked its way across the Newfoundland muskeg, we drank the best part of a bottle of rum together.

At Grand Falls, the headquarters of the Anglo-Newfoundland Development Corporation, we joined a huge crowd of men at a splendid lunch, after which there must have been at least a dozen speeches, one of which was made by Mr Cahill. As he passed me on the way up to the rostrum to give his speech, looking very much the worse for wear, I heard him mumble, 'I'm blowed if I know what I am going to say.' As he began to speak, he meant to say, 'Grand Falls is the corner stone of prosperity on the Island of Newfoundland,' but instead found himself saying 'Grand Falls is the Corner Brook of posterity on the Island of Newfoundland.' Miles Murray, one of Newfoundland's ministers, and I exchanged glances, but nobody else seemed to notice; they all cheered and roared at the racy stories Cahill went on to tell.

By that time, I had been appointed a director of the British Newfoundland Corporation, or 'Brinco' as it had come to be known, and for the remainder of this trip I travelled around the province with Val Duncan, of Rio Tinto, Eric Hinton, Bowater's hydroelectric expert, and Monty Lewin, Bowater's manager at Corner Brook and a vice-president of Brinco. It was a thrilling journey, and from Eric Bowater's home I wrote a report on Brinco's progress on the business side and – which nowadays seems to me rather more interesting – some notes of my first impressions of Newfoundland's inhospitable terrain.

'From the air base near Stephenville, we flew across Deer Lake and up to the north coast, and thence past the scattered settlements along the shore to St Anthony's. Part of this territory is available to Brinco, and a party of geologists is currently traversing the peninsula to see if there is anything worthwhile. There are very few trees inland, a considerable amount of rock, as well as a lot of ponds, muskeg and swamp. Northern Newfoundland is a pretty desolate place. After St Anthony's, where there is a hospital run by the Grenfell Mission, we crossed the straits to the mainland and saw icebergs below.

'The coast of Labrador is rugged and barren, but inland, and along the river valleys, there are plenty of trees, taller and larger than those in Newfoundland. We flew past Cartwright, and in beautifully clear weather flew along the great Hamilton inlet at Lake Melville, the shores of which are covered with dense stands of timber. We landed to refuel at Goose airport. It is one of a string of air bases at strategic intervals up to Baffin Land and the North Pole, manned twenty-four hours a day.

'From Goose airport we took a trip over the Siegheim Forest, now known as the "Brinco Limits". Imagine a carpet of deep green interspersed with a few lighter patches, gently rolling for mile upon mile, patterned with the blue and peaty-brown threads of the streams and rivers. That is the timber limits. Except for about 150 square miles that has burnt out, most of the rest, which is very dense, appeared to be in prime condition. It seems it may be an asset of considerable worth to Brinco. Monty Lewin told me that he had had one enquiry for possible amounts of up to 10,000 tons of newsprint per annum.

'After a night at Goose airport we took off for Knob Lake. It is the opening of the iron ore railway to Knob Lake, from Sept Iles in Quebec, that has made the prospect of developing the hydroelectric power of the Hamilton River a real possibility. And what a tremendous spectacle the Hamilton River is. Near its mouth it looked as wide as the

Channel at Dover, and even at its narrowest point, near the Muskrat Falls, about the width of the Solent. It drains a vast tableland, desolate and almost totally uninhabited, of swamps and long, wide lakes, the greatest of which, Lake Michikamau, is over 700 square miles in area.

'We flew over Lake Michikamau. It is so wide that even flying at 2,000 feet one could not see the lake shore. It acts as a kind of giant cistern, fed by the whole tableland, an area about the size of Wales, with its main outlet at Hamilton Falls. It has two overflows, one at the top north-east corner of Michikamau, and one leading from Ossokmannuan Lake down the Unknown River. Seven hundred feet of dam might suffice to plug the former, but the latter could require a dam as long as 35 miles, which could be constructed from local earth and rubble. The Unknown River presented a fine sight of falling cataracts, the largest about 100 feet high.

'Hamilton Falls are often compared to Niagara. They are, in fact, 60 feet higher, and the whole fall of water, over a distance of some 16 miles of torrents and rapids, is three times as high. The spray rising from the Falls themselves can be seen at least 20 miles away, and the thundering noise of the water could easily be heard above the sound of our aeroplane's engines. Below the falls are immense canyons, and the river tumbles down in a succession of rapids. One other sizeable waterfall, the Muskrat Falls, occurs before the Hamilton River finally empties its waters into the sea at Lake Melville, near Goose airport.

'After visiting some of the camps, which seem to be comfortable and at least adequately catered for, we returned to Knob Lake to inspect the railway and the digging operations, and to get an idea of the standard of life of the community who stay all year round in this part of Labrador – exactly what the maintenance parties would have to do at the Falls' power-house.

'The railway is a fine feat of engineering and, as it is a common carrier, of inestimable value to Brinco. One of the Brinco personnel has been trying to find an approach route to the Falls from the railway. He spent three weeks on one route supplied by helicopter and sea-plane and managed to trace out a route, sounding the muskeg as he went. He thought he had found a route with a hard bottom, 12 feet below the surface in places, but it ran out 20 miles short of the Falls, so he is now working on another. Monty Lewin estimates the rough cost of building a track at around $1 million, or $10,000 per mile.

'We flew on to Sept Iles on the northern shores of the St Lawrence seaway. We were met by M. Georges Blouin, the local Brinco agent, and he showed us round the harbour. Charts of the harbour show it to be suitable for large ships for ten months of the year, and with an ice-breaker probably the whole year round. The Iron Ore Company have put down steel plates for a waterfront, but have found that with winds blowing strongly their ships have difficulty loading. On the other side of the bay Clarke City offers more shelter and is ice-free, factors which make it a promising site for industrial development.

'The radio network has been a great success. The operator at Sept Iles has been particularly good, and all the camps have had constant contact with the head office in Montreal. For example, a geologist and a pilot set off in a helicopter from one of the camps in southern Labrador. They failed to return and immediately the camp radio made contact with North West River, which in turn transmitted to Sept Iles via Hamilton Falls, and so Montreal was able to contact the Federal Government in Ottawa for search parties. Luckily it proved unnecessary, as the helicopter had only run out of gas and the two men had walked to the nearest settlement.

'From Sept Iles we flew down the coast to Lake Allard, and looked at the Titanium lakes and the countryside in which ilmenite occurs. It is pretty, hilly and wooded, and the natural port of exit for the ore is Havre St-Pierre. It may not be practical to build a railway along the coast due to the many large rivers which would have to be bridged. If power is needed to extract titanium from the ore, Havre St-Pierre could be the place to carry this out, with power from the Hamilton Falls or the Muskrat Falls. Val Duncan said that if titanium is in great demand, Kennecot Copper might use the existing refinery as their pilot plant.

'We flew back to Stephenville and down the south coast of Newfoundland. Here, beyond the Annieopsquotch mountains, the country is grim to a degree, rocky and treeless with towering cliffs along the shoreline. The only human habitations are the scattered fishing communities, the boat being their only means of communication. We flew along the Baie d'Espoir and saw what might turn out to be a useful ice-free port with a good source of power from the river and lake system inland. But Eric Bowater is insistent that any scheme here, which could be put into operation quite quickly, must not detract from the one at the Falls.'

It was to be three years before I visited Newfoundland and Labrador again, and by then it had emerged that the hydroelectric potential of the Hamilton Falls was going to provide by far the best resource for development in the whole concession area.

6

Exbury

That evening the two girls wandered round with mixed feelings, bemoaning the fate that had landed them into a place where there was nothing operational going on and which was ten miles from the nearest movie. At the same time, they were forced to realise that the Navy had sent them to one of the most lovely country houses in England. It was a stone-built, fairly modern country house in the grand style, with a flagstaff flying a white ensign on the lawn in front of it. All afternoon the two girls wandered up and down the woodland paths between thickets of rhododendrons in bloom, each with a label, with water piped underneath each woodland path projecting in stopcocks here and there for watering the specimens. They found streams and pools, with ferns and water lilies carefully preserved and tended. They found a rock garden half as large as Trafalgar Square that was a mass of bloom; they found cedars and smooth grassy lawns. They found long ranges of greenhouses, and they learned with awe that the staff of gardeners had been reduced from fifty to a mere eighteen old men. And finally, wandering entranced through the carefully tended woods, they found the Beaulieu River running up between the trees, still tidal. The path ended in a private pier with a hut and a small dwelling house at the shore end.

Nevile Shute, *Requiem for a Wren* (1955)

When my father was alive, I took no real interest in the gardens at Exbury; indeed, I was almost discouraged from doing so. The gardens were very much my father's domain; any chance remark I made about them would usually be met with a dismissive response. None of us, not even my mother, was permitted to do much more than help show them off to cousins and house-party guests during the height of the flowering season in April and May.

But when I returned home to Exbury in 1946, I went for a solitary walk along the woodland paths. And – rather like Janet and Mary, the two Wrens recently arrived at HMS *Mastodon* (Exbury House) in Nevile Shute's novel *Requiem for a Wren* – I was moved by the beauty of my father's legacy. Although I could see that there would be a huge task ahead – acres of brambles and weeds to be cleared, hundreds of dead branches to be cut away and many sickly plants in need of uprooting – I decided, there and then, to try to restore the gardens.

Almost as soon as my father had acquired Exbury towards the end of 1918, he set armies of men to work clearing the 250-acre woodland site he had designated for ericaceous shrub cultivation. The undergrowth, including thousands of unwanted saplings, was uprooted, and the soil was enriched and prepared for new planting. At selected sites, a 'trenching team' of 150 men dug the ground to a depth of two spits, mixing peaty leaf-mould – though no manure or fertilisers – with the soil as they returned it. Open glades were formed where sunlight could reach the new shrubs which my father was in the process of collecting from all over the world. Some 30 miles of paths were laid out, 10 miles of which were designed to be wide enough for my father to drive along in his Armstrong-Siddeley.

Once the ground had been prepared, a further workforce of sixty trained gardeners embarked on a years-long programme of nearly one million new plantings. Because, for geographical reasons, Exbury lacked the necessary rainfall for good rhododendron cultivation, boreholes were sunk – to a depth of around 270 feet – to tap underground springs which otherwise drained into the Beaulieu River. An irrigation system, spreading out from a water-tower by the stables containing two 20,000-gallon tanks, was installed to carry in the region of a quarter of a million gallons a day to the gardens through some 26 miles of underground piping. Hydrants were positioned along the paths at intervals of roughly twenty-two paces, and surface pipes linked them to sprinklers, which could regularly be moved around the garden.

At a site near an old gravel pit deep in the woods, where there was a shallow ravine overlooked by oaks, a rock garden was constructed to accommodate alpine plants from the Himalayas and elsewhere. Vast blocks of sandstone brought from Wales were built up into terraces and low cliffs under the skilful supervision of Mr Edward Balls, of Clarence Elliott Ltd. Pipes were sunk behind the stones to enable watering from below ground, and spraying mechanisms installed to water the whole area from above once a week. To ferry the materials from the estate yard through the woods, my father built a small railway – and engaged an engine-driver, Mr Alfred Thomas. The project took four years to complete.

My father also planned an extensive arboretum, where, with the advice of his friend W. J. Bean, the Curator of Kew Gardens, he began to plant a collection of every tree sufficiently hardy for the English climate. To prepare the arboretum for planting, teams of men used dynamite to blow holes in the ground. But during the war the arboretum was turned over to vegetable cultivation, Brussels sprouts in particular, and since then it has been turned over to agricultural production.

Two acres of greenhouses were constructed from the finest teak, cut to the desired length and shape at the estate sawmill. All the metal greenhouse fittings were manufactured under the supervision of Pullen, the estate blacksmith, from approximately 50 tons of steel, and glaziers installed 60,000 square feet of glass. One vast greenhouse, the Rhododendron House, measuring 100 by 50 feet, was designed for growing tender rhododendrons from the warmer climes; another was specially heated for growing tropical plants, including bananas; another was set aside for my father's fabulous collection of orchids.

By the time my father died, his cymbidium collection was considered to be of such importance that we were granted a special oil allowance to maintain the necessary degree of warmth in the orchid house. It would probably be true to say that until the late 1940s or early 1950s, the collection was the finest and most valuable of its kind in the world. Throughout the war, the orchids continued to be tended by Benjamin Hill.

For many years my father helped to finance the expeditions undertaken by George Forrest, Reginald Farrer, Frank Kingdon-Ward and other intrepid plant-hunters to the Far East – to China, Tibet, Burma, Assam and all over the Himalayas: that 'immense reservoir of hardy plants', as Kingdon-Ward describes it, 'where the wind sobs and raves over the high passes, where the rain mist smokes over forest and moor and snow blankets the landscape for months on end' – where many species of the rhododendron and azalea occur naturally. Seeds and specimens were sent back to Exbury for cultivation, and the plants were then used to produce new hybrids.

When George Forrest died during an expedition to China in 1932, his guide had to walk for twelve days to the nearest telegraph office to

send the news of his death to England. My father then made whatever arrangements he could, at such a distance, for Forrest's funeral –
in a burial ground, chosen by Forrest, overlooking the great mountains of the Salween divide. He also succeeded in getting the plants
and seed which Forrest had collected brought back to England.

In all, my father made rather more than 1,200 rhododendron and
azalea crosses, from among which over 460 new varieties were indi-
vidually named and registered by the Royal Horticultural Society.
Francis Hanger, then one of the under-gardeners, recalled how 'a telephone message would be received from London to gather perhaps a
dozen different rhododendron blooms with pollen to be ready for Mr
Lionel's first [weekend] morning at Exbury, and before the day's tour
ended a plant of *R. discolor* in a basket or a tub would be married to all
those flowers.'

My father was always anxious to get down to Exbury as early as
possible on Friday afternoons, and he used to tell the story of how he
once managed to wind up a complicated Creditanstalt meeting in time
to catch the 4.35 train from Waterloo. Presented with a lengthy agenda,
he took the items in quick order, but on item No. 9 Mr Tyzer, of
Lazards, began to raise an objection. 'You disagree with that, Mr
Tyzer? Well then, we'll strike it out,' said my father. 'By the way, Mr
Tyzer, is that a boil you've got on the back of your neck? I've got a
sovereign remedy for boils; I'll write it down for you. And I tell you
what – if it doesn't work, I'll pay £5 to any charity you care to name.
Any other business?' And he got up and went off for his train.

Hybridisation is the process of crossing one variety with another.
Two plants are chosen for whichever of their characteristics one
hopes to combine. The closed bloom of a female plant of one variety
is then selected (the bloom must be closed in order to ensure that
pollination has not already taken place); the petals are carefully
removed, and the pollen-bearing portions are cut out so as to leave the
stigma exposed. Then the pollen-bearing anthers from the desired
male parent plant are selected, and the pollen dabbed on to the stigma
of the female. It is a very uncertain process, as one can never be sure
that the resulting cross will turn out to possess the exact characteristics
one wants; to achieve a satisfactory result can take years.

However, by using specimens collected in the wild and plants
already in cultivation, my father steadily enhanced and extended the
flowering season. He also improved the form of the plant, obtained a
greater abundance of flowers, and bred plants better suited to the

English climate. One of his finest crosses, and one of his own great favourites, he named *R.* 'Naomi' (after my younger sister), and it has sometimes been said to possess all the characteristics that a rhododendron should have, from its sturdy form and full growth to the profusion of scented and nectar-laden pink flowers it reliably produces. Furthermore, in America *R.* 'Naomi' is rated to resist temperatures down to $-15°F$. Crossed with what was perhaps one of Frank Kingdon-Ward's finest discoveries, *R. wardii*, *R.* 'Naomi' produced *R.* 'Idealist', a particularly beautiful plant.

Of the innumerable crosses my father made – and he did nearly all the hybridisation himself – he allowed only the best to be kept. He always remembered two pieces of advice he received from his gardening friend J.C. Williams: 'Plant your shelter first, before attempting to build up your garden,' and 'Lionel, please give great thought to the crosses you are about to make. There are far too many rhododendron hybrids made indiscriminately.'

In preparation for his weekend visits (which might begin as early as Thursday afternoon), specimen plants would be lifted from the nursery plantations, wrapped in hessian bags filled with peat, and lined up along the pathways to await ruthless inspection. Second-rate plants went straight to the sandpit for burning. 'I shall have a glorious bonfire,' my father wrote in 1934, 'of my seedlings of this cross [*R. cinnabarinum* x *R. ambiguum*] when I have something to fill the space they now occupy.' Over the years, hundreds, if not thousands, of young plants were burned as part of his rigorous programme of selection.

Approved stock, on the other hand, would be planted out according to my father's sense of colour and design. Writing about the planting of one particular type of rhododendron (subsection *Argyrophylla*) in *The Rhododendron Year Book* of 1933, he declared that 'they must be regarded more as the Queen Anne walnut table, which just fits into the drawing-room beside the armchair and helps to make the room feel comfortable and homely and sets off the Reynoldses and Romneys that grace the walls.' And just as one might rearrange a room, so my father regularly moved plants around the gardens to improve the look.

The gardens themselves comprise three main woodland areas: the Home Wood (which includes the Winter Garden), Witcher's Wood and Yard Wood.

The first area to be developed was the Home Wood, which covers an area stretching from the house down towards the Beaulieu River. The entrance to it is at the west end of the house, via a spacious glade, guarded by a great cedar of Lebanon. On an oak tree near the entrance to the glade hangs an old Burmese temple bell, which used to be used to summon my father from the gardens into dinner. Further on, by a crossroads in the wood beyond the glade, there is a bank of yellow *R*. 'Hawk' var. 'Crest', the hybrid in which my father's desire to create a pure yellow rhododendron bloom was finally realised – although sadly he never saw it, as it did not flower until the early 1950s.

R. 'Crest' is the result of the second and better hybridisation he undertook of *R. wardii* x *R*. 'Lady Bessborough' (from *R. discolor* x *R. campylocarpum* Elatum). The story goes that at a gathering of his gardening friends one weekend, he invited them to help themselves to some rhododendron seedlings from a tray. By the time they had finished, one small seedling remained, which my father left to take its chances in the garden – and it was this that became *R*. 'Crest', the best of his yellow *R*. 'Hawk' hybrids.

Many of my father's hybrids were named after friends and important acquaintances, of which *R*. 'Lady Bessborough' is one, and *R*. 'Lady Berry' (*R*. 'Rosy Bell' x *R*. 'Royal Flush') another. ('Lady Berry' was so named because my sister Rosemary's first husband was a son of the Kemsleys.) In 1949 Roberte Bessborough came to stay at Exbury during a visit by Princess Mary, the Princess Royal, and joined us all for a walk in the gardens. When we came across a beautiful small tree, cascading with a profusion of pale rosy-opal, trumpet-like flowers, I announced to the party, 'Here is the pride of the garden: "Lady Berry".' Casting a quizzical look at the tree, Lady Bessborough responded, 'I am not jealous. She droops.' *R*. 'Lady Bessborough', one of my father's earliest and most successful hybrids, is a big, upstanding shrub, whose apricot buds produce blooms of a deep rich cream, marked with a dark red eye.

The Home Wood also boasts some fine examples of *R. yakushimanum*, the background to which is intriguing. When my father was in the process of building up his plant collection, he was in touch with the Japanese plantsman, Mr Koichiro Wada, who owned and ran the Hakoneya nurseries at Yokohama. Numerous species of rhododendron, azalea and camellia are native to Japan, and in the 1930s Mr Wada sent my father a good number of fine specimens. Among these was *R. yakushimanum*, named after the mountainous, windswept island to the south of the Japanese mainland (at one time used by the

Japanese army to toughen up raw recruits), where it grows in the wild. When Francis Hanger, my then head gardener, left Exbury for Wisley, he took one of the plants, or a layer, with him – and in 1947 it won a First Class Certificate (FCC) from the RHS.

R. yakushimanum, perhaps the most important rhododendron species to be cultivated in Europe in the last fifty years, forms a dense, mounded shrub about three feet high. Its leaves, about three and a half inches long by one and a half inches broad, curl downwards and inwards along their margins, giving them a somewhat tubular appearance. When young, the leaves and petioles are almost completely covered with a white felt; gradually they turn dark green on the upper surface, while the underside develops a heavy, woolly, cinnamon-coloured indumentum. In May, *R. yakushimanum*'s deep rose-pink coloured buds open into clusters of bells of a paler pink, which, as they expand fully, turn almost completely white. In relation to the plant as a whole, the flower trusses are enormous, and it is a prodigious flowerer.

The main path through the Home Wood leads by St Mary's Spring and over a Japanese bridge to the Top Pond, which is stocked with golden orfe and carp, and then on to Middle and Lower Ponds. Just above Middle Pond there is a fine example of *Emmenopterys henryi*, an extremely rare flowering tree which W.J. Bean sent to my father from Kew. My father wrote to Bean a number of times complaining that the tree had not flowered, but when I returned in 1946 I heard that at last it had flowered for the first time, and that the Admiralty had granted special permission for horticultural experts from Kew to come down to see it. However, the day before they arrived, a naval rating had apparently sneaked out and picked the solitary bloom for his girl-friend, and everyone had then been confined to barracks until the young man owned up. I should perhaps say, though, that until the first authenticated flowering of *Emmenopterys henryi* in Europe at the Villa Taranto, in Italy, in the 1960s, almost every garden with a specimen of the tree had some colourful story to explain its lack of blooms. I am still waiting to see ours flower, although since, later in the war, it was damaged by a bomb, I am afraid it may never do so.

The Winter Garden was developed beyond the ponds in a stretch of woodland running down to the Beaulieu River. As its name implies, it was designed primarily for the rhododendrons which flower in January and February, but also as home to several camellia species, including the wild form of *C. reticulata*. Among the rhododendrons are *R. sinogrande*, with leaves up to two feet long, and the pale yellow *R. macabeanum*, the young shoots of which resemble suede gloves. The Winter Garden is also now home to some notable groups of my father's superb hybrid *R.* 'Fortune' (*R. falconeri* x *R. sinogrande*), which won an RHS First Class Certificate in 1938. In flower, it has large, well-knit globes, each about nine inches high (roughly the size of a human head), and composed of anything up to twenty-five large honey-gold bells, each with a small crimson patch at the throat.

Recording the first appearance, in 1938, of *R.* 'Fortune', my favourite rhododendron of all, my mother wrote: 'As we walked into the woods we saw this magnificent plant holding up its glorious blooms to a deep blue sky. In the evening Lionel gathered his family to a round-table conference to discuss the merits of the new seedling. There it stood in the largest vase available, looking most majestic. Not only was the flower outstanding, but its stance and bearing were bold and commanding. Its great leaves were disposed so as to remind me of the Discobolus, the Greek thrower of the discus with arm stretched out and poised for the throw.'

Witcher's Wood, named after a family of charcoal-burners called Witcher who used to live in the New Forest, is linked to the Home Wood by a daffodil meadow, which affords spectacular views of the Beaulieu River as it nears the Solent. The wood was planted with many fine specimens of ornamental trees, including a Chinese Empress tree and a cucumber tree (*Magnolia macrophylla*), which has the largest leaves and flowers of any tree or shrub hardy in the British Isles. A path through Witcher's Wood is known as the Lady Chamberlain Walk, after a pretty salmon-coloured *R. cinnabarinum* hybrid (*R. cinnabarinum* Roylei x *R.* 'Royal Flush' orange form), which was awarded an FCC in 1931. My father named it in honour of Ivy Chamberlain, the wife of his friend Sir Austen, and of his three great *R. cinnabarinum* hybrids (the other two being *R.* 'Lady Berry' and *R.* 'Lady Rosebery'), *R.* 'Lady Chamberlain' has become the best known.

Yard Wood was the last part of the gardens to be developed before the war. To reach it, one must cross over Gilbury Lane by a stone bridge, the construction of which was so costly that my father dubbed it 'Lionel's Folly'. Yard Wood boasts many ancient yews, and derives its name from the use of yew wood to make the yardsticks for long-bows in medieval times. Running over the bridge and through Yard Wood is the broad Azalea Drive.

One of my father's finest achievements was the development of a range of deciduous Exbury azalea hybrids, though he also raised evergreen azaleas of great charm. Since I took over Exbury, we have succeeded in improving the deciduous azaleas still further with our Solent range. Plantings of the Exbury azalea *R*. 'Cécile', which produces large salmon flowers with a yellow flare and is named in honour of my first cousin, have lent an extra touch of colour to Park Avenue, in New York.

Several more detailed accounts have been written of the creation and scope of Exbury gardens, and of the significance of the plant-hybridisation work carried out by my father during the twenty years before the war. The best and most detailed of these are contained in *The Rothschild Rhododendrons*, by Peter Barber and Lucas Phillips, and in the chapter devoted to Exbury written by my son Lionel for our cousin Miriam's book *The Rothschild Gardens*.

Having made the momentous decision to continue with my father's work, I realised that in order to carry the plan through, I should have to do so on a strictly commercial footing. The financial pressures weighing down on me in 1946 made it inconceivable that the enterprise could be funded in any other way.

My father had lived, as I have indicated, in great style. Indeed, had he lived at his accustomed rate for much longer he would without doubt have been obliged to make some very serious economies, as I was. Although for much of the 1930s, when new business at New Court dried up, he had continued to derive a good income from the gold bullion business of the Royal Mint Refinery, it turned out that he had also run up a considerable overdraft at the bank. Consequently, by the time he died I was saddled with a debt to the bank of about £500,000 (the exact sum he could have raised by selling his Rhokana mining shares before the war), and on top of that I needed to borrow a further £200,000 to pay the estate duty. Tony helped me out with a further loan from the bank to settle the latter, but the burden of repaying the debts was to remain with me for many years.

Moreover, the state of affairs that I inherited had a further important consequence for me. My father and Tony, as working partners of NMR, had each owned fifty per cent of the bank, and I inherited my father's share. But in 1947 Tony put forward proposals to change NMR from being a straightforward partnership into an entity over which a limited liability company would exercise control. The firm was recapitalised with £1 million of preference capital (non-voting shares) and £500,000 of ordinary (voting) shares. Broadly speaking, 60 per cent of the ordinary shares were then taken up by Tony, 20 per cent by Victor, and 20 per cent by me.

On top of the debts and estate duty, I also inherited my father's responsibility to continue to provide salaries and pensions for the large number of estate staff and servants he had employed. This included the thirty or so wartime staff on the Exbury payroll at the time of my father's death, and extended to the surviving band of Uncle Alfred's retired retainers from Halton, for whom my father had continued to provide pensions since disposing of the Halton estate.

In 1942, to raise funds for an initial payment of £41,000 estate duty on account, I had called in Christie's to organise an immediate sale of the contents of 18 Kensington Palace Gardens. The sale lasted two days and, as it took place in the middle of the war, most things went for a song. One gratifying aspect was that many of the items were bought by a family friend, Ambrose Congreve, a nephew of Lady Bessborough's. Ambrose had been inspired by my father with a love of horticulture, and has created a magnificent garden at Mount Congreve, his house in Ireland. After the war I sold the lease on 18 Kensington Palace Gardens – which had for a time been occupied by the Free Poles – to the Soviet Embassy. The sale price was £10,000.

One item with which we were unable to deal when we left Kensington Palace Gardens was my parents' safe – because my mother had forgotten the combination. For some reason she decided not to have it blown open, I suppose in the hope that her memory would return. Eventually, after the Russians had already been in occupation for some time, it did; my mother suddenly recollected the formula. Straight away, I contacted the Russian Ambassador's office, and was invited round to open up the safe; but of course it was completely bare.

After the Christie's house sale, I was obliged to proceed with the sale of many more treasures, including two large marble groups of sculpture, *The Four Muses*, by Antonio Canova, a pair of Rembrandts and a long list of other Old Masters.

Of the more valuable pictures, I sold a number to Agnews and to the dealer Tancred Borenius. One with which I was particularly sad to part was Pieter de Hooch's *Lady in a Courtyard*, which my father had bought through Agnews from my cousin Victor's sale of the contents of 148 Piccadilly. When I decided I should have to sell the picture, I first approached Agnews; but at the time they were not in a position to buy it. So Borenius bought it for £12,000, which was a good price for a painting in those days. Subsequently, Borenius sold it, along with other pictures he had bought from me, including a seascape by Willem van der Velde the Younger, to a Yorkshire ice-cream millionaire, Enrico Fattorini. When Mr Fattorini's collection came up for sale in London recently, Pieter de Hooch's *Lady in a Courtyard* sold for £1.5 million.

But there is certainly some consolation to be had from the fact that some of the very best pictures I inherited are now on permanent view to the public. *The Castle of Valkhoff at Nijmegen*, a beautiful golden river landscape with horsemen and country folk painted by the seventeenth-century Dutch master Aelbert Cuyp, can now be seen in the National Gallery of Scotland, and another large Cuyp, *The Watering Place*, in the Rijksmuseum in Amsterdam. The Rembrandts are in the Metropolitan Museum in New York; and two still-life paintings, by Jan van Huysum, which belonged to my great-grandfather Baron Lionel and came to Exbury as part of my father's inheritance from Uncle Alfred, are now in the Getty Museum in California, where I have been to see them. Baron Lionel had two pairs of paintings by Jan van Huysum, and when he died they were incorrectly divided, so that the two now in the Getty, while they match well enough, are very slightly different in size. Both depict a profusion of flowers and fruit in vases, with insects painted so realistically that people sometimes try to flick them away.

Two favourite items which I declined to sell, and which I still enjoy seeing on my way down to breakfast in the morning, are a pair of enamel elephants, roughly the size of mastiffs (I pat them on the head as I pass by), which were given by the Chinese Emperor Ch'ien Lung to Tipu Sultan in the eighteenth century. They were brought to England by Warren Hastings after the Battle of Seringapatam in 1799, in which Tipu Sultan was killed by the Redcoats at the fort I visited on my way to Bangalore in early 1939. After Warren Hastings's impeachment, the Government held a sale of his property, and Baron Lionel bought the elephants.

Notwithstanding the art disposals, it was quite clear that in order to keep Exbury at all, not only the gardens but the whole estate would have to be run along proper commercial lines, and would have to begin to pay for itself. So when Peter Barber, whom I had come to know at the Artillery School at Eboli, had been down to stay at Exbury once or twice, and had seemed to get on with my mother, I invited him to try his hand at acting as my estate manager.

Peter and I had become good friends, and in Italy I had been impressed by his efficiency and sympathetic handling of the men in our charge. As he had no firm plans of his own, he agreed to give Exbury a try, and he and his Italian wife Marina moved into a house on the estate. A great bonus of the arrangement was that my mother took an immediate liking to Marina. Although in different eras, they had both been brought to live in England with scant experience of the English or the English way of life, and this provided a strong common bond.

The Admiralty were still in occupation of Exbury House, and were to remain there until 1955. Although HMS *Mastodon* had closed in July 1945, it had been recommissioned the next year as HMS *King Alfred*, and then again, after only a few months, as HMS *Hawke*, a training establishment for Upper Yardsmen. As *Hawke* it was also used by the Admiralty Interview Board.

In the meantime, fortunately, a clause in the Admiralty's lease allowed us to keep the gardens in repair. During the war, such work as it had been possible to carry out with a skeleton staff of elderly men had been supervised by Francis Hanger, who, having been passed unfit for active service, was appointed head gardener after Arthur Bedford's death. Hanger had started, in a junior capacity, in Exbury gardens in 1927, before which he had worked in the Dowager Countess of Derby's household as a 'foreman decorator'. One of his responsibilities had been to decorate the Derbys' London house with flowers and plants for their parties, and for their great Derby Day celebrations. Before taking over as head gardener, he had been in charge of Exbury's greenhouses, excluding those devoted to the orchids.

Hanger's wartime task had not been easy, especially in the period leading up to the Normandy landings in 1944, when HMS *Mastodon*, as a Combined Operations Base, was at the centre of the planning and preparations for D-Day. Thousands of men were encamped in the district, many of them involved in the construction of the mysterious concrete structures which turned out to be components of the famous Mulberry harbour. There were twenty-three Nissen huts in the grounds of the house, and altogether some 1,500 officers, ratings and Wrens were accommodated there and in various houses in Exbury village. In the autumn of 1943, William Rattue wrote to me: 'If you saw Exbury now you would think you had come to the wrong place. The population is going up in leaps and bounds. You can hardly go down to Gilbury, all stopped off, sentries everywhere, not a bit like Exbury. But I suppose it will all end one day and when you return you will see some alterations about here. It will take some getting back as it was before.'

Perhaps the disruption had proved too much for Hanger. In May 1945 I received a letter from him which filled me with depression. 'Now that the war in Europe is over,' the letter began, 'the Council of the RHS are appointing a Curator at Wisley at a good salary and pension. I have asked for the details and received some, with a definite offer from the Council, which after much thought I find myself bound to accept. This means, Sir, that I am writing to ask you to relieve me of my engagement here at Exbury about the end of October. After eighteen years it is not easy for me to form this decision.'

It was a hard blow; Hanger had been at Exbury since the days when the gardens were still under construction, and so had built up an intimate, practical knowledge of the running of the place, and also great horticultural expertise. Early on, he had become involved in propagating hardy shrubs for my father's ambitious planting schemes, and his exceptional talents as a gardener had been rapidly recognised. The strides he made in the hybridisation of rhododendrons and camellias in later years earned him a series of medals and awards. When he was only 38, the Royal Horticultural Society appointed him an Associate of Honour; and later they awarded him the Victoria Medal of Honour, one of only sixty-three – the number of full regnal years of Queen Victoria's reign – held at any one time.

The RHS, I subsequently discovered, had approached Hanger in part because they thought it inconceivable that I should attempt to carry on with the gardens at Exbury; and as, in 1945, I had formulated no clear ideas on the matter myself, I regretfully agreed to let him go. So when, on my return the next year, I resolved to carry on after all, Hanger's departure left me with the daunting task of finding a suitable successor to supervise operations in what had developed into one of the most extensive and specialised private gardens in the country.

In setting about finding a replacement for Hanger, I approached a number of my father's old gardening friends for help and advice, including Sir William Wright Smith, the Keeper of the Botanic Gardens in Edinburgh. The huge Rhododendron House my father built at Exbury was designed by the firm of Mackenzie & Moncur, who designed a similar one for Edinburgh.

Sir William recommended a man named Harold Comber, the son of the Messels' head gardener at Nymans, in Sussex. He had trained at the Edinburgh Botanic Gardens, and before the war had visited South America, New Zealand and other countries on plant-hunting expeditions which my father had helped to fund. Coming with excellent references, and having expressed a keen interest in building up Exbury's lily and alstroemeria collections, he seemed to be an ideal candidate for the job and I duly appointed him. Unfortunately, it soon transpired that he was by no means suitable. He turned out to have little interest in rhododendrons, and failed to establish any kind of useful rapport with the existing garden staff – in fact he rapidly reduced them to a state of turmoil. He also had a very awkward manner with my mother, contradicting whatever she said and making her feel unwelcome in her own garden.

So in 1948 Comber was replaced, after rather less than a year, by someone whom we already knew – Freddie Wynniatt, who had worked at Exbury as a journeyman gardener from 1938 until his call-up. During the war he had been captured by the Germans, and had been consigned to two years' incarceration in a salt-mine, without once seeing daylight.

Wynniatt's pre-Exbury gardening experience had included stints in Sir Ernest Wills's gardens at Littlecote, in Wiltshire, at Mrs Ronnie Greville's at Polesden Lacey, and on Lord Derby's garden staff at Knowsley Hall, near Liverpool. He was, I should say, a natural gardener, though in 1948 he was none the less in need of training for his new responsibilities. Knowing our predicament, Francis Hanger kindly volunteered to help out, and for a period came down to Exbury from Wisley at the weekends to give Wynniatt his advice and encouragement.

In the meantime, we had begun the long, slow process of clearing away all the weeds and brambles which had taken hold during the years of neglect. Every year before the war, at the end of the flowering season, parties of women from Southampton used to come to Exbury to clear away the debris, but that tradition had come to an end in 1939. Consequently, our now much smaller staff would spend their days hacking away at the undergrowth with billhooks, saws and shears;

and at the weekends, my mother and I – and any guests who happened to be staying with us – would be cutting away at the jungle all day long. One richly rewarding aspect of our labours was to discover some of the wonderful crosses, such as *R.* 'Crest', which my father had bred but never seen.

We also began to make some new crosses ourselves and, in view of the need to make the whole enterprise pay, commenced the development of a nursery of shrubs for sale, at home and overseas. This got off to a good start: in 1948, in a single shipment, we supplied very nearly 600 rhododendron grafts and scions to Henny & Brydon, at Brooks, Oregon, whom I had been to visit after my banking *stage* in New York a year earlier. John Henny, who was one of the greatest rhododendron experts in America and familiar with my father's hybrids, then introduced us to Wayside Gardens, Ohio, who went on to become customers too.

America also provided a good market for the orchid collection, which I had regretfully decided I should have to sell. The greater part of the collection consisted of cymbidiums, cattleyas and cypripediums, among which the cymbidiums took pride of place. I sent Peter Barber to America to see what he could achieve, and the plan worked out very well: one bulb alone, of my father's cymbidium hybrid, *C.* Rosanna 'Pinkie', was sold to a collector for a world-record price of £10,000.

The timing of Peter's trip was just right. Within a very few years American orchid growers – in particular the remarkable Dos Pueblos Orchid Company – were leaving their English counterparts far behind. By the mid to late 1950s, American orchid production was outstripping domestic outlets, and the Americans themselves were looking for overseas markets.

At home, I continued with my father's practice of exhibiting at the RHS flower shows, including Chelsea. In 1950, I remember, we had a large stand made up of mainly yellow and flame-red azaleas, with a particularly fine *R. yakushimanum* as the centre-piece. We were awarded a silver medal, beaten to first place in our category by the Royal gardens at Windsor – to which, over the years, my father had sent more than one truckload of rhododendrons.

I was married by then, and early one morning my wife and I went to Chelsea to meet the Royal party, including the King and Queen and the Princess Royal. Walking by our stand, the King took my wife by the arm and confessed how his own love of gardening had been encouraged by my father. He also said how pleased he was to see that I was carrying on with the gardening, instead of spending all my time hunting and shooting.

Just before D-Day, the King had visited Exbury for an inspection, and the officer in command of *Mastodon* had carefully planned a tour through the gardens to the Middle Pond, where the azaleas were in full bloom. But before they set off, the King had said he would rather go alone, down the path he knew through the Home Wood, and sit by the pond for a while. And for twenty minutes or so, he sat there on his own, thinking of what the armed forces were shortly to undergo on the beaches of Normandy.

Prior to the inspection itself, I later learnt, it had been decided that there was not enough room on the lawn for the Wrens; they were told that if they wished to watch, they should do so from the ha-ha. Consequently, the King, inspecting the rear rank, had been somewhat surprised to see a lot of young faces peering up at him from ground level at the edge of the park.

The gardens, of course, were only a part of the responsibilities I inherited at Exbury. Beyond the rhododendron plantations, the estate was divided up among four farms: Lepe, near Inchmery; Lower Exbury, near the Beaulieu River; East Hill, at the far end of the estate; and Gatewood Hill, bounding the New Forest. When I returned from the war we had something like 1,500 acres in hand.

The farmland was poor, mostly red loam or a mixture of clay and gravel, and the soil had to be limed for arable use, and treated with large quantities of fertiliser. Corn crops did not on the whole do well, averaging only 8 to 10 sacks per acre, with exceptional crops on a few acres yielding more than 12 sacks of any cereal.

Moreover, my father had never taken much interest in the agricultural side of things, and when he died all four estate farms were already suffering from years of poor management and neglect. Just after his death – a fortnight before my regiment was posted overseas – the whole Exbury farm enterprise was given an unimpressive 'C' classification by the Hampshire War Agricultural Committee.

However, in August 1943, shortly before my father's old farm bailiff Mr Watson was due to leave, I received a hopeful letter from the faithful William Rattue. 'They have had a nice time this week to get on with the harvest,' Rattue wrote. 'I think they have got 16 ricks up, but they haven't got any more than a third of it in yet. They finished the cutting last Friday, so I expect all hands will be on carting next week. We shall want a month of fine weather for the corn, and a shower for the green crops; and a good shower wouldn't do the potatoes any harm.

'I expect by the time this reaches you we shall be having some changes here. Watson will have gone and Mr Honey will be coming in. I do hope he will be a sportsman. It makes all the difference if the farmer is interested in shooting; he can do a lot towards helping to pre-serve the game on the farm. I don't think he will have any rabbits to complain of, especially while the troops are here, for they are every-where and it's no use trying to keep them out.'

And then soon after Honey's arrival, Rattue wrote again. 'We shall soon have to start on the rats; I see there are a few getting about and I must not let them get into the ricks, or I'll be having Mr Honey com-plaining. I don't think things will be allowed to go on as before. He seems a very energetic young man. He has been very busy since he has been here getting the potatoes up, also getting ready for wheat sowing. He has got a very great task ahead to pull the farms round, but I should think he is the right man for the job. I am pretty sure you will like him. He is fond of a bit of sport, he likes to see a few pheasants and partridges about. I think we shall get on very well together.' Rattue's judgement was vindicated; the quality of the farming improved, and by 1947 the land had been re-classified from a 'C' rating to an 'A'.

During the war, Francis Hanger had acted as agent for the estate as well as head gardener. As agent, he succeeded Mr Johnson, the man whose hat my father had knocked off into the Beaulieu River when Queen Mary arrived at our pier from the Isle of Wight during Cowes Week in 1925.

To assist Hanger, we had found a manager-cum-accountant called Haskell, and to some extent the running of the estate's affairs had also been overseen by John Tarver, my father's erstwhile tutor and my grandmother's, and then Tony's, agent at Ascott. But Tarver was getting old, travel was difficult during the war, and his visits to Exbury had been infrequent. A consequence of this rather unsatisfactory arrangement was that when I returned home and began to take a close interest in estate affairs, the estate office, temporarily housed in a wooden hut containing all the estate records, was mysteriously burnt down – and very soon afterwards Haskell took his leave of us. Fortunately, Peter Barber then engaged an accountant, a Mr Arthur Thomas, whom we had both met in the Army in Italy, and he turned out to be the most efficient book-keeper one could have asked for.

But profits from the farms, despite Honey's improvements, were still non-existent. 'Peter Barber,' I noted in September 1947, 'is most gloomy about the farms; he considers that they are making an outrageous loss. So we shall have to alter our policy and go in for livestock. We have, however, made quite a bit of progress, cleared a lot of land, and generally prepared the ground for livestock.'

The land clearance began in earnest after the 1947 harvest. We had asked a water diviner to walk over some derelict fields running down to the Solent foreshore, on Lower Exbury farm. In one field, when we dug at the point indicated by the diviner's hazel twig, we found a water source which produced 900 gallons a minute when pipes were connected up; and at another spot selected by the diviner, in a field by the sea which had always been rough and infertile, we dug 12 feet down and found an ancient brick cistern, which produced 1,200 gallons a minute. Both fields came into cultivation the next year.

Part of the problem with the farms' profitability was that Mr Honey, for all his excellent points, seemed to us extravagant – 'he behaves more as if he were dealing with the Rockefellers than the Rothschilds,' my mother used to say – and in 1948 he left. His departure was followed by an unsatisfactory twelve months with temporary help, until we engaged Mr Rainford – always known as 'Honest' Rainford – who proved to be a conscientious and hard-working bailiff.

But by then the estate already looked better than I ever remembered having seen it before. The hedges were properly cut, the ground was decently cultivated, and we were slowly introducing new livestock, including dairy cattle. Also, we had embarked on a programme of renovation of all the existing farmhouses and cottages. Besides undertaking general repairs and redecoration, we equipped all of them with electricity and running water – including flush lavatories.

In the late summer of 1949, I was proud to record that 'the barley was fairly good; the wheat well above expectation; some of the oats exceptionally good, some medium; and the linseed about the same as last year. The only light crop is the sugar beet, but there is still a chance for that if we have some rain. The hay is excellent and the straw abundant – we have enough for two years' supply. The hedges are now being tidied up, posts have been cut which are to be creosoted for the double fencing for the "attested" herd; by the middle of November, the whole farm will be much tidier. Our milk has kept up surprisingly well, and now the autumn calvers are coming in, we should have 200 gallons of milk a day going away. There are sixty little pigs in Lepe yard, and they seem to be doing very well. Rainford is making great strides.'

By 1952, we had built up a herd of 240 cattle, made up of Ayrshires, Guernseys and Shorthorns, and a flock of more than 500 sheep (Leicester crosses as tegs and, for breeding ewes, Cheviots crossed with Suffolk rams). We also had more than 1,000 head of poultry, and had reclaimed nearly 100 acres of derelict grass and scrubland, and a further 50 acres by drainage of marshland.

In January 1948, I had become engaged to Elizabeth Lentner, six months after we had met at Peter Trehearne's engagement party.

Elizabeth, a friend of Peter's then bride-to-be Sybil, came from a family of prosperous Austrian Jews. Before the war, her father Marcel had owned a firm of outfitters called Löwy, well-known in those days for their sporting clothes, skiing outfits especially. There was a large store in Vienna, where the family also lived. When things began to look bad for the Jews in Austria, Marcel, who had been a highly decorated officer in the Austro-Hungarian army during the First World War, changed the family name from Löwy (the equivalent of Levy) to Lentner.

Elizabeth's mother was born Henriette (though she was always known as Harriet) Gellert, and her family owned a paper factory at Budweis (Ceske Budejovice) in Czechoslovakia, which made stiff, corrugated packing paper. The Gellerts were reasonably well-off, and then in the 1920s two Gellert brothers, Oswald and Leo, married two sisters of the much richer Petschek family, who owned coal-mines and a bank in Prague. Several large mansions built by the Petscheks in Prague were later occupied by foreign embassies. As a result of the two marriages into the Petschek family, the Gellerts' paper business expanded, and they acquired a further, much larger paper factory at Neusiedl, in Austria.

In 1938, the whole family, including Elizabeth and her parents, left Austria and Czechoslovakia for England. The Gestapo had been to call, and had told Marcel that from now on he would be sweeping the streets of Vienna. When he had then produced his First World War military uniform, and the medals for bravery he had won fighting the Serbs, the Nazis let him off – but only, he realised, for the time being.

Having arrived in England, most of the family then left for America, though not until 1940. But Marcel and Harriet decided not to go. Although Harriet's brothers had assured her and her husband of financial support in America, Harriet was worried that this would not be enough. So instead, she and Marcel made the extraordinary decision to return to mainland Europe – to live in Prague, in one of the Petschek houses which was vacant, but still fully staffed. Among the staff was Mr Cervenka, one of the best chefs in Prague, though how great a part that factor played in their mad decision is impossible to say. The only sensible thing they did was to leave Elizabeth at school in England, in the care of Harriet's mother, Augusta Gellert.

Although the political situation in Europe was rapidly deteriorating, Marcel and Harriet could probably have got out again without much difficulty before Hitler arrived in Czechoslovakia in 1939. But by that time Marcel had fallen fatally ill with a brain tumour, and was too sick to travel. His death soon afterwards left Harriet in an even more vulnerable situation, but at that point she came into her own. With the help of non-Jewish friends in Prague, and after several bold visits to Gestapo headquarters (which were located in the old Petschek bank building), she obtained the papers which enabled her to leave Czechoslovakia on one of the last trains out. By a circuitous route, via Spain and Cuba, she finally made her way to the United States. After the war, she came to join Elizabeth in England, settling at the Berystede Hotel, at Ascot – a largely residential hotel of a kind which now barely exists.

By the time full-scale war broke out in 1939, Elizabeth was in her last year of school. Thereafter she worked mostly as a nursery attendant for the local WVS until 1945. By the time Elizabeth and I met two years later, she was a student at the Central School of Art and Design, in London. In search of ideas for textile design she used to go to the Royal Horticultural Society hall, where she had come across floral exhibits from Exbury – never for one moment supposing that she would one day live there herself. As a girl, she had once visited a fair in Austria, where a fortune-teller told her that she would one day marry someone from a well-known foreign family – a prediction which her parents had naturally enough pooh-poohed.

When we got engaged, Elizabeth was 25, I was 32 – 'of an age,' she later said, 'when we were quite sensible about these things and sufficiently old-fashioned to consult our families'. Soon after we had announced our engagement, Elizabeth came down to stay at Exbury one weekend, and there was a small, very touching party given in her honour at the Exbury village club. As she and I walked into the hall, I remember, a band struck up with the tune 'Daisy, Daisy, give me your answer do' and all the estate staff present applauded. Before the dancing began, William Witts, who was still employed as my mother's butler, made a short speech, and presented Elizabeth with a tremendous bouquet of carnations.

Elizabeth and I were married in London by the Chief Rabbi, on 22 June 1948, at the New West End Synagogue. Elizabeth was given away by her uncle Egon Gellert, and my brother Leo was best man. The ushers included Jock and Philip Colville, Griff Llewellyn, Julian Layton and my cousin Evelyn. Afterwards we held a reception at Claridge's, where, so one of my friends reported afterwards, a waiter was more than once seen to come through the swing doors with a tray of champagne, only to turn around smartly and disappear back with it.

We spent our honeymoon on the Continent, driving through France and Switzerland in a motor car provided by Mr Follett. We spent the first part of the honeymoon staying near Cannes, in a house with a first-rate chef, all arranged for us by my cousin Cécile. In Switzerland we made our base at Flims.

Unlike my parents, we were not travelling with a complement of drivers, mechanics and servants, and Elizabeth showed her mettle when we were having an anxious time getting up the Stelvio Pass. About three kilometres outside Trafsi, I stopped the car to take a photograph – and noticed that the radiator was boiling. When I started gingerly to unscrew the radiator cap, I was almost blown away by the escaping steam. From then on, at every second hairpin bend on the way up the pass, I had to get out to let the steam out of the radiator and to top it up with water. Each time, Elizabeth dutifully got out too, to place chocks of wood behind each wheel. There were forty-nine hairpin bends, so it was quite a testing time for us both.

As Exbury House was still occupied by the Admiralty, when we returned from our honeymoon we moved back into my childhood home at Inchmery. During the war, Inchmery House had been requisitioned for occupation by Free French and Polish forces and, during preparations for D-Day, by the Commandos – among them George Lane, who had married my cousin Miriam. George and Miriam wrote to one another regularly, but George was not allowed to say where he was stationed. However, after Miriam had received a letter clearly postmarked 'Exbury', they managed to arrange a surreptitious meeting in Exbury church.

After the war, Inchmery had been let to tenants, and then my mother had moved back there for a time. A month or two before Elizabeth and I were due to move in, my mother returned to the converted laundry (since named Marise Cottage in her honour), and in the meantime Peter Barber and I had done our best to tidy up Inchmery for Elizabeth's arrival.

One newspaper article which appeared at around the time of my engagement had declared that at home in the country 'Mr Edmund de Rothschild maintains a hospitality befitting a millionaire,' while another described Inchmery as 'a small house at Exbury in the New Forest'. The true picture fell well short of the first statement, while the second was something of an understatement. In any case, we were fortunate to begin our married life at Inchmery with a cook, a housemaid and a butler, named Summersell. In London, I had bought a small house in Ovington Street from my sister Naomi, and there we had a live-in housekeeper and cook. It took me a little time to adjust to my new, married status, and to all the changes that came with it. Signing a pile of cheques at New Court one day, I came to one made out to Elizabeth de Rothschild. 'Who is she?' I asked.

We furnished Inchmery with many of the wonderful things that had been in storage during the war; as Elizabeth was very interested in art and antiques, I left the arrangement of the house and the choice of pictures to her. She had a particular success with one of the panelled rooms which had come down to Exbury when my grandfather's London house in Hamilton Place was sold. The carving on the panels consists of hunting trophies and monkeys, and Elizabeth had these picked out in realistic colours. One panel opened to reveal our best Sèvres dessert service, decorated with bird portraits. Elizabeth herself was an accomplished artist, drawing and painting animals, birds and landscapes, and she often designed our Christmas card. She also learned to etch and engrave on glass with great skill.

Only one potential problem clouded our move into Inchmery. Almost as soon as we had settled in, the Air Ministry unveiled a proposal to establish a bombing range at Warren Flats, a short distance from the house. The proposal was made not long after plans had been abandoned to turn the Beaulieu River area into a permanent Combined Operations training centre for assault landings. So Edward Montagu (Lord Montagu of Beaulieu) and I teamed up to obtain the services of Ewen Montagu KC to represent us in opposing the implementation of the proposed scheme. Ewen was the younger son of Lord Swaythling, one of the Montagus of the merchant bank Samuel

Montagu, and had worked in naval intelligence during the war. Based on his wartime experiences, he wrote the official version of *The Man Who Never Was.*

Once we had lodged our objections, an Air Commodore came down from the Ministry to inspect the foreshore at Lepe, the preservation of which was a major plank in our case. In return for a nominal rent of £1 per annum from the parish council, my father had opened the beach to the public, and I had transferred the lease to the Rural District Council. Thousands of people came down each year to enjoy the views across the Solent and to watch the bird life on the flats.

The Air Commodore was predictably unimpressed when this was pointed out to him, and it seemed as if there would be no escape from the roar of low-flying aeroplanes overhead and the thudding of bombs and flour-bags. However, as Ewen Montagu was standing on the foreshore, he pointed to a small coastal cargo vessel and said, 'Air Commodore, do you see that small boat proceeding from east to west? Would that be within range of the site you are intending to bomb?' The answer was, 'Yes. The boat would simply have to move out further from the shore.' 'Well,' said Ewen Montagu, 'what do you suppose would happen to that boat? I will tell you. It would be proceeding backwards where it is proceeding forwards because there are double tides of great strength in the Solent.' And on those grounds Lord Montagu and I went on to win our case.

In 1949, Elizabeth gave birth to our first child, Kate, and that year we also received our first Royal visitor since before the war. Princess Mary, the Princess Royal, came to stay for a weekend in May, and showed a keen interest in all the work which was under way in the gardens and on the estate. Young Kate took a great fancy to the glass cherries in the Princess's hat.

As the Princess was an enthusiastic gardener, during her visit we naturally showed her over the greenhouses, and this gave rise to an amusing incident. When Peter Barber had explained how my father used to say that it was often the puniest-looking seedlings which grew into the best plants, Ben Hendy, who was in charge of the green-houses, backed this up with a story of his own. He told the Princess that one day he and my father had been pricking out a box of seedlings, and that when they had got down to the smallest and most sickly among them, Hendy had asked my father if they should be thrown away. 'Yes,' came the reply; but then, after a moment's further thought, 'No. We will send them to Windsor.' Hendy added that he knew they had gone on to do extremely well, some of them indeed turning out to be the best.

On Sunday, when the Princess attended a service in Exbury church, the rector forgot to say the prayers for the Royal Family, and had chosen as the text for his sermon, 'Put not thy trust in princes.' Afterwards, my mother told us of a surprising experience she had had on a visit to church when staying with the Bessboroughs at Stansted towards the end of the war. On Sunday morning she accompanied Lord Bessborough to morning prayer, and on the way out put half a crown in an offertory box by the church door – before she had noticed that it was labelled 'For the Conversion of the Jews'.

Our son Nicholas (named after my friend Nicholas Fitzgerald) was born in 1951 – on Yom Kippur, the Day of Atonement, a most auspicious day in the Jewish calendar. The twins, Charlotte and Lionel, arrived four years later, and their birth, together with the opening of Exbury Gardens to the public, made 1955 something of a landmark year in our lives.

I opened the gardens for the first time on the Whitsun bank holiday, and so many people came to look round that there was a line of cars stretching nose to tail all the way across the Forest from Exbury to Beaulieu. As, in those days, we had no car park, the visitors had to park their cars all over the lawns; but this is a state of affairs which we have long since remedied – a necessity in view of the number of coach parties we are now able to welcome. The present car park at Exbury was opened in 1986 by the Prince of Wales – and, as the Prince remarked, is very possibly the only car park anywhere to have been so launched.

On the weekend of Elizabeth's birthday, 20 May, in 1955, we were honoured by an overnight visit to Inchmery from Queen Elizabeth the Queen Mother. When young Nicholas was presented to our guest, I remember him asking, 'Where is your crown?' – to which the Queen Mother replied, with a lovely smile, 'I will put on my tiara for you tonight.'

7

Senior Partner

One June afternoon in 1955, Tony left New Court to attend one of his governors' meetings at St Mary's Hospital. Shortly after he arrived at the hospital he suffered a very severe stroke, and although officially he remained senior partner of the bank for a further four years, he was never again fit enough to return to work. My first act on assuming the role of acting senior partner of Rothschilds was to send for the stalwart Michael Bucks, on whose assistance I knew I should be able to depend, and to raise his salary by £2,000.

My brother Leo joined the partnership in January 1956, and in 1960, when I finally succeeded Tony as senior partner (a few months before he died), my cousin Evelyn, then aged 34, arrived to join us in the Room. Evelyn and Leo set about expanding the bank's investment department, and in the summer of 1961 the public was for the first time offered shares in an investment trust managed and owned by N.M. Rothschild: Rothschild Investment Trust (RIT) was launched, with £3 million capital, two thirds of which was raised from the public. It was to be the first of a series of similar, publicly-quoted Rothschilds investment trusts, including Equity Income, Equity Consort and the Five Arrows Fund. By the time of my official retirement from the bank in 1975, RIT, having absorbed a number of other investment trusts, was enjoying pre-tax revenues of approximately £3 million, and Rothschilds' stake in it had been diluted to less than 10 per cent.

Evelyn also oversaw the demolition of the old New Court buildings in October 1962, and supervised the three-year rebuilding project, while the bank was temporarily relocated to City Gate House, in Finsbury Square. We had already spilled out of New Court into another building on St Swithin's Lane, and the layout of the old bank, including the Room, no longer suited our needs. The thought that after the war we had turned down the offer of the Salters' Hall site, on to which we might now have expanded, was galling – and the disappearance of Baron Lionel's New Court extremely sad.

David Colville and Michael Bucks gave sterling service and, in July 1960, I made David a partner. Although he was the first non-Rothschild to join the partnership, his appointment was, as Leo described it at the time, 'a *de jure* recognition of a *de facto* situation'. In October 1961, I also made Michael Bucks a partner, and in April 1962 we were joined in the Room by yet another, though this time by one who was neither a Rothschild nor a New Court employee. This was Philip Shelbourne, a barrister in his thirties who had built up an outstanding reputation for himself as a tax lawyer at the Bar – on the strength of which a number of his former clients subsequently became clients of the bank.

When, after a *stage* with Morgan Stanley in New York, my cousin Jacob, Victor's elder son (now Lord Rothschild), was admitted to the partnership in 1963, he and Philip Shelbourne together began to build up the bank's corporate finance business through our new Finance Department. To attract business, we established a branch in Manchester in 1964, and two years later formed Yorkshire Industrial Trust (Holdings) at Leeds. Partly as a result of this, we undertook issues for Evans Outsize Garments (manufacturers of clothing for large women), and for the vintners Seager, Evans. Issues for C.T. Bowring, the insurers, for Associated British Foods, and for Beaverbrook Newspapers also came our way, and by the end of the decade Rothschilds ranked in the top half-dozen most active issuing houses.

From the early 1960s, we also became much more involved in the developing mergers and takeovers business which had got off to an explosive start with Siegmund Warburg's battle, on behalf of American clients, for control of the British Aluminium Company in 1958–9 – after which, for better or worse, the City never seemed to me to be quite the same again. Rothschilds were not involved in that saga, but a number of other leading institutions were. Warburgs teamed up with Schroders and Helbert Wagg on behalf of the Americans; British Aluminium, keen to resist the takeover, retained Hambros and Lazards to represent a consortium of British

Aluminium shareholders, including Samuel Montagu, Morgan Grenfell, M. Samuel, Guinness Mahon and Brown Shipley. Siegmund won the day, leaving a lot of people feeling very sore – but at the same time aware that a decisive blow had been dealt to the unhurried, 'gentlemanly' style of business which had until then prevailed in the City. The new style was perhaps reflected in Warburgs' modern building on Gresham Street, where there was no partners' room and a notable absence of fireplaces and family portraits.

Siegmund used to compare the role of the merchant banker to that of the family doctor, and there was one occasion when I experienced his bedside manner at first hand. Not long after my uncle had had his stroke in 1955, leaving me as the sole working partner at New Court, Siegmund called round to see me. Once or twice in the past, my uncle had given him a dressing-down for the aggressive way in which he felt Siegmund conducted his business, so I was surprised and pleased to see him. I saw him alone in the Room and, after some polite enquiries as to Tony's health, he quickly came to the point. 'Si par hasard [if by any chance],' he said, 'you would ever like to be joint with me, I would be honoured and delighted.' I have always thought it was kind of him to make the offer, but neither of us ever mentioned the matter again.

Rothschilds' first notable success in the field of mergers and take-overs came in 1963 when, acting for the Welsh steel group Richard Thomas & Baldwins, we defeated a rival bid, orchestrated by Morgan Grenfell and Schroder Wagg (Schroders having absorbed Helbert Wagg) for the Whitehead Steel Company. Subsequently, in the 1960s, we advised Sun Alliance (successor of the Alliance Assurance Company, and now a 21 per cent shareholder in Rothschilds Continuation) in its bid for London Assurance, and Polycell, against an unwelcome bid by Wall Paper Manufacturers. With Morgan Grenfell we organised the Chartered Consolidated merger, and we advised a number of other well-known companies. Within a period of about five years we participated in deals worth £350–400 million.

With things proceeding well at New Court, and with such a capable team on board, I spent an increasing amount of my time abroad, trying to sort out old problems and to generate new business. I had my fair share of disappointments, but in South America I succeeded in obtaining the Brazilian government's agreement to honour all out-standing payments due on their pre-war bonds; and as a result of a visit to Chile, at the time of the Queen's State Visit in 1968, I was able to arrange the financing for the sale to the Chilean government of its first atomic power plant – a small British 'swimming-pool' nuclear reactor.

I should say that our real specialist on South America was Leo, who did much to revive and expand the bank's relationships there, especially in Brazil. When I was presented to the Duke of Edinburgh in Santiago during the Queen's State Visit, he remarked that there seemed to be rather a lot of Rothschilds on the continent at the time – as he had only just met my brother in Rio de Janeiro. Leo was there in connection with the construction of the Rio–Niterói bridge, for which he led the financing.

The greater part of my time overseas was spent in Canada and America, dealing almost exclusively with Brinco's affairs. Surveys conducted during the first two summer exploration seasons in Labrador had shown that at a single site below the Hamilton Falls a potential of 4 million continuous horsepower could be developed. Although this figure was in fact well below the eventual capacity, it indicated that the Falls were going to be by far the best resource of the whole concession area. From an engineering standpoint, moreover, studies by Montreal Engineering and Shawinigan Engineering showed that the topography of the Falls area was suitable for the creation of a large reservoir, and of an underground power-house which could be fed by diverting the waters above the Falls into a man-made channel, ending in a 1,000 foot drop to the turbines. The reports concluded that the cost per horsepower of the development would be very low.

Consequently, by the time of my second visit to Newfoundland in 1957, Brinco had embarked on the building of an all-weather tote road, 105 miles long, from Esker, a siding at 'Mile 286' on the Quebec North Shore and Labrador Railway, to the west bank of the Hamilton River above the Falls. This project involved the construction of three earth dams across the Atikonak River and a foot-bridge and cable-way across the river above the Falls.

I was accompanied on the visit by my friend John Tweedsmuir, the elder son of Canada's former Governor-General (the author John Buchan, who was created the 1st Lord Tweedsmuir). We had the use of a single-engined aeroplane and flew around the whole concession area, visiting all the people working for Brinco.

We visited all but one of the men's camps – at one of which I remember getting quite a surprise on finding that the hot water had been connected up to the lavatory by mistake. After a day spent trudging through the muskeg, we would sleep out under canvas, with the

Northern Lights flickering in the sky and the timber wolves howling in the forests. The one camp we missed was to have been the last on our itinerary, but John persuaded me to go on a short fishing expedition instead. This turned out to have been a lucky change of plan for us, though not for others. The camp was nearly out of food and we had provisions to supply them. The next day the camp was cut off by low cloud, and for a whole week the men had to live off one unfortunate moose.

Years later, when Brinco's work at the falls was nearing completion, and I looked back to my fishing trip with Tweedsmuir, I asked Joseph Smallwood for a commission – at which he looked at me rather sharply. So I explained to him that in the early days of Brinco, one of our pilots had got into difficulties, and had had to land his amphibious plane on a lake. As he was taxiing the aircraft towards a kind of jetty, an American GI appeared out of the blue and told him that he could not land there, and then proceeded to threaten him with a gun. It turned out that an American general had taken the local fishing rights, and did not want anyone else to interfere with his enjoyment. 'This was a grave infringement of your sovereignty,' I told Mr Smallwood. 'And my commission is therefore going to be the right for myself and my sons to fish free of licence [which would have cost $5] on any river or lake anywhere in Newfoundland and Labrador.' 'Done,' he said, and my request subsequently received the unanimous assent of Newfoundland's legislature.

While the reports had concluded that the cost per horsepower of the falls development would be low, the key question of finding a market for the power had still to be resolved, as it was clear that Newfoundland alone could not possibly absorb even the minimum power output that was going to make the project viable. The provinces of Quebec and Ontario, and the north-eastern United States, including New York, seemed hopeful candidates: they were all consuming increasing quantities of power, and for a number of reasons nuclear-generated power was even then unlikely to supply their growing needs. But there was the difficulty that Brinco's power transmission line was going to have to follow an overland route, via Quebec, and this became a seemingly intractable problem which stymied the progress of the project for many years.

The chief stumbling block was the left-wing Liberal government of Quebec, under Premier Jean Lesage, which, maintaining that Labrador rightfully belonged to Quebec in any case, insisted on conditions for co-operation over the transmission line which were completely unacceptable to Brinco. This became especially frustrating when, in 1962, Consolidated Edison of New York declared that they were willing to buy large quantities of power from the Hamilton Falls for delivery to New York State.

Egged on by his resources minister René Levesque, Lesage, whose government had nationalised Quebec's private power companies, demanded that in order for a deal to be done, Newfoundland must nationalise Brinco, and develop the Hamilton Falls in partnership with Quebec. He was also adamant that the power from the falls would have to be delivered to Hydro-Quebec, his province's hydroelectric power utility, on the Quebec side of the Labrador boundary, so that the power itself would be sold on from Quebec – and Quebec, instead of Newfoundland, would earn huge tax rebates from the Federal Canadian government. Furthermore, the president of Hydro-Quebec, Jean-Claude Lessard, made public statements to the effect that all or most of the workers and materials for the Hamilton Falls project must come from Quebec; and it proved almost impossible to agree a price for the power.

Robert Winters, a gifted engineer and businessman who became chairman of Brinco in 1963, was driven to the verge of despair by the difficulties posed by Lesage's government. Negotiations broke down completely in 1964, and it was not until Lesage had lost the Quebec elections in 1966, to be replaced by Premier Daniel Johnson and his Union Nationale party, that an agreement was finally signed on power transmission, so enabling the development of the falls to go ahead. But by then Consolidated Edison of New York had dropped out of the picture, leaving only Quebec as a potential customer for the huge output.

My principal task all along was to ensure that the financing of the project remained on a sure footing. This involved regular, and sometimes hair-raising visits to our financial agents in New York, Morgan Stanley, and to other banks and potential investors in Canada and America. But I also got to know all the politicians involved, including the French Canadians in Quebec; and, looking back, I have the impression that it was simple chauvinism, on the part of both the Newfoundlanders and the Québecois, that was the root cause of the obstacles which for so long held up Brinco's progress.

For example, while a French Canadian presence on our board – and so on our side at the negotiating table – would, I always felt, have been an invaluable help in moving matters forward, none such of any real stature was ever appointed. I got to know well a Quebec lawyer called Marc de Goumois, who was on friendly terms with all the people with whom we had to deal in the Quebec government and at Hydro-Quebec, and who would have welcomed closer involvement with Brinco. But for no good reason that I could make out – except the fact of his French-Canadian background – my fellow directors refused to accept that he was a suitable candidate for a board appointment.

Marc de Goumois had even arranged for me to meet Levesque at a private lunch, at which Levesque had explained to me that he would like to sit down with Brinco to work out a deal whereby Newfoundland and Quebec could develop the Hamilton Falls jointly. But when I passed on his proposal to Brinco's head office, my colleagues all but ignored it; my strong impression was that they could not accept the idea that an Englishman could succeed where they were failing. I should also say that Lesage, the head of Hydro-Quebec – by whom I was always personally well received – was also set against doing any such deal.

When Sir Winston Churchill died in 1965 and the Brinco negotiations were still at a critical stage, Premier Smallwood telephoned me in London to ask if I thought he should come over for Churchill's funeral. I said I thought that he certainly should. So he came over to England and before the funeral John Tweedsmuir made arrangements for Mr Smallwood and me to go to the Lying-in-State in Westminster Hall. We were both very moved by the experience, and as we walked out into the wintry January sunshine, I took Smallwood by the arm and said, 'Mr Premier, we still have a lot of unfinished business.' He took a little time to reply, and when he did, his reply was quite unexpected. 'Yes. I wonder. By Jove, I think I can do it,' he said. 'Let them be called the Churchill Falls.'

So when, in October 1966, Brinco was finally able to announce the start of the construction – on what was then the Western world's greatest hydroelectric project ever undertaken – the name everyone heard was the Churchill Falls. It was to be the biggest venture ever to be financed entirely by private enterprise, and it followed the government of Quebec's confirmation of an agreement for the sale of all the Churchill Falls' power output to Hydro-Quebec, for onward transmission.

The ground-breaking ceremony took place on 17 July 1967, and ended with a tremendous fireworks display. Joseph Smallwood, wearing a gilded miner's helmet, used a gold-plated spade to turn the first sod of earth. Among the spectators were representatives of the Federal government, all the Newfoundland legislature, and members of Hydro-Quebec. The Brinco contingent included myself, Bob Winters, Don McParland (the mining engineer brought in to supervise technical aspects of the project, who went on to become Brinco's president), and Donald Gordon, the then newly-appointed president of the corporation (whose acceptance of the job six months earlier had been greeted by Joseph Smallwood with a telegram reading 'Hurray Stop Joey'). Winston Churchill, grandson of the Prime Minister, attended the ceremony too.

The official opening of the Churchill Falls development did not take place for a further five years, but in the autumn of 1967 the detonation of the first explosive charges signalled the start of the vast power-house excavation, an operation which someone compared to that of a mine working at a rate of 3,000 tons a day for three years. Altogether, the excavation of the whole power-house complex involved the removal of 2,300,000 cubic yards of rock, enough to fill a 550 mile-long column of 35 ton trucks. When completed, the power-house was 972 feet long, up to 81 feet wide in places, and 154 feet high – more than five times the size of the concourse of Central Station in Montreal.

Another cavern, almost as large, was excavated between the power-house and the Churchill River. This was the surge chamber, designed to collect the water after it had spun the turbines and to direct it into two 'tailrace' tunnels, and to protect the power-house against surges of water resulting from its flow through the turbines. The surge chamber was 763 feet long, in places 60 feet wide, and 150 feet high. A third underground chamber, 856 feet long, was built to house the transformers, which were designed to step up the electricity from the 15,000 volts produced by the generators to a transmission level of some 700,000 volts.

The transformers and generators were built by three Canadian companies, General Electric of Canada, Marine Industries and Dominion Engineering, who joined up to form the Churchill Falls (Machinery) Consortium. The shafts connecting the turbines to the generators – the bolts alone of which each weighed 350 lbs – were manufactured in England; other parts were made in Scotland, France and America. One of the turbine runners, which were cast in Canada, was, at a finished weight of 80 tons, the largest piece of stainless steel casting that had ever been undertaken. The transformers were the heaviest items of all, the largest of them weighing 240 tons; special cranes and equipment had to be designed and manufactured to get them to the site, including a 250-ton railway truck and two 700-hp tractors.

The construction of the principal reservoir, christened the Smallwood Reservoir, resulted in one of the largest man-made bodies of water in the world. It covered an area of more than 2,000 square miles and at its maximum level reached depths of up to 1,500 feet. At the peak of construction work, Brinco had as many as 5,000 men working in the area; and the total costs of the project, which remained comfortably within budget, just exceeded $1 billion.

The power output of the Churchill Falls development was once described to me as being sufficient to light a line of 40-watt light-bulbs standing next to each other, with no gaps in between them, the whole way round the Equator.

At the inauguration ceremony of the Churchill Falls power station in 1972, Premier Frank Moores of Newfoundland, whose Progressive Conservative party had recently replaced Joseph Smallwood's Liberals in government, described the project as 'proof of what can be achieved when private enterprise works in co-operation with governments'. He went on to say, 'Long before the first physical work was done on the site, there was a group of men, most of them world-known financiers and bankers, who took the initiatives that made even the idea of a hydroelectric project in this sub-Arctic region possible. They were the men who were willing to put their money on the line for something that had never been tried before and which carried an element of real risk.'

Two years later, when the finishing touches to the project were within a few months of completion, Moores's government set in motion the machinery for the nationalisation of Brinco. 'The resources of Newfoundland are the property of our people,' he said. 'It follows that control over these resources must rest with the people's government.' In fact a compromise was reached whereby the province agreed to buy the Churchill Falls company we had established, together with all Brinco's remaining water rights in Labrador, for $160 million.

Over the whole period of the Brinco project, I made more than 400 trips across the Atlantic, and in the 1960s I also began to make regular visits to Japan. At one stage, I was spending so much time overseas that the Governor of the Bank of England, Lord Cobbold, called me into his office to ask if I thought it wise to be away so often from New Court. My answer, that my highly competent fellow partners were well able to get along without me, did not altogether placate him, but thereafter he none the less left me alone.

My family's links with Japan date back to the second half of the last century, to the early years of the reign of the Emperor Meiji. He ascended the throne in 1868, a decade and a half after the arrival at Uraga, at the mouth of Tokyo Bay, of the American naval squadron of twelve black warships under the command of Commodore Matthew Perry, which led to the opening up of Japan to Western ships and trade. And it was Emperor Meiji and his ministers who began the whirlwind process of Japan's transformation from a feudal to a modern state.

My great-grandfather Baron Lionel and his brothers joined with Parr's Bank in underwriting a loan for the construction (supervised by British engineers) of Japan's first railway, running between Edo (Tokyo) and Yokohama, which opened in 1872. Then in 1881 Emperor Meiji sent an imperial mission overseas to study the constitutional arrangements of Western industrialised countries, including Germany, France, America and England. Demands for some kind of representative government in Japan were growing, and the emperor had decreed that a form of elected assembly was to be established in ten years' time. During the Japanese delegation's visit to London, they called on Lord Rothschild and his brothers, my grandfather Leo and Uncle Alfred, at New Court, though more to elicit their views on the British monarchy and the constitution than on merchant banking.

But when the Japanese began to build up their navy, NMR was able to offer more concrete help – in the shape of a loan for the construction of Japanese warships building in British shipyards. In 1911 we issued the Japanese National Bond, and in 1923, when virtually the whole of Yokohama and most of Tokyo (already the third largest city in the world) were destroyed by an earthquake, Rothschilds joined in the international effort to fund the rebuilding. We made two loans, the 1924 Imperial Japanese Government 6 per cent sterling loan of £25 million, and then, two years later, a further loan of £6 million to the City of Tokyo. An unexpected consequence of this – or so I have heard tell – was that when the Japanese took Shanghai during their war with China, they were not so harsh in their treatment of the colony's large population of German-Jewish refugees.

Prior to Japan's entry into the last war, during the period of ultra-nationalism which the Japanese now call *kurai tanima* (the dark valley), Japan's debts to the United Kingdom were re-scheduled, in 1934. Three years later, when the Japanese military had persuaded the government to ban all overseas investment, NMR broke off all direct dealings with the country, though we kept open a line of communication through a Dutch bank, which acted as our correspondent. Until the 1860s, Dutch merchants had held special trade concessions in Cipangu, as Japan was then known; they sold the Japanese the guns with which they fired on foreign ships entering their waters, and they continued, to some extent, to enjoy 'favoured nation' status with the Japanese.

During the early years of the Military Occupation of Japan by America after the Second World War, the Americans laid down that all foreign business undertaken by Japan must be transacted in US dollars. With the strict Bank of England exchange control regulations of those days, it was a policy that effectively ruled the British out of the picture, though two British overseas banks – the Chartered Bank of Australia, India and China, and the Hongkong and Shanghai Banking Corporation – continued to maintain a presence in Japan. However, one day in 1949, Roland Williams came across an article in the *Evening Standard* which reported that the American authorities in Japan were considering a relaxation in their foreign currency policy, and that they were on the point of allowing the Japanese to do business in sterling as well as dollars.

So Roland got in touch with our Dutch contacts in Tokyo (at that time the Nederlandsche Indische Handelsbank and the Nederlandsche Handelsbank Maatschappij) and they confirmed the accuracy of the report in the *Standard*. Roland then suggested to Tony and me that perhaps he ought to go out to Japan, with the idea of reviving the foreign exchange and silver bullion business which Roland's father Sidney had done with the Japanese in the 1920s and early 1930s – and also, of course, to pick up any new business. We naturally agreed.

Before the war, Japanese finance and industry had been completely dominated by the great *zaibatsu*, the huge family-owned financial and industrial conglomerates which dated from the Meiji era. The heads of the Mitsubishi, Mitsui, Sumitomo and other families ran their businesses like little kingdoms, and were among the richest men in the world. But during the Military Occupation, the Americans broke up the *zaibatsu*, and supervised the formation of new banks and public companies in their place. (After the Occupation, the *zaibatsu* re-emerged, but in a very different form, and no longer concentrated in the hands of a few families.)

Our Dutch friends in Japan introduced Roland to a number of the newly constituted banks, most of which were keen to do business in sterling. Rothschilds consequently became correspondents for some half-dozen institutions, including the Daiwa and Sumitomo banks, the Bank of Yokohama and the Industrial Bank of Japan, and we opened up sterling letters of credit for them in London. All the relationships established at that time were in the commercial banking area, and they proved highly remunerative. Roland was also introduced to officials at the Ministry of Finance, which proceeded to open the Japanese government's main sterling account with Rothschilds in London.

When the peace treaty between Japan and the Allies was signed in 1951, and when diplomatic relations between Japan and Britain were restored, we assisted their envoy in London, Mr Takashi Ihara, to find a new home for the Japanese mission. At that time, of course, the Japanese were still immensely unpopular in Britain, but Takashi Ihara, a Japanese aristocrat who was distantly related to the Imperial Family and had been imprisoned for his opposition to Japan's entry into the war, was an inspired choice. First as the treasury representative of the Japanese government's overseas agency, and then, after the peace treaty came into effect in 1952 and full relations were restored, as Financial Counsellor at the Japanese embassy, Ihara worked hard to rebuild bridges. He also became my closest contact and friend in Japan after he returned there in 1954.

By the end of the war Japan's sterling debts accounted for something like three quarters of the country's total external debt. Takashi Ihara set about achieving a fair settlement of these debts, and in doing so he helped to establish a renewed good faith, at least from a financial point of view, between Britain and Japan. Almost certainly his most important achievement was to obtain instructions from Tokyo to deposit £20 million with the Bank of England. This served as a sign of his country's good intentions in respect of the repayment of Japanese government sterling bonds which had been issued in London in the 1930s.

Soon after his arrival in London, Takashi Ihara came to have lunch at New Court. One of our other guests was Lord Ivor Spencer-Churchill, who had a message to convey to Ihara from his cousin Winston. Churchill was once again Prime Minister, and the message was – and for some reason I remember the Churchillian phraseology exactly – 'Mr Ihara, my uncle has charged me to let you know that if he can do anything to heal the breaches of war you are to let him know.' Ihara had learnt all about Rothschilds' connections with Japan and, after he had relayed Churchill's message to Tokyo, we were more or less besieged by Japanese banks and security houses desperate to re-establish connections in London. So we advised them on opening up London branches, and I used regularly to accompany Japanese bankers to interviews with Mr Hilton Clark at the Bank of England. Hilton Clark, who had worked closely with Governor Montagu Norman, was the official who authorised the establishment of branches in London by foreign banks and finance houses.

In this process, I got to know Tsunao Okumura, the president of the leading Tokyo stockbroking house Nomura Securities, and a close friend of the then Japanese Finance Minister Hayato Ikeda. Okumura was one of the shrewdest and best-connected businessmen in Japan, whose relatively lowly, and thus untainted, status at Nomura before the war made it possible for him to rise straight to the top afterwards. He got Nomura back on its feet in the 1950s, and through personal contacts solicited important government support for the growth of the Japanese stockmarket and stockbroking houses in general.

Although Tsunao Okumura came from a very different background from Takashi Ihara – Okumura's father had been a rich tradesman – he also became a great friend of mine. He had risen through the ranks of Nomura, gaining the reputation of a great playboy along the way – a reputation he certainly deserved. When he died in the 1970s, he left a wife and four mistresses. Between them, Ihara and Okumura knew everyone in the Japanese government and the business community; when Ihara left the diplomatic service, he became chairman of the Bank of Yokohama, the only bank in Japan which had no foreign borrowings.

In 1962, at the instigation of Tsunao Okumura, a group of Japanese businessmen – the president of Mitsubishi Bank, the chairman of Tokyo Electric, the president of the Japan Chamber of Commerce and Industry, and Okumura himself – invited a delegation of senior bankers from the City of London to visit Tokyo for meetings with bankers, brokers and government officials. Among those who received invitations were Siegmund Warburg and Sir Alexander Hood, of Schroders; and so I was especially flattered to be asked to head the delegation. However, although I was by then the senior partner of NMR, I felt it would be more appropriate for an older man to be the leader – and if possible one with a title. So I proposed Alexander Hood as a more suitable candidate, and everyone fell in with my suggestion. What I cannot have known at that time – or so, at least, I like to think – is that the titular head of a Japanese mission is not, *de facto*, the most senior individual. This is so that if anything goes wrong, it is not the senior man who loses face; and when we got to Japan, I, as the *de facto* leader in the eyes of our hosts, was certainly treated with an almost embarrassing deference.

En route to Japan, Elizabeth and I broke our journey in India, to stay at Mysore for the Desara festival, as guests of the Maharajah, His Highness Sri Jaya Chamarajendra Wadiyar Bahadur, with whose predecessor, Maharajah Sri Krishmraja Wadiyar IV, Peter Trehearne and I had stayed in 1939. During a visit to London the Maharajah – who had succeeded his uncle in 1940, and was to be the last ruling member of a dynasty which was established in Mysore at the end of the fourteenth century – had come to have lunch at New Court, and a week or two later I had received the invitation to the festival. We flew from Bombay to Bangalore, where we were collected by one of the Maharajah's drivers in an ancient green Rolls-Royce. At Mysore, a house in the palace precincts was placed at our disposal, with our own cook, bearer, chauffeur and other household staff.

It must have been one of the last of the old-style durbars, and it was a fabulous occasion. On the night of the festivities, we sat in the Maharanee's box in the vast durbar hall of the palace, and witnessed one of the most colourful ceremonies one could have wished for. In the centre of the durbar hall the Maharajah sat on a dais, cross-legged on a silver throne covered with golden cushions. He was surrounded by courtiers dressed in gorgeous scarlet costumes and bodyguards with swords and Indian scimitars.

Outside, on the parade ground, his troops were drawn up, and as Mysore was a 21-gun state, the number of troops he was permitted was large. The soldiers marched past as a band played 'The British Grenadiers' and other regimental tunes, and a detachment of Gurkhas marched to 'Scotland the Brave'. During the war the Maharajah had followed his uncle's example in giving strong support to the Allied cause, and in the later stages of the war Mysore provided great facilities for the massing and preparation of troops for the expulsion of the Japanese from Burma.

There was also a parade of elephants, and six of these magnificent creatures, all heavily caparisoned, advanced towards the Maharajah. One of them was specially trained for the occasion, and in front of him was placed a huge silver platform, to one side of which there was a silver tub filled with rose petals. The elephant, with his mahout, walked solemnly forward, placed one foot on the silver platform, and with his trunk sucked up rose petals from the tub. He then put his trunk above his head and trumpeted shrilly, blowing a stream of rose petals into the air. All the elephants trumpeted, everybody clapped and huzzahed, and the band struck up with the Mysore national anthem. I wore my miniature campaign medals for the occasion and met a number of Indian Army officers who had fought in the same campaigns as I had.

The Maharajah's senior subjects, all dressed in vivid uniforms, in turn went up to their sovereign, seated on his silver throne, and presented him with a symbolic gold rupee. After the durbar we were invited to attend a special ceremony inside the palace. We were ushered into an audience chamber where the Maharajah, magnificent in jewel-studded costume and with a huge row of pearls, mounted another throne, surrounded by his courtiers. The Maharanee brought in a large silver bowl and washed her husband's feet. There was then an audience at which we exchanged gifts. We gave him an eighteenth-century *étui* (a small sewing kit), and he gave me a magnificent ivory chess set and many other gifts to my wife.

Before setting off, I had decided that I should learn some Japanese, and so through the Japanese embassy I arranged for a young woman, Keiko Nakamura, to come to teach me some basic phrases and vocabulary – at my mother's house in Thurloe Square, for the sake of propriety. In my ignorance at the time, I did not appreciate that there are several ways of speaking Japanese – that there are different grammatical voices, depending on the gender and relative status of the speakers. For example, a man of lowly status speaks a more deferential version of the language when addressing his superior. In the days before the Japanese adopted Western dress, when two people met they would ascertain their respective rank by looking at the *tongs*, or ideograms, on their sashes, bowing to the appropriate depth and speaking in the fashion required.

With the help of Keiko Nakamura I mugged up a little speech to make on my arrival, and when eventually I arrived at Tokyo airport, at 2 o'clock one morning, I duly delivered it to Tsunao Okumura and the welcoming party which had come to meet me. But as I spoke my piece I could not help noticing first the look of surprise on the assembled faces, and then the suppressed amusement. The Japanese I had learnt was the deferential form in which a woman addresses a man.

My Japanese never progressed far beyond the rudimentary level of polite words and phrases, though I learnt to chat about plants and gardens in a simple way. At business meetings – where I spoke in English – I used to understand enough Japanese to sense when the interpreter was not properly translating my remarks, and when to exclaim *tondemonai!* or *bakarashi!* (roughly translated as 'Nonsense!'). Every now and again I would get over-confident and run into difficulties. On one occasion I was in Tokyo with a young colleague from New Court, Michel de Carvalho, who used afterwards to relate teasingly how one morning I insisted on ordering breakfast room-service in Japanese. Feeling rather smug, his story went, I sat back and waited – for almost an hour. Eventually, there was a light tapping at the door; I opened it, and there, standing before me, were two beautiful kimono-clad ladies bowing politely and saying, 'You ordered geisha girls?'

After several days of meetings, receptions and dinners with our hosts in Tokyo, I felt I had had a sufficiently interesting glimpse of Japan and the Japanese to report back my first impressions to my partners at New Court. Anyone familiar with Japan would, I imagine, have found my observations simplistic, but, except for Roland Williams, none of my colleagues at Rothschilds in those days had had the chance to observe the Japanese in peacetime.

'Most people,' I wrote, 'would agree that for industriousness, orderliness and cleanliness the Japanese are a race far above most. They are thrifty, yet at the same time they have learnt to like many Western comforts. They suffer from no "war-guilt" complex; to them the Emperor – no longer a god-like figure – purged the nation in his broadcast in 1945. He had been led astray by his Ministers, and told his people that they must turn their thoughts to other things.

'Many leaders of industry were taken by the Americans to "rehabilitation" centres where they too "purged" themselves and were "democratised". The *zaibatsu* were disbanded, but it is still evident that the great concerns like the Mitsubishi, Fuji, Sumitomo, Sanwa and Daiwa still have extraordinary power, owning so many of the industries and all that goes to make up the structure of these industries – rather like Ford of America, though on a smaller scale.

'The Japanese like to be led in a paternal way, and this can best be illustrated by the way labour is either not free to or does not move from one industry to another. Once in a job, then there the employee stays, no matter whether the industry is going through a difficult period.

'General MacArthur, who was considered a *shogun*, greatly offended the Japanese (and they do take offence quite easily) by saying that they were an immature people and had a childlike mentality. But this is true insofar as few Japanese think for themselves. An order is an order; a thing to be done cannot be varied to suit different circumstances. They do not easily change their views of their own accord, but they will adapt themselves very quickly once they have been told by the authority above them what is needed.

'In the pre-war days it was the *daimyo* or feudal lords who really still ruled. Today the system has been abolished and there are no titles. However, many of the *daimyo* have taken leading positions, and they are still accorded the highest respect; their decisions are usually carried out to the letter.

'However, there is another side to the Japanese mind. Sir Robert Black, the Governor of Hong Kong, told me of how he had been interrogated during the war, and of the ruthlessness and seeming inflexibility of purpose shown by his captors. But he discovered that this could be deflected. He described how he escaped "breakdown" in his interrogation by making the Japanese interrogator lose face. Immediately, he said, the train of thought would change and his captors were unable to go back to pick up the threads.

'Face is all-important. The president of any corporation is sheltered by those below him who can "take the rap" if necessary, and they in turn have others below them. The Japanese will go to great lengths to avoid any circumstance where this loss of face can occur, and many are the devious and ingenious ways whereby this can be overcome with honour satisfied on all sides.

'There is an inherent politeness which sometimes, by its formality, can be maddening. But it can also be the most convenient cloak for not understanding a question or evading an issue. Hospitality is considered a virtue, and the meticulousness of planning every available moment for one's guests is sometimes disconcerting.'

I ended the report with some simple observations on the Japanese women I had encountered. 'They are charming, elegant and well-mannered, and appear docile and subservient to their men. They are uncomplaining, know when not to talk, or when to make conversation if conversation is required.'

The primitive attitude of some Japanese men to women was brought home to me when, some years later, I was in Japan with my wife Elizabeth, and together we went to a party given by Tsunao Okumura, who was then seriously ill with cancer. The moment came when he wanted to talk to me about some piece of outstanding business, and so turning to Elizabeth he said, 'Woman, leave the room.' She was sufficiently startled to do so – but it was by no means the last I heard of it at home.

On my first, and almost every subsequent, visit to Japan, I used at some point to have meetings with the Japanese prime minister of the day and his minister of finance. This, I noticed, gave me a standing among Japanese bankers and businessmen which would not normally be accorded to foreign visitors, or *geijin*. In 1962, I and my fellow delegates from the City were invited to a meeting with Mr Ikeda, Tsunao Okumura's friend who had by now become Prime Minister, and his Minister of Finance Mr Tanaka – who was also, later on, to become Prime Minister. We were received with great cordiality, and the Prime Minister told us how he wanted us to help build Japan's future prosperity; he stressed his government's desire to be more closely associated with Britain and Europe, and was at pains to emphasise that he did not want Japan to be dependent solely on the American economy. A day or so later, when the *Times* correspondent asked Mr Ikeda what he thought of the British bankers' visit, he said that bankers are traditionally cautious, and he found this to be particularly so of British bankers.

Most of our meetings took place in a large conference room at the Okura Hotel, located on a hillside overlooking the Imperial Palace and the western edge of downtown Tokyo. The hotel, built by the nobleman Kishichiro Okura, had only just opened, and was the first in Tokyo to have been designed to de luxe Western standards. The London contingent sat in a row along one side of a long table covered with a green baize cloth, with the Japanese opposite us. We were especially impressed by the thoughtful and friendly tone of our meeting with the Governor of the Bank of Japan, Masamichi Yamagiwa, and by the president of the Mitsubishi Bank, Makoto Usami (later also a president of the Bank of Japan). Both men stressed the Japanese shortage of capital, and the need for money to satisfy the tremendous upsurge which was taking place in their country's economy.

Kiichi Miyazawa, Japan's director-general of Economic Planning, told us of the dissent within the Japanese cabinet as to whether or not the country should solicit foreign aid at all, but explained that he and Prime Minister Ikeda took the view that there was a need for foreign capital and investment. They were determined to build their country into a top-class industrial power, and said that they would have liked to trade with China, but were hesitant because of American feelings and the (understandably) difficult terms on which the Chinese wanted to trade. The Japanese seemed to address all questions to me, but Alexander Hood always replied for our side by saying what a thoughtful speech we had just heard, and how much we should like to study the transcripts.

Mr Miyazawa later took up the reins at the Ministry of International Trade and Industry, which Prime Minister Ikeda himself had used as a springboard to the Ministry of Finance and so to the top office. MITI was a powerful and highly influential organisation; every large Japanese company had a research team, which was obliged to pass on its findings and any worthwhile new ideas to MITI, whose officials then distilled all the material relating to a certain sector of business or industry, and passed it on to the relevant corporations. Companies competed ferociously among themselves, but they still had to share their knowledge.

During our stay, our Japanese hosts arranged for us to visit the gardens of the imperial palace, the former residence of the Tokugawa *shogun* from whom Emperor Meiji reclaimed political power in the 1860s. At a pavilion in the grounds of the palace we were entertained to a show put on by the Emperor's guards – mock-combat with long wooden staves – and were invited to a performance of classical dancing and music in a small theatre. I enjoyed the guards' display, and the highly stylised dancing, called *bugaku* – performed in honour of the first Japanese emperor, Jimmu Tenno – as well as the performers' elaborate costumes and strange head-gear. But the ancient *gagaku* music I found excruciating, almost painful, to the ear.

Touring the imperial gardens after the musical entertainment, I came across the most magnificent camellia tree I had ever seen. Although it was not in flower, it had large, deep-green, glossy leaves and was laden with seed. I asked one of our guides if I might be permitted to take some seed, but after a consultation with his colleagues he informed me, with much bowing and apology, that this would not be possible – because the seed from this very special camellia tree was used exclusively to make hair oil for the Empress. Not to be put off, I then did something which I strongly discourage visitors to Exbury from doing. I dropped my camera lens and stooped down to retrieve it in my handkerchief, scooping up a few seeds from under the tree in the process.

But I got my come-uppance in the end. I had to wait seventeen years for the camellia to bloom in Exbury gardens; and when it did eventually produce some flowers, in 1979, I showed it to Sir Giles Loder – one of the greatest camellia growers of our time – who confirmed my suspicions that the plant was no more than a fine, strong strain of the common-or-garden *camellia japonica*.

On subsequent visits to Tokyo, on the say-so of the Grand Master of Ceremonies – *Shikibu-Shoku* – of the Imperial Household Agency, I was allowed to visit parts of the imperial gardens where visitors are not normally permitted to go, and where once or twice I caught a distant glimpse of the Empress Nagako and her ladies-in-waiting. In time, a small part of the gardens was devoted to a collection of deciduous azaleas which I sent out from Exbury, and which, so I was told, the Emperor Hirohito would visit once a year at the height of the flowering.

The primary purpose of my next visit to Japan, in 1964, was to attend meetings of the International Monetary Conference, and on my arrival I was asked to give a press conference. The account of it, as reported in the *Asahi Evening News* (Japan's only English language evening newspaper), gives an idea of how the Japanese perceived me and my family, and must, I feel sure, go some way to explain the extraordinary cordiality I always experienced.

The world's wealthiest man, the banker who lords over the world's financial circles, the man who manipulates the world's gold at will, the head of the Rothschild family of England which is still looked upon in mystical awe by the people of the world opened his mouth and spoke fluently in Japanese. '*Nippon wa nikai-me, sukoshi Nihongo wo benkyo shitaga muzukashi-idesu.*' (This is my second trip to Japan. I have studied some Japanese, but it is still very difficult.)

Rothschilds act as merchant bank, issuing house, acceptance house and bullion broker, and also as agent for the Bank of England in transacting gold bullion. 'The official gold price of the Bank of England is set every day at my office; we have been doing this since 1806.' So saying he smiled. When mention was made of the sudden leap in the gold price from $35 per ounce to $40 at the time of dollar uneasiness in October 1960, 'When the price of gold went up, my house sold it,' he said with indifference.

The family which at one time made loans to the Emperor of France and forwarded the lump sum to the British Government for the take-over of the Suez Canal seems to have been experiencing unfortunate decline in the twentieth century. Forced to relinquish a portion of his huge and unfathomable assets in the post-war period as inheritance tax, one of his mansions is now used as the Soviet Embassy.

In similar vein, at the time of the reconstruction of New Court as a modern six-storey building, Japanese press reports spoke of a new sixty-storey building.

During the two years since my first visit to Japan, Rothschilds, in partnership with Nomura Securities, had completed Eurodollar bond issues for Hitachi, Teijin, and Toyo Rayon. Consequently, my Japanese friends pushed the boat out, and I was invited to a geisha party every evening for more than a week. This had its hazards: being invited to so many parties in such a short space of time I would find myself at a restaurant where I had already been entertained, perhaps only the night before. So when I arrived at the geisha house, I used to caution the Mama-san, the woman in charge of proceedings, not to show any signs of recognition, so as not to give offence to my solicitous hosts. As true geisha girls can only be hired at considerable expense, an invitation to a geisha party is, or used to be, quite an honour.

Luckily for me, as the parties tended to go on for some time and I was already getting a little stout, I was not often required to sit Japanese-fashion – resting on the heels with one's feet crossed – but would be placed at a conventional table with my host. When the food was being served, sometimes all at once, though usually with the more delicate dishes first, small bottles of slightly warm *sake* would arrive, together with a good deal of Asahi, Kirin or (more often in the winter months) Sapporo beer. As *sake* tends to make one thirsty, I always enjoyed it best when I had a glass of beer to hand. The *sake* cups were filled up continually by the geisha girls, and there were a great many toasts of *kamp-pei*, or Good Health. A guest would pass his cup to the host, who would drink from it, rinse it in a small bowl of water, and hand it back, and then offer his cup in return.

After dinner we would be amused by the geishas, who are professional entertainers, though by tradition they sometimes go on to become the mistresses of their regular patrons. They undergo a strict training, and an educated geisha will be an accomplished musician, singer and actor, and will be well-versed in the classical literature of the East. Dressed in their beautiful kimonos, and wearing their distinctive make-up – a very white face and an elaborate wig with large combs – they perform dances, act out little plays and sing songs, the words of which I got to know very well. One geisha girl I remember even had an extensive repertory of card tricks. Sometimes, when the *sake* was beginning to have its effect, my host would perform a sword dance, or we would together mime or play the games described by Ian Fleming in his novel *You Only Live Twice*. Luckily for me, the Japanese love of flowers and gardens made the conversation relatively easy; I could always talk about Exbury, or the gardens and flowers I came to know in Japan, or about *ikebana*, the Japanese art of arranging flowers.

At one geisha party given jointly by Sohei Nakayama, the chairman of the Industrial Bank of Japan, and Kenichiro Komai, the head of Hitachi, during my visit in 1964, I was the only European guest to be invited. With the First Bank of Boston, Rothschilds were then managing the Eurodollar bond issue for Hitachi, which was sponsored and guaranteed by the Industrial Bank of Japan. I was seated at the top table, flanked by my hosts, while everyone else sat cross-legged on the floor. Towards the end of the meal, when my Japanese friends were engaged in animated conversation among themselves, a pretty little geisha girl came up to refill my *sake* glass. 'Rothschild-san,' she said to me, 'I don't call you Rothschild-san; I call you Spoilt-child-san because you have so many parties.'

Tsunao Okumura's geisha parties were the most lavish. To a great extent he had built up his and Nomura's connections with prominent Japanese businessmen and politicians, notably Hayato Ikeda, by entertaining, and he knew the value of a good party. Takashi Ihara's parties tended to be rather more restrained affairs, and were sometimes attended by Yusuke Kashiwagi, an important and greatly respected figure in Japan at that time, who later succeeded Takashi Ihara as head of the Bank of Yokohama. In the course of the evening there would often be a discussion on the future direction of world finance or politics, and my companions would turn to me for my views. By chance, the predictions I was called upon to make sometimes turned out to be right, for example on the movement of the gold price, and earned me a quite undeserved reputation as a man of foresight.

In 1972, I received a letter from Tsunao Okumura which began, 'Prime Minister Eisaku Sato now cherishes your friendship, especially your wisdom and foresight and also the great influence of the Rothschild group.' It went on to explain that the biggest issue then facing Japan was the problem of how to deal with China. 'During my last interview with the Prime Minister, he asked me to enquire whether Mr Edmund de Rothschild would be kind enough to send me a letter so that I can pass it on to the Prime Minister with (a) EdeR's personal views on Communist China and (b) a friendly suggestion from EdeR as to how Japan should cope with Communist China.' I dread to think what I advised.

One of my partners at New Court, Philip Shelbourne, returned from a visit to Japan in 1968 convinced that, in view of the spiralling growth of the Japanese economy and the continuing need of Japanese companies to borrow abroad, Rothschilds should do everything possible to strengthen its position in Japan. So in 1969 I made my third visit to the country, accompanied by two young colleagues from New Court, Tony Hillier and Nick Eeley; and on my arrival I gave an interview to *Nihon Kezai Shimbun* (*Japan Economic Journal*), the Japanese equivalent of the *Wall Street Journal*, about a new investment fund we had recently launched with Nomura Securities and Pierson, Heldring, Pierson.

'When I was looking at the maps of the American continent,' I said, 'it occurred to me that the countries surrounding the Pacific Ocean are growing fast. Why shouldn't we invest in these countries?

'We have been doing business with Japan since we undertook the Japanese National Bond in my grandfather's day in 1911, and since the Second World War we have contributed to the reconstruction of the Japanese economy, though it may only be a small contribution. In the future we should be delighted to assist the enterprises in your country through the Pacific Seaboard Fund. NMR accepted the National Bonds before the war and the bonds of Nippon Rayon after the war. Most recently we accepted the Pioneer Electric Corporation CDR issue.

'We have established National Provincial and Rothschild (International) jointly with the National Provincial Bank, one of London's clearing banks. This will extend Rothschilds' credit network in line with the increasing demands for funds from various parts of the world.'

Opening the European equity market through the Pioneer CDR

issue had been a valuable exercise for Rothschilds, and already the Pacific Seaboard Fund had been a great success, both technically and as a public relations venture – so much so, indeed, that the financial press in Tokyo was recommending equities specifically on the grounds that they were likely to be chosen by the fund.

The Japanese whom we met on that visit were, as usual, very cordial; but my colleagues and I sensed that there was a danger of NMR trying to do too many pieces of business with too many different people. The Japanese take great pride in their loyalties, and we had to be careful not to upset them. So Nomura Securities remained our Number One contact in the investment field, and we were careful that any visit we made to any other security house was made known to Nomura. It seemed to be acceptable for us to pass certain orders for private clients through other houses, but we cleared any major piece of business brought to us by them in the issuing field with Nomura.

'There is no doubt that our name stands very high in commercial circles,' I wrote to my partners. 'We got an excellent press and I stressed, I think with some success, that our firm was "go-ahead" in its policy with its young men, and I tried to play down the Personality Cult which seems to surround me.' On the other hand, the presence of Tony Hillier and Nick Eeley beside me at meetings seemed if anything to add to the respect with which I was treated.

The success of the Pacific Seaboard Fund encouraged us to launch, with Merrill Lynch and Nomura, a second fund, Tokyo Capital Holdings; and in November 1969, Tony Hillier and I had to make a two-day visit to Japan to sort out some teething problems. I flew to Tokyo from Canada, where I had been attending a Brinco board meeting, and on the second evening in Tokyo, by which time we had sorted things out, Tony and I were taken out to dinner by Tsunao Okumura. During dinner I suddenly felt a sensation like a cold draught of air, which made me feel very uneasy. I asked Tony if anything was wrong; he assured me that all was well, but I felt curiously sombre and unsettled for the rest of the evening. When we got back to England, I was telephoned early in the morning with the dreadful news that Brinco's chief executive, Don McParland, together with the company treasurer Eric Lambert and three other Brinco executives, had been killed when their aircraft crashed at Churchill Falls – while I was dining in Tokyo.

I was appointed chairman of the supervisory committee of Tokyo

Capital Holdings, and thereafter visited Japan at least once a year for board meetings and other business. Visiting banks and other companies, I soon became familiar with the peculiar Japanese way of conducting negotiations. Meetings always began with an exchange of business cards between an advance party of middle-ranking company representatives; a few minutes later the top man would arrive and the meeting proper could get under way. The Japanese would take an inordinately long time to reach any commercial decision, and so as to buy time there would often be one man in the room whose role was simply to shake his head and say 'No' to everything proposed by my side. But if, then, there was a dinner in the evening, the same man would have been briefed to say 'Yes' to everything. I also learned to judge the seniority of a company official, which was not always revealed by the exchange of cards, by the way in which his office was equipped; if the office was uncarpeted, you knew that you were not dealing with a man of much consequence – except in the case of government officials, where a less discernible system of privileges seemed to apply.

Several times I was invited to attend seminars arranged by *Nihon Kezai Shimbun*, and on one occasion, at a session on Japan and America, I had an object lesson in the Japanese fixation on saving face. As background, it is perhaps worth mentioning that until 1945 the Japanese had never been defeated in all their history, and that they identified the Americans, who had dropped the atomic bombs and occupied the country, as the cause of their dreadful humiliation.

At one seminar we were divided up into groups; mine included the president of Esso, and an unrepentantly nationalistic old Japanese professor of economics. Every word the professor said was translated meticulously into English, but whenever we spoke, the professor ostentatiously removed his earpiece so as not to hear the translation. At the end of our deliberations, the Japanese chairman of our group produced a statement, which was read out by the chairman of *Nihon Kezai Shimbun*. It amounted to a summary of the professor's anti-American talk, and attributed his views to us as well; so I got up and announced that neither I nor my friend from Esso would have any part in this, and that we were now going to leave – which was awkward for the organisers as they had invited various members of the Finance Ministry to meet us at a reception afterwards. So they quickly agreed that I should draft a summary of our contribution to the discussions, and that a summary would be printed in full in the English edition of the journal. But in the Japanese edition, they explained, it might appear with some slight variations.

Whenever possible on my visits to Japan, I used to try to fit in a few days for sightseeing or plant-hunting around the country. On several occasions, with Takashi Ihara, I went searching for wild azalea seed in the mountains; and with another friend, Mitsunari Yamada, head of the credit-card company Nippon Shinpan and a devout Buddhist, I went to visit the great shrines and temples at Kyoto and other places. With the British Ambassador Sir John Pilcher, I visited Nikko, where a fortune-teller threw some beans and told me that in old age I would become very rich. There is a Japanese saying, 'Never say *kekko* [wonderful] until you have seen Nikko', and it is certainly a very beautiful place.

Mitsunari Yamada once took me to see the great ninth-century Buddhist monastery complex at the summit of Mount Koya, in the Kinki region of Japan, not far from Osaka. There we were introduced to a form of the Japanese tea ceremony (*chanoyu*) in a little pavilion – in sight of the greatest and oldest *Cryptomeria japonica* 'Elegans' I have ever seen – at the top of a great flight of steps built into the monastery's exquisite hillside gardens. I was also invited to meditate with the monks, but as I found it uncomfortable to sit cross-legged on the floor for more than fifteen minutes, and impossible to empty my mind of the thought of my discomfort, the exercise was not altogether successful.

The tea ceremony is as much an exercise in refined manners as tea-drinking, and is intended to be conducive to a feeling of serenity. In 1964 Tsunao Okumura took me and my agent Peter Barber to a special tea-house of Nomura's on an island in a lake near Kyoto, where an elderly tea-master explained how he made the tea from specially selected leaves, which, boiled up two or three times, produced a thick green liquid, astringent to the taste. It was not, I found, as conducive to serenity as intended; but we were also given little sweet cakes, as usual with much bowing and smiling.

When I stayed in Japan over a weekend, Tsunao Okumura used to take me to play golf at the 300 Club outside Tokyo; but one Friday afternoon, when he asked me what I would like to do for the weekend, I said I should very much like to make an expedition to Beppu, a hot-spring resort on the north-eastern coast of Kyushu, the southernmost island in the Japanese chain. Tsunao Okumura was curious to know why I had chosen Beppu, but I said that I would let him know the reason once we were there.

The reason was that one evening I had been playing bridge with Ian Fleming at the Portland Club, and at dinner the conversation had turned to his James Bond book *You Only Live Twice* – and he had said to me that when I next went to Japan I must pay a visit to Beppu. So we arrived at Beppu in the dark one Friday evening, and 'went Japanese', which involved my being rigged out in the traditional male *kimono*. The next morning, when I pulled back the curtains of my room, there, sure enough, was the fantastic castle surrounded by clouds of steam issuing from the bubbling volcanic mud springs. We took a special bath, sitting in a series of large communal pools of hot water at different temperatures, and the pools were surrounded by lush foliage, and aquaria full of exotic fish. And so I was able to explain to Tsunao Okumura how Ian Fleming had drawn on Beppu for inspiration for his book, and how he had embroidered on it by adding poisonous plants and man-eating piranhas in the castle moat.

As a result of my involvement with Japan, in 1971 I accepted an invitation from the British Department of Trade and Industry to succeed Mr Michael Montague as chairman of the Asia Division of the British National Export Council. The BNEC was organised into twelve divisions, each of them headed by an industrialist or a banker, and we met regularly to discuss ways of promoting British exports, by overseas exhibitions and suchlike. The Asia division's 'parish' was huge, incorporating Japan, Burma, Thailand, Malaysia, Singapore, Korea, Indonesia, the Philippines, Taiwan, Hong Kong, the Pacific islands, and India and Pakistan. The main part of my job was to visit the chambers of commerce in the various countries, to ascertain their plans for development and to promote British exports.

On my way to a British engineering exhibition in Singapore that year, I visited Thailand. In between discussing British export opportunities in Thailand, I took an afternoon off to visit the British war cemeteries at Kanchanaburi and Chung-kai, the site of the infamous bridge over the River Kwai, built by Allied prisoners of war. The bridge had been rebuilt, but no trains ran over it into Burma; Burmese insurgents were in control of the other side. But the train which was used in the film *The Bridge on the River Kwai* was there, as well as another which the Thais had rescued from the jungle.

To reach the cemeteries I went down the Kwai in a sampan over the sandbanks, and when I arrived at Chung-kai there were gardeners trimming the grass around the graves and planting flowers, and there were masses of huge butterflies in the air. Walking through row upon row of gravestones, my colleague from the BNEC, Bill Bailey, told me how he had been a POW there, and how a prisoner's average life-expectancy was about twenty-nine days. When dysentery and cholera broke out, the Japanese left the camp in the charge of sadistic Korean guards, who meted out regular beatings to those who did not or could not work. Apparently the Japanese arranged for a doctor to be sent up from Singapore, and for those prisoners most seriously ill the doctor rigged up a kind of saline drip fashioned from bamboo shoots. The fact that this one man was doing something positive to help them gave the prisoners new hope and the will to survive.

As the boat took us back past the poor raft-houses of the Thais, each shack with lovely sprays of orchids cascading down from the roofs, gracefully bowing to the flowing stream, I thought of the service and dedication which so many had given to our country, and how lucky were we who survived. That evening we went to dinner with Prince and Princess Piya Rangsit at their old house near the Royal palace in Bangkok, beside a lake surrounded by tropical scented trees.

The exhibition in Singapore was a great success; the British exhibitors sold all the engineering equipment they had brought out with them. Consequently, a further BNEC-sponsored exhibition took place in Tokyo in the early part of 1972 – even though by that time, much to the chagrin of myself and others, the BNEC had been wound up by the Conservative Government.

From Singapore I went on to Japan, where I had been invited to chair a seminar at a conference in Kyoto which had been organised by the futurologist Professor Hermann Kahn, of the American Hudson Institute. Professor Kahn, a man of such huge proportions that special seating arrangements had to be made for him whenever he travelled by air, had written several books on Japan, and was in the process of collating some monumental work on the Year 2000. The stodgy subject of his conference was the Corporate Environment 1975 to 1985, and the seminar I chaired was concerned with Japan's Future and Potential.

Professor Kahn had lined up four distinguished and interesting men to speak: Finance Minister Takeo Fukuda, who later went on to become Prime Minister; Konnosuke Matsushita, the founder and head of the Matsushita Electric Industrial Company; Eikichi Ito, head of the great trading house Ito & Co.; and Shinzo Ohya, the head of Teijin. Eikichi Ito and I were at Cambridge together, and Shinzo Ohya, who immediately after the war served as a cabinet minister under Prime Minister Yoshida, had been to London – and visited New Court – in 1934, as a member of the Japanese mission to renegotiate the re-scheduling of the country's debts. Konnosuke Matsushita rose from the humblest of roots to become perhaps the greatest business leader of Japan this century (the refrain of the Matsushita company song was, 'Like water gushing from a fountain, grow industry, grow, grow, grow; Harmony and Unity'). My only disappointment was the absence from the conference of another Japanese friend of mine, the great innovator Akio Morita, head of the Sony corporation, who contributed so much to Anglo-Japanese friendship that he was given an honorary knighthood.

However, I became good friends with Shinzo Ohya, and also with his wife Masako, a remarkably accomplished woman who danced, sang opera, appeared on Japanese television cookery programmes, and was one of the first women in Japan to run a successful business. She owned a golf club, at which I was often invited to stay, and where she played round the course in bright pink slacks. She used to put me in a bedroom at the very top of the building, where I had great difficulty sleeping in an extremely uncomfortable bed with pillows filled with rice instead of feathers.

The 1972 BNEC exhibition in Tokyo was to promote British medical equipment, and a few months before it was due to take place, one of the Emperor's physicians, Dr Taro Takemi, came on a semi-official visit to Britain. Unfortunately, there was some confusion over the time of his arrival, so that there was no one at Heathrow to meet his flight – on top of which he experienced a hostile reception from one of the airport immigration officers. Consequently, he returned to Japan in a fury, and I was so concerned that he might try to intervene to put a stop to our exhibition that I went to deliver a personal letter of apology to him in Tokyo. To my relief, he could not have been nicer, and even invited me to dine with him at his home, where we were waited on by his wife and I talked rugby football to his son. Later on, it was Taro Takemi who discovered my wife Elizabeth's heart condition.

The exhibition in Tokyo was opened by the staunchly Anglophile Princess Chichibu, the widow of Emperor Hirohito's younger brother. She was the daughter of a Japanese diplomat who was more than once posted to London, and she herself had been born at Walton-on-Thames. She spoke the best English of any Japanese I ever met, and was utterly enchanting in every way. The exhibition, at which

some thirty British surgical and pharmaceutical products manufacturers took stands, was held in Tokyo's Science Museum. In support
of the exhibitors, we arranged a programme of seven symposia held
over six days in the museum's theatre. The subjects covered were
obstetrics and gynaecology, neurosurgery, intensive care, cardiology,
oncology, pharmacology, and toxicology; and each symposium was
conducted by a prominent British specialist.

After I retired from NMR at the end of 1975, I continued to make
an annual trip to Japan, in my capacity as honorary life president of
the Twin Lakes Club, a magnificent country club and golf course
near Maebashi in central Japan, built by Hitoshi Matsuura, chairman
of the Nitto Kogyo Corporation, one of Japan's largest golf-course
construction companies. One afternoon he was watching a golf
match on television, but play was suspended when a storm blew up.
Before the match resumed, a short film was shown to fill in time – and
the film was about Exbury Gardens, *The Glory of the Garden*, made by
my elder son Nicholas. Hitoshi Matsuura so much enjoyed it that he
contacted me to ask if I would help him plant up and landscape the
new course he was preparing to build at Twin Lakes. Although, owing
to the nature of the soil and the climatic conditions, the Twin Lakes
site was unsuitable for rhododendrons (ninety-eight out of the one
hundred complimentary plants that I sent out on trial died), Hitoshi
and I became firm friends, and my second wife Anne and I have spent
many happy days over the years at Twin Lakes.

8

The Home Stretch

In Nicholas's award-winning film *The Glory of the Garden*, I describe how my father used to take hold of a plant that had failed to flower, give it a good shake and say to it in his most severe tone of voice, 'You must flower.' If the plant then failed to flower the next year, he would prune its roots, so as to give it a sharp shock; and if, after a further year's trial, it failed again, he would dig it up and burn it.

As this rigorous regime in the gardens at Exbury lapsed with my father's death in 1942, during the late 1950s and 1960s we continued to discover the odd rhododendron species he had acquired, and a good number of his hybrids, which had for years remained hidden in the undergrowth. One species, for instance, a turkey red form of the species *R. haematodes* ssp. *chaetomallum*, which was found by Freddie Wynniatt in 1959, had grown from seed gathered by George Forrest on an expedition in 1924–5. Another, *R. traillianum* var. *dictyotum* 'Kathmandu', a plant with glorious white flowers, crimson-eyed and spotted, which had grown in a distant part of the woods, from seed from the same expedition, we only found in 1965.

One of my father's best hybrids, *R. lacteum* x *R.* 'Naomi', remained unnoticed, growing at the back of the estate yard, until it bloomed for the first time in 1954. Rose-pink in the bud, the flowers open to a deep, rich, Cornish cream colour, flushed opaline pink on the margins, with little crimson flashes in the throat. It flowered just two days before the RHS Rhododendron Show, and straight away won an Award of Merit (in 1974 it was promoted to FCC). A big, hardy plant of commanding appearance, I named it *R.* 'Lionel's Triumph'. Yet another find, *R.* 'Revlon', a superlative *cinnabarinum* hybrid in the R. 'Lady

Chamberlain' mould, had been growing unobtrusively at the side of the drive up to the house until it burst into flower, with lovely, brilliant carmine trumpets, in 1957.

Building on such discoveries and utilising the many other well-established plants in the gardens, my head gardeners and I have produced several hundred further new crosses, some more successful than others, and by no means all of them of sufficient quality to name and register. Although I have not attempted to go in for hybridisation on anything like the same scale as my father did, I have always found it an exciting process, partly because of its inherent uncertainty. Because it is a sexual method of propagation, one can never be sure that the cross will turn out to possess the precise characteristics for which one aims. In a sense, it is not unlike two people having a child: no one can predict what the child will look like, or in which particular respects it may resemble either of its parents, or its siblings. As the flower of a hybrid opens for the first time, one waits with a tremendous feeling of expectancy to see the result.

I have always borne in mind my father's guiding principle that any worthwhile hybrid must be an improvement on at least one of its parents – though preferably both – and that if the result is no better, it should be destroyed. But in addition to being ruthless in the destruction of inferior plants, I have learnt two other important lessons: that a cool appraisal for quality of flower and good plant habits in a new hybrid is essential, and that no hasty judgement should be made after only one year of flowering. Experience has taught me that even if a plant appears to be of a very high standard in the first year of flowering, it will not necessarily be as good in the years to come.

Purity of colour is always an important factor in making these assessments; so, too, is the size of the flower, the compactness of the truss, the time of flowering, the scent, the plant's hardiness and other factors. Among my father's aims there was also the consideration of prolonging the flowering season; he would have liked to see rhododendrons in flower in the gardens, and as cut flowers on the table, all the year round. In this last respect I have diverged from his programme, as I explained in a contribution I made to a symposium on aims in breeding rhododendrons, which was published in *The Rhododendron Year Book* of 1960.

What then should one attempt to do in crossing a rhododendron? Many tell us they wish to prolong the flowering period. My father was continually working to that end and he had some success, but I wonder if this is really worth while. We have rhododendrons from Christmas until the end of May and early June in abundance. Then a few continue through the latter part of June and July. Some of these late hybrids can be rated fairly high, but in the strong July sun they do not seem to have the beauty and certainly not the excitement of the mid-season rhododendrons; and in a drought period they look anything but happy. In July we have our roses, geraniums, herbaceous and bedding plants, and so many other flowers with intense colours that the softer hues of spring flowers such as rhododendrons tend to pale into insignificance. We all like daffodils, but would we think them so wonderful if they flowered in mid-summer? I believe that the existing flowering period from January to the end of June is long enough.

Of the various goals I have at different times set myself in rhododendron hybridisation, the accomplishment of three has given me particular satisfaction. Many years ago, I decided that I should like to raise another butter-yellow flowered rhododendron, similar in colour to my father's *R.* 'Crest' (*R. wardii* x *R.* 'Lady Bessborough'), but different in form and habit. I also wanted to produce a plant with large, bold red flowers, similar to my father's rich redcurrant red *R.* 'Kilimanjaro' (*R. elliottii* x *R.* 'Dusky Maid'), but more hardy. *R.* 'Kilimanjaro' was probably my father's best red rhododendron (as a parent, *R. elliottii* has produced a fair number of the best red hybrids), though he also bred the very fine, deep crimson *R.* 'Queen of Hearts' (*R. meddianum* x *R.* 'Moser's Maroon') and the crimson-scarlet *R.* 'Leo' (*R.* 'Britannia' x *R. elliottii*).

Thirdly, I decided I should like to breed a good *R. yakushimanum* cross. We, and other enthusiasts, had been finding consistently that *R. yakushimanum*, though one of the most beautiful of all known rhododendron species, did not make a good parent, and so it was a challenge to find the right plant with which to marry it.

Attempts to produce the yellow rhododendron eventually resulted in *R.* 'Pearl Betteridge' (*R.* 'Damaris' x *R. lacteum*), which I named after the late wife of my head gardener Douggie Betteridge (Freddie Wynniatt's successor), and registered with the RHS in 1993. I cannot put my hand on my heart and say that it is more beautiful than *R.* 'Crest', but it does produce a wonderful, vivid yellow flower, and it won an AM in 1993. The red flowering rhododendron I had hoped for was achieved in a hybrid – *R.* 'Kilimanjaro' x *R.* 'Fusilier' (*R. elliottii* x *R. griersonianum*) – which has ended up being called *R.* 'Edmund de Rothschild'. Bred from two of my father's prize-winning hybrids, it produces well-built trusses of deep red blooms, quite untinged by blue, and in 1993 it won an FCC. It is a plant of which I can confidently say that my father would have been proud.

The parentage of the successful *R. yakushimanum* cross we finally made was, from my point of view, even more satisfying, as it was produced with pollen from one of my own hybrids, *R.* 'Elizabeth de Rothschild' (*R.* 'Lionel's Triumph' x *R.* 'Exbury Naomi'), a plant with lovely pale yellow flowers, spotted with chestnut in the throat, which grows as high as 20 feet (FCC, 1992). We named the cross *R.* 'Lady Romsey' (AM, 1982), and in my opinion it ranks alongside Wisley's *R.* 'Seven Stars' (*R.* Loderi 'Sir Joseph Hooker' x *R. yakushimanum*) as one of the two outstandingly good *R. yakushimanum* crosses so far made – a reflection, in both cases, of the careful choice of parents.

As a rule, it is difficult to surpass the beauty of an original species; however good a hybrid is, it nearly always lacks something of the subtlety of the parent species. Except in the two cases I have mentioned, this has nearly always proved the case with *R. yakushimanum*, which after a good deal of trial and error, I have concluded tends generally to be more successful as a grandparent – or even as some remoter ancestor – than as a parent.

Another post-war cross of which I am very proud is *R.* 'Fred Wynniatt' (*R. fortunei* x *R.* 'Jalisco'), a tall, compact plant which produces large maize-yellow blooms in May. We used one of the better-known of my father's yellow rhododendron hybrids, *R.* 'Jalisco' (*R.* 'Lady Bessborough' x *R.* 'Dido'), which, though registered in 1942, was one of the plants which did not reveal its full glory until some years after my father's death.

The same cross – *R. fortunei* x *R.* 'Jalisco' – has produced a number of other good, award-winning varieties, ranging from yellow through apricot and orange to pink, including *R.* 'Douggie Betteridge', *R.* 'Bach Choir' (of which my brother Leo is the chairman), *R.* 'Stanway' and *R.* 'Trianon'. For other yellows, I have used the wonderful American hybrid *R.* 'Hotei' (named after a Japanese deity), which with *R.* 'Crest' is probably one of the two most important, if not necessarily most beautiful, post-war yellow rhododendrons bred anywhere. With *R.* 'Hotei' we have made another splendid hybrid, *R.* 'Duchess of Rothesay' (*R.* 'Hotei' x *R.* 'Decorum'), a title of the late Diana, Princess of Wales, which earned an RHS Award of Merit in 1983.

One other rhododendron I sought for some years to raise was an improved, frost-hardy, broad-leaved form of *R.* 'Jocelyne' (*R. lacteum* x *R. calophytum*), a superb early flowering (March–April) hybrid with mother-of-pearl coloured blossoms marked with crimson. Although I have never been altogether successful in this aim – the quality of frost-hardiness has eluded me – *R.* 'Our Kate' (*R. calophytum* x *R. macabeanum*), named after my elder daughter, comes quite close. Seed from *R.* 'Our Kate', a cross between two giant Asiatic rhododendrons, did not flower for fifteen years after sowing; but it finally produced good-sized, loose trusses of beautiful pale pink flowers, lit up with a ruby-coloured throat. It won an RHS Award of Merit in 1963. My daughter Kate, having inherited her mother's artistic eye and studied at the Courtauld Institute, is now a well-known figure in the world of Old Master drawings.

The hit-and-miss quality of hybridisation is well illustrated in the case of another of my favourites, *R.* 'Jungfrau' (*R.* 'Marie Antoinette' x *R.* ?), a tall shrub with dark green foliage, which bears very large conical trusses of white flowers in late May. It is the result of a cross between one of my father's less distinguished hybrids and an unidentified mate, and it always reminds me of a remark P.D. Williams once made to my mother during a tour of the gardens. After dinner the evening before, my father had shown his guests a film, as he often did; but instead of the usual Western, he unwittingly showed a rather risqué 'Don Juan' film which had somehow found its way down from London – and which was greeted with a stony silence. Tramping around the rhododendrons with my mother the next day, PD brushed away a large bumble-bee from one of the blooms, saying, 'These large Don Juans with their big hob-nailed boots fertilise all the wrong rhodos.' *R.* 'Jungfrau' is living proof that sometimes they do the right thing.

There are two ambitions with rhododendrons which I have failed altogether to achieve. One is to breed a rhododendron with a scent as fragrant as that of the Javanese types which my father used to cultivate in his great Rhododendron House, but one which would thrive out of doors in our climate. Secondly, I should like to have produced a general purpose plant as hardy, free-flowering, beautiful and popular as my father's favourite hybrid *R.* 'Naomi' (*R.* 'Aurora' x *R. fortunei*).

Besides hybridisation work with rhododendrons, we have made considerable strides since the war in the development of azaleas. By careful crossing of the Waterer family's Knap Hill strain of deciduous azaleas with other species, my father created the Exbury azalea, in a remarkable range of colours; and building on that we have succeeded in raising a still hardier and more tightly-trussed type – with larger flowers and in a more intense range of colours – which we have named the Solent Range, and which now line Lover's Lane in the gardens. Probably my favourite among these is a butter-yellow azalea which we named *R.* 'Princess Margaret of Windsor', on the occasion of a visit by the Princess to Exbury.

I have always thought it a great privilege to be able to name plants, and I hope I have not abused it by naming a fair number of new hybrids after members of my family and other people whom I admire. Of my children, only my son Lionel, who now knows more about rhododendrons than I do, has yet to have a hybrid named after him – an oversight which I hope to correct. I must also admit that from time to time it can be rather useful to have the power to name a hybrid up one's sleeve. This has never been brought home to me more clearly than in 1962, when we had been invited by the RHS to represent Britain at the Valenciennes International Flower Show.

Having put together the finest display of rhododendrons and azaleas we could muster – with some difficulty, since Freddie Wynniatt had fallen out of a tree and hurt his back – my agent Peter Barber and I were very chuffed to be awarded first prize for our exhibit, particularly as it was the first time that Britain had won. But almost straight away the Belgian entrants objected; technically, they said, we should have shown in three classes, not two (they were showing orchids as well as rhododendrons and azaleas). It just so happened that one of the new rhododendron hybrids we had brought with us, more or less by chance, flowered for the first time that morning, and so when I went to see the show's organiser, Mme Zelia Plumecocq, I asked if we might be allowed to name the new hybrid in her honour. We heard no more of any complaints from our competitors – and we kept the prize. *R.* 'Zelia Plumecocq' (*R.* 'Rosy Morn' x *R.* 'Crest') has large, saucer-like flowers of yellow tinged with pink, though I have to admit that it has not quite lived up to its extremely promising start.

Freddie Wynniatt, when he was not falling out of trees, was responsible for some of Exbury's most splendid post-war show exhibits, for instance a very colourful garden at Chelsea in 1959, which won a gold medal. That same year Freddie himself was awarded the RHS's A.J. Waley medal, in recognition of his contribution to hybridisation work with rhododendrons.

In due course, Freddie was succeeded as head gardener by Douggie Betteridge, and Douggie in turn by our present head gardener Paul

Martin; Douglas Harris eventually took over from Peter Barber as managing director of Exbury Gardens. In different ways, they have all been of invaluable help, and I feel extremely fortunate to have had them to work for me. With them, over the years, I have continued to replace old plants with new, and also to develop previously neglected parts of the gardens.

In the last half-century we have replanted approximately three quarters of the whole acreage. Unlike such celebrated gardens as Bodnant, Stourhead, Sheffield Park or Windsor, Exbury has no great vistas or commanding elevations, and consequently we have to be particularly sensitive in our planting. In going about this, we have tried our best not to lose sight of my father's acute sense of landscape, striving always to maintain the illusion of height and distance within confined spaces, and to get the best out of each modest fold of the land. Foliage is always, in my view, extremely important: the variation of leaf shape and colour can as much enhance a particular view as a great bank of colour.

Although my father had planned to extend the gardens further to the north, into an area of woodland called Steerley's Copse, we have kept within the boundaries of the gardens as he left them. Indeed, it was not until the mid-1970s that we finally cleared the weeds and brambles away from the last derelict area, the Rock Garden.

Then in 1976 it seemed for a time as if our efforts might have been in vain. Rhododendrons are thirsty plants – some, in their natural habitat, get as much as 80 inches of rainfall a year – but for three months in the summer of 1976 there was a drought so severe that the water table at Exbury fell by about nine feet. In the autumn this was followed by torrential rains; the roots of trees and shrubs which had been struggling to reach down for water during the summer became water-logged, as a result of which we lost thousands of plants (the weaker ones to fungus), and even well-established trees.

Once more we had to set about clearing out the dead growth and replanting; but much of our work was again undone by the great gale of October 1987. The winds that swept up the Solent during the night of 16 October hit Exbury at about midnight, and the gardens took the full force of the gale. When I arrived from London two days later – once the road to Exbury had been cleared of fallen trees – I was met with a scene of extraordinary devastation. Oaks, beeches and evergreen trees had fallen in all directions, and the huge root-balls that had been pulled up out of the ground as the trees fell had shattered parts of the underground irrigation network which my father had had so carefully laid. In all, we lost 360 oaks and 150 other trees, among them some important and rare specimens.

However, by nature an optimist, I soon recognised that this apparent calamity might well be a blessing in disguise. I noticed that the trees seemed to have fallen slowly, and that their branches had saved many of the rhododendrons and other shrubs from being crushed by the full weight of the tree-trunks. New vistas had been opened up, and the storm had removed trees which , although no one would have had the heart to fell them, were past their prime. Also, the heavy canopy of leaf that had covered the majority of the gardens had been blown open, allowing light to reach the plants below, and so to improve, given time, the quality of the flowering. And some areas, such as the Rock Garden and the Azalea Walk, were more or less untouched.

Chain-saw gangs quickly removed the smaller trees and debris; and to remove the huge root-balls my then agent, Charles Orr-Ewing, arranged for them to be blown up *in situ* – so as not to have to bring heavy lifting machinery into areas already badly damaged by the storm. Army explosives experts detonated small charges among the roots, which could then easily be gathered up. In this way, over the next six months, almost all the storm damage was repaired, and the gardens were open to the public as usual in the spring of 1988.

Scarcely two years later, in January 1990, we were hit by yet another storm, less spectacular than that of October 1987, but in some ways more damaging to the gardens. The trees which fell this time were mostly firs, which, having no spreading branches to break their fall, did more damage to the shrubs below. Among the trees we lost were three great cedars of Lebanon which grew near to the house, and the two famous specimens of *Cupressus sempervirens* which had grown from the seed of the wreath from the Duke of Wellington's funeral carriage. To make up for the loss of the two cypresses, when the present Duke of Wellington paid us a visit he gave me an oak tree grown from an acorn picked from the tree which grows on the grave of Copenhagen, the 1st Duke's horse, at Stratfield Saye.

Today, with all the storm damage cleared away and new plantings well-established, a visitor to Exbury would probably not notice a great deal of difference – unless he knew where to look. Wholesale new plantings include the evergreen azaleas around the Middle Pond (the so-called Azalea Bowl), and the Solent Range of deciduous azaleas which flank either side of Lover's Lane. We have also created a

Bog Garden, and have developed the area around a huge beech tree north of Yard Wood. Currently, we are in the process of tackling the northern parts of the gardens generally, planting them out with summer-flowering trees and shrubs so as to put on a better show for visitors once the rhododendron season is over. In 1993 we received 170,000 visitors, a record number for Exbury, though the more usual (and manageable) annual figure is in the region of 100–150,000.

To safeguard the gardens for posterity, in the late 1980s I separated them completely from the commercial side of the Exbury estate. I placed them (all the trees and shrubs) in one of my charitable trusts – Exbury Gardens Trust – to which my brother Leo contributed a generous and substantial endowment. Since then the gardens have been run and maintained on behalf of the charitable trust by Exbury Gardens Ltd, of which Leo is the chairman. The board of directors includes other family, as well as non-family, members, and, although I have no official role, I help them with advice on planting and in any other way I can. All the visitors' entrance money goes towards the gardens' upkeep, but the greater part of the maintenance cost is funded by Leo's endowment, together with contributions from my charitable trusts.

The commercial wholesale and retail side of the gardens, Exbury Enterprises, is the preserve of Nicholas, my elder son, who lives full time at Exbury with his family. Under his aegis we have recently built an extensive range of new, state-of-the-art greenhouses to replace the old-fashioned, and by now somewhat dilapidated, greenhouses built by my father.

When the gardens are open, I still like to drive along the paths in my small car, and it gives me real pleasure to stop and talk to the (sometimes rather surprised) visitors along the way. Armed with a good pair of secateurs and a stout rhododendron stave, I continue to enjoy knocking off old blooms and 'brashing out' the dead wood. Nowadays, we have eight gardeners, including the head gardener, and two dead-headers. I like to think of myself as the eleventh member of the team.

Inspired by my son Lionel, we have recently returned to one of my father's interests – the cultivation of nerines. My father built up a small but important collection of nerines, some of which I showed after the war. The plants are native to South Africa, and so in England they flower in the autumn. However, in the 1970s we sold the bulk of the collection, keeping only a few back in the greenhouses so as to be able to send the Queen Mother a bouquet of them every year.

Having been sold *en bloc*, the nerine collection was subsequently dispersed – some of the finest hybrids being acquired by Sir Peter Smithers, who then proceeded with the kind of rigorous breeding programme of which my father would have approved. Sir Peter produced some top-class hybrids, and when he decided to dispose of the Smithers Collection in 1995 he kindly approached us first – and we acquired it for Exbury.

Until I retired from N.M. Rothschild in 1975, business kept me away from home and the family a great deal. My wife Elizabeth and I lived at our small house in London during the week and, as when I was a child, our children stayed down in the country, at Inchmery House, and later went to boarding school. My mother, who lived on until 1975, divided her time between Marise Cottage at Exbury and her London house in Thurloe Square. She was adored by our children, who called her Didi. When I was not travelling abroad, I tried to make it a rule to dine with her at Thurloe Square once a week. Elizabeth would stay at home, sometimes down at Exbury for an extra night, and treat herself to a real Austrian dinner – with lashings of sauerkraut – which I was always happy to miss.

I have never been very good with small children, and in London we only had room for one child to stay with us at a time. Now that I am older, of course, I sometimes feel uneasy about this, though the children seem to have got along well enough without seeing too much of me in their young days. A year or two ago, I was very pleased to learn from my daughter Charlotte that she remembers her childhood as 'sheltered and totally lovely, with Nanny, games and lots of love'. She and Lionel remember me visiting them in the nursery on the top floor on Sunday afternoons, lying on a sofa in the corner and pretending to be asleep, with my labrador sprawled on top.

During summer weekends we all used to play tennis and croquet, and make the most of the swimming pool Elizabeth built for us at Inchmery. In the evenings I would show films (a cine-camera my father gave me on my twenty-first birthday lasted me well for forty years), usually concluding with an early, silent Mickey Mouse cartoon which my father used to show me, and which Lionel now shows to his three children. We would also play a lot of games, especially word games, such as Bali and Scrabble, which Elizabeth used to enjoy, as well as mah-jongg and card games – bezique, bridge, Slippery Anne (or Hearts) and misère. Bridge remains one of the few activities at which I can honestly say I have not yet been outdone by my children. An evening a week at the Portland Club helps me to stay ahead.

We also went on tremendous family holidays, to the South African game parks, the Austrian lakes, Brazil, India and Israel. When Nick and Kate were young we used to go every summer to the Ile de Porquerolles, off the French coast near Toulon, and for several years we took all four children to Austria (to which Elizabeth always remained very attached), renting a house near St Gilgen, on the Wolfgangsee. Twice we chartered a boat round the Greek Islands. Perhaps the best holiday of all, and the one that the children recall most vividly, was to Kenya, for a safari one Christmas time – the only Christmas I have not spent at Exbury since I married.

Kenya has a special place in my affections, not only because I had a wonderful time there as a young man in 1938, but also because after the war, in 1948, my sister Rosemary and her husband Tony Seys settled there to farm in the White Highlands. With great determination they built up a highly productive farm – which they called *Rhodora* – and the finest herd of Guernseys in the country. Before they returned to England in 1962, I went out to visit them a number of times, taking advantage of the opportunities for butterfly hunting in the near-by Bahati Forest, where I caught several unusual and lovely swallowtails. In 1993, Rosemary published *The Rhodora Letters*, a fascinating record of her and Tony's day-to-day life on the farm.

The children's abiding memory of me on holiday is of my rushing off with a butterfly net, dressed in shorts and knee-length socks, whether in the African bush or on a piranha-infested river in South America. There is, I should say, an element of caricature in this, but also some truth. During a trip with Elizabeth (though no children) to Paraguay in 1968, we were provided with a car and a driver by President Stroessner to visit the Iguaçu Falls, one of the most beautiful places I have seen on my travels. In the forest around the falls, besides the flocks of brightly coloured parrots and the hummingbirds, there were thousands of butterflies. In all, I caught seventy different species, of which three specimens are now in the Natural History Museum. The rarest turned out to be a little brown one, which I had almost ignored.

Although Elizabeth was largely responsible for bringing up the children, I have tried to instil in them two things: an understanding of the obligations which go with the lucky life into which they, and I, have been born, and an appreciation of the natural wonders around them. On the latter count, in 1970 I took all the family on a trip to South Africa to visit two game reserves, Umfolozi and Hluhluwe. The parks were looked after by the conservationist Ian Player, who then worked for the South African National Parks Board. He became a good friend and, in the early days of rhinoceros conservation, I helped him to send seventeen white rhinos to Whipsnade Zoo. He went on to found the World Wilderness Leadership organisation, and Anne and I have been on a trek with him in the African bush. Before Nick went up to Trinity, Cambridge, I sent him to the wilds of Newfoundland to work for Brinco. And at the same stage in his life Lionel went to Africa for eighteen months, half of the time spent working at a school in Botswana, the other half, through Ian Player, helping to catch live game for game farms in South Africa and Namibia.

Butterflies aside, my own interest in the natural world has for many years centred largely on water. Dating from the time when I helped to arrange for the sale of the atomic power plant to Chile in the 1960s, I have been keenly interested in the possibilities of producing potable water by desalination (the heat generated by a nuclear reactor can easily be harnessed to run a desalting plant). Although I have had more failures than successes in getting across my ideas for using desalination plants to transform the world's arid zones, I remain hopeful that one day, as the population continues to grow, more may be done in this direction.

My biggest disappointment came in 1967, when, after the Six Day War, I proposed in a letter to *The Times* that Israel and Jordan should be given large-scale atomic desalting plants. Partly inspired by President Johnson's second Water for Peace conference, which I had attended in Washington in 1965, my idea was that these plants could provide each country, as well as the Gaza Strip, with the water so badly needed to bring agricultural prosperity to the region – and in the process improve the prospects of peaceful settlement. The United Kingdom Atomic Energy Authority had published a design study for a plant capable of producing slightly more than 100 million gallons of potable water a day, at an estimated cost in the region of $170–210 million. In my letter to *The Times*, I suggested thinking in terms of constructing three such plants, to provide Jordan and Israel with 100 million gallons a day each, with 50 million a day for the Gaza Strip.

'Surely,' I concluded, 'now is the time to seize the chance and try to implement these major schemes. There is now a wonderful opportunity of turning the present situation of turmoil in the Middle East to one in which all efforts are devoted to promoting the economic and social welfare of all the peoples of the area.'

The initial response was encouraging. The next day's *Times* carried a full-page analysis of my proposal by Michael Ionides, a Middle-East water resources expert, who considered that the idea deserved a full and immediate feasibility study. He pointed out that if the money given by the world community to provide food were used to supply people with water, so that they could grow the food themselves, there would be far more for the same cost; and that, in any case, 'the costs suggested by Mr de Rothschild are insignificant compared with waging a war every ten years and a running economic sore in between times.' His conclusion was that 'if it turns out that money can indeed buy as much water for agriculture as the [international] community is prepared to pay for, an unprecedented means of moving towards a peaceful settlement will have been achieved.' The article ended by saying that if the United Nations 'were to take it for granted that they have every right to initiate a feasibility study without asking anyone's permission, it could be on the table by Christmas? Why not?'

After this, I got into correspondence and had meetings on the subject with politicians in Britain, America and the Middle East, including Harold Wilson, Golda Meir, Vice-President Hubert Humphrey and General Eisenhower. But while almost everybody seemed to agree with me in principle, and while the experts confirmed that my plans and costings were feasible, apparently insurmountable political difficulties continued to stand firmly in the way. In the end, the only notable result of all my leg-work was that whenever I ran into Harold Wilson he addressed me as 'Mr Desalination'.

From my Brinco days, I have been fascinated by the possibilities of power generation from water, and have been involved in several projects, including the construction of the world's largest tidal power unit, using a straight flow ('straflo') turbine, at Annapolis Royal in the Bay of Fundy. This was really intended to be a test site for a much more ambitious scheme, and I remain hopeful that these straflo turbines will one day be used to harness the enormous potential of tidal power in the Bay of Fundy or, nearer to home, in the Severn estuary – or even, on a more modest scale, in the Medway.

But it is not only the large-scale projects that have caught my attention. I have also been involved with Micro Hydro, utilising the AUR Water Engine (named after its inventor, Mr A.U. Reid), a portable reciprocating engine which operates in low heads of water of three metres or less. It can be used not only to produce electricity from a generator, but also, if anything more efficiently, power for pumping or heating.

Since attending a conference organised by Ian Player's World Wilderness Leadership, in conjunction with the United Nations, in Colorado in 1975, I have also been interested in wider environmental problems, in particular pollution control. In recent years, the main focus of my interest in this area has been on the possibilities of using different kinds of algae to clear up agricultural and industrial waste, such as slurry, oil spills, steel mill tailings and effluent from sugar production.

In 1980, a few hours after I had left Exbury on a trip to Alberta one Sunday afternoon, Elizabeth died. We had been due to meet up in America a few days later for a holiday, and before I set off we had been for a walk in the gardens and had kissed goodbye. That evening she was watching television with Charlotte at Inchmery, and when she got up to switch off the television set she had a heart attack, dying almost at once. She had had a heart condition for some years, and in 1974 had undergone open heart surgery for a new aorta valve. In other people this might easily have meant living the life of an invalid; but Elizabeth had resolved to continue to enjoy life to the full, so far as her strength allowed, although she fully realised that in doing so she risked shortening her life.

Charlotte, who was 24 at the time, was quite magnificent in the crisis, and for nearly two years afterwards helped to keep me cheerful, and to look after the domestic side of things at home. I should add that R. 'Charlotte de Rothschild' (*R. discolor* x R. 'St Keverne'), a lovely, large pink rhododendron, was one among those of my father's hybrids which it was left to me to show for the first time and name. In 1992, the RHS awarded it an FCC.

Between Exbury House and the Home Wood, not far from my father's memorial, Nicholas – in consultation with Kate and the twins – has created a beautiful rose garden in Elizabeth's memory. In May 1980, we also held a concert in her memory at Goldsmiths' Hall; Charlotte sang songs by Mozart, Schumann and Bach, and the Arion

Trio played two movements from Schubert's E flat major piano trio, *op.* 100.

In the spring of 1982 I married Anne Harrison, at whose home near Middlesbrough I was billeted during the war. Her husband, my old friend Mac, had died about six months before Elizabeth. After our marriage, we decided to make some improvements to Inchmery House; but we soon found that the whole structure was in need of major renovation – during wet weather and at very high tides the cellars were regularly flooded – and also that since my children had grown up it was too big for us. So we resolved instead to make a fresh start and to move back into part of Exbury House, empty since the Admiralty had finally left in 1955. The ground-floor rooms, simply furnished, had been used for parties during the flowering season, but otherwise the house was untouched and unused. Exbury also offered the advantage over Inchmery of being much more conveniently sited, right at the heart of the estate – and a few steps, rather than a drive, from the gardens.

It was an enormous undertaking, but I was fortunate to have the help and advice of an excellent team led by the architect James (now Sir James) Dunbar-Nasmith. James has been a friend of my brother Leo since prep school days, and designed and built a superb modern house for him at Exbury in 1965. Anne and I discussed our plans with him, and fell in with his suggestion to convert the top floor into a flat for my son Lionel, to have private apartments for ourselves on part of the first floor (the old guest bedrooms remaining closed off), and to restore all the ground-floor rooms. The only significant change we made to the ground floor was that, having decided to abandon the old kitchen in the basement, we turned my parents' dining-room into a modern kitchen, with views across the lawns and into the Italian garden, and converted my father's library into a new dining-room.

We sold Inchmery in 1987, and under the direction of my curator Michael Hall, the house was dismantled and the works of art and pictures were put into store. Michael took charge of the restoration of the main rooms of Exbury, pictures were cleaned and reframed, furniture was restored and all manner of carpets, curtains and interior decoration were organised by Anne. We renovated the north wing, formerly the housekeeper's quarters, and lived there while the restoration was under way. The work took nearly two years, and was carried out with military precision under the eagle eye of Ron Cromie, of the firm of

Ernest Ireland. Despite the complexity of the work, it was finished on time, and we were able to take up permanent residence in the summer of 1989 – after a break, in my case, of almost exactly fifty years.

In the 1990s, I seem to have spent much of my time – very willingly – assisting in the commemoration of a succession of different kinds of anniversary, beginning with D-Day in 1994. I have always taken a great interest in the welfare of ex-servicemen, and have for many years had close links with the Not Forgotten Association and the Association of Jewish Ex-Servicemen and Women. So in 1994, as part of the nationwide D-Day remembrance, I offered Exbury for use by the Normandy Veterans' Association, on account of the wartime role of the house and estate as HMS *Mastodon*.

The Association accepted, and on 29 May 200 ex-servicemen came to take part in a service of commemoration, conducted by the Rector of Exbury on the lawn in front of the house. A guard of honour was supplied by the Army, and a detachment from HMS *Collingwood*, the weapons engineering school at Gosport, came to hoist the White Ensign, which the Queen had given us special permission ('the sole and exceptional privilege') to fly from our flag-pole for the day. The BBC Big Band came down to play for us as tea was being served in the garden, and a cadet force of the Royal Marines beat the retreat and played the Last Post and the National Anthem as Anne and I stood by the flag-pole. It was an especially moving occasion for Anne, whose brother Alfred was killed, aged 23, at Catania in 1942, and it brought back many memories for me. In the last remaining Nissen hut in the grounds we staged a display of Second World War memorabilia, ably organised by my son Nicholas, and when the White Ensign was lowered it was entrusted to me for safe-keeping.

The other great event of 1994 was the dual commemoration in Frankfurt of the 1,000th anniversary of the city's foundation and the 250th anniversary of the birth of my great-great-great-grandfather Mayer Amschel Rothschild, the Frankfurt banker and father of N.M. Rothschild and his four brothers. Frankfurt's city authorities decided that to mark the anniversaries they would like to honour the Rothschilds, and consequently nearly a hundred members of the family, including Guy and Elie and one or two other survivors of my own generation, assembled there.

We attended the opening of an extensive exhibition of Rothschild art and memorabilia, much of it lent by family members, at Frankfurt's Jewish Museum, which is housed in an old Rothschild property. The exhibition opening was accompanied by the publication of a book of learned essays on different aspects of our family and its legacy. Also, we all took part in an intensely moving family ceremony in the old Jewish cemetery, where, miraculously, the gravestones of Mayer Amschel and of Elchanan, one of our sixteenth-century forebears, had escaped the appalling desecration wrought on the cemetery by the Nazis.

In 1996, my cousin Evelyn and his wife Victoria staged by far the best party I have ever attended: a dinner at Exbury to celebrate my eightieth birthday. Having only recently recovered from emergency heart by-pass surgery the year before, I felt especially fortunate to be there. And the arrangements were out of this world; no detail was overlooked. Victoria and her friend Nicholas Haslam had masterminded the most beautifully decorated marquee imaginable: the tables were arranged around huge cork-bark trees, painted silver and gold, with lanterns hanging from their branches; the roof was lined with dark blue velvet set with brilliant star-like lights. Outside the marquee, as the guests arrived, a band of the Royal Artillery played from an elegant little bandstand, decked out in our blue and yellow colours. All my immediate family were there – Rosemary, Naomi, Leo and all my children, as well as Anne's – and many other friends and relations.

After a magnificent dinner – at which we were treated to a fine vintage of Château Lafite sent over by the family from France – we were entertained at the piano by Mr Richard Stilgoe, who composed – off the cuff and with a bit of help from the guests – the following words about me:

> I'm Exbury Eddy, I'm eighty already,
> I've lived an incredible life,
> I've harnessed a fountain, I've climbed a mountain –
> Ben Nevis it was, with my wife.
> I've built a power station for every nation,
> I know about algae and desalination,
> I'm Ed, Ed, my shield is red,
> I'm a dab hand with spade, fork and hoe.
> I never have failures (well, sometimes azaleas),
> I'm Exbury Eddy you know.
>
> I'm Exbury Eddy, my pulse rate is steady
> Though last year my heart tried to sneeze,
> I had a by-pass so incredibly vast
> That protesters sat up in the trees.

My butterfly collection I hold in affection,
I keep them for show, and some for dissection.
I'm Ed, Ed, I see a blonde head
In the woods, I approach and say 'Oh,
Come up and see my moths, child, I'm Edmund de Rothschild,
I'm Exbury Eddy you know.'

The years since we moved back into Exbury House have been among the happiest of my life. With the dedicated support of a small staff, I have been able to enjoy life at Exbury to the full. I still spend two to three days a week in London at New Court, where Evelyn – under whose forward-thinking stewardship N.M. Rothschild & Sons has again become a major force in the investment banking world – is most tolerant in continuing to allow me the use of an office. But Exbury is very much the centre of my life, and by Thursday afternoon I am more than ready to leave London and return to the peace of Exbury Gardens.

Looking back, I realise that I have been extraordinarily fortunate in my lot, and above all in the wonderful family I have always had around me. Since marrying Anne, who has been the most loving, tolerant and understanding companion, it has been a particular pleasure for me to see how well her children and mine have got on together. All of them have houses or cottages on the Exbury estate, and we continue to see them and our grandchildren as often as we can. It is for them that I have attempted to record my story, and from the bottom of my heart I wish them all the same good fortune, health and long life that I have been so fortunate to enjoy.

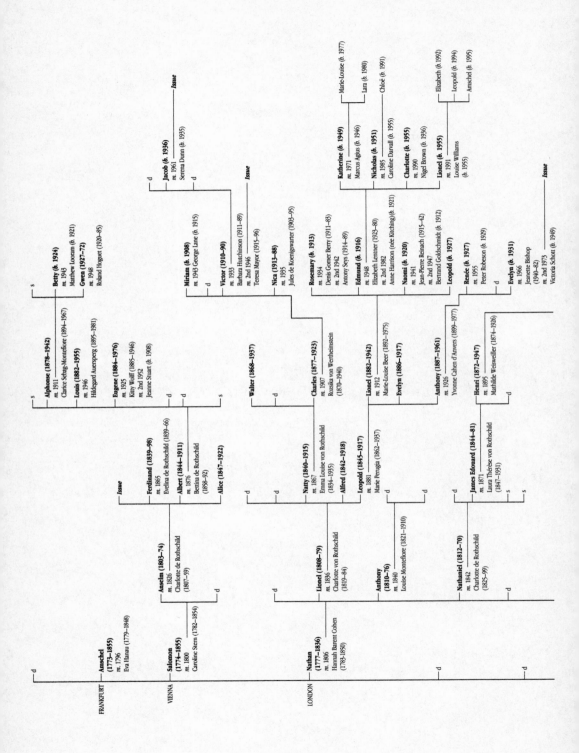

FRANKFURT **Amschel (1773–1855)**
m. 1796
Eva Hanau (1779–1848)

VIENNA **Salomon (1774–1855)**
m. 1800
Caroline Stern (1782–1854)

Anselm (1803–74)
m. 1826
Charlotte de Rothschild (1807–59)

Ferdinand (1839–98)
m. 1865
Evelina de Rothschild (1839–66)

Albert (1844–1911)
m. 1876
Bettina de Rothschild (1858–92)

Alice (1847–1922)

Alphonse (1878–1942)
m. 1911
Clarice Sebag-Montefiore (1894–1967)

Louis (1882–1955)
m. 1946
Hildegard Auersperg (1895–1981)

Betty (b. 1924)
m. 1943
Matthew Looram (b. 1921)

Gwen (1927–72)
m. 1948
Roland Hoguet (1920–85)

Issue

Eugene (1884–1976)
m. 1925
Kitty Wolff (1885–1946)
m. 2nd 1952
Jeanne Stuart (b. 1908)

Walter (1868–1937)

Charles (1877–1923)
m. 1907
Rozsika von Wertheimstein (1870–1940)

Miriam (b. 1908)
m. 1943 George Lane (b. 1915)

Victor (1910–90)
m. 1933
Barbara Hutchinson (1911–89)
m. 2nd 1946
Teresa Mayor (1915–96)

Nica (1913–88)
m. 1935
Jules de Koenigswarter (1903–95)

Rosemary (b. 1913)
m. 1934
Denis Gomer Berry (1911–83)
m. 2nd 1942
Antony Seys (1914–89)

Edmund (b. 1916)
m. 1948
Elizabeth Lentner (1923–80)
m. 2nd 1982
Anne Harrison (née Kitching)(b. 1921)

Naomi (b. 1920)
m. 1941
Jean-Pierre Reinach (1915–42)
m. 2nd 1947
Bertrand Goldschmidt (b. 1912)

Leopold (b. 1927)

Jacob (b. 1936)
m. 1961
Serena Dunn (b. 1935)

Katherine (b. 1949)
m. 1971
Marcus Agius (b. 1946)

Nicholas (b. 1951)
m. 1985
Caroline Darvall (b. 1955)

Charlotte (b. 1955)
m. 1990
Nigel Brown (b. 1936)

Lionel (b. 1955)
m. 1991
Louise Williams (b. 1955)

Marie-Louise (b. 1977)

Lara (b. 1980)

Chloë (b. 1991)

Elizabeth (b. 1992)

Leopold (b. 1994)

Amschel (b. 1995)

Issue

LONDON **Nathan (1777–1836)**
m. 1806
Hannah Barent Cohen (1783–1850)

Lionel (1808–79)
m. 1836
Charlotte von Rothschild (1819–84)

Natty (1840–1915)
m. 1867
Emma Louise von Rothschild (1844–1935)

Alfred (1842–1918)

Leopold (1845–1917)
m. 1881
Marie Perugia (1862–1937)

Lionel (1882–1942)
m. 1912
Marie-Louise Beer (1892–1975)

Evelyn (1886–1917)

Anthony (1887–1961)
m. 1926
Yvonne Cahen d'Anvers (1899–1977)

Renée (b. 1927)
m. 1955
Peter Robeson (b. 1929)

Evelyn (b. 1931)
m. 1966
Jeanette Bishop (1940–82)
m. 2nd 1973
Victoria Schott (b. 1949)

Issue

Anthony (1810–76)
m. 1840
Louise Montefiore (1821–1910)

Nathaniel (1812–70)
m. 1842
Charlotte de Rothschild (1825–99)

James Édouard (1844–81)
m. 1871
Laura Thérèse von Rothschild (1847–1931)

Henri (1872–1947)
m. 1895
Mathilde Weisweiller (1874–1926)

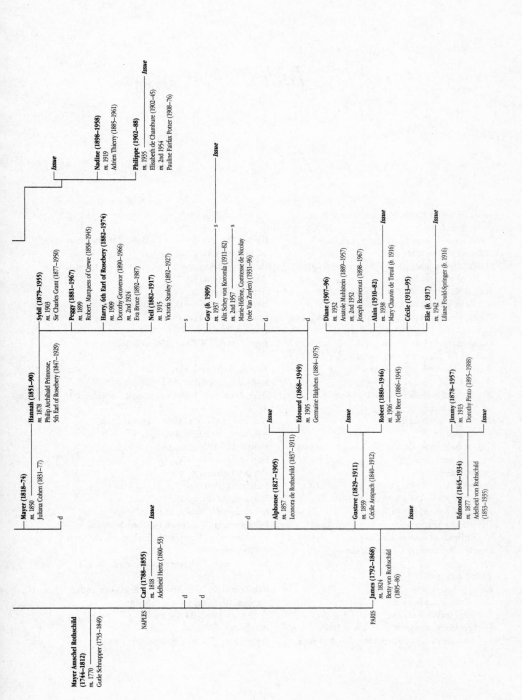

Mayer Amschel Rothschild (1744–1812)
m. 1770
Gutle Schnapper (1753–1849)

NAPLES
Carl (1788–1855)
m. 1818
Adelheid Hertz (1800–53)

d

d

Mayer (1818–74)
m. 1850
Juliana Cohen (1831–77)

d

Hannah (1851–90)
m. 1878
Philip Archibald Primrose,
5th Earl of Rosebery (1847–1929)

Sybil (1879–1955)
m. 1903
Sir Charles Grant (1877–1950)

Peggy (1881–1967)
m. 1899
Robert, Marquess of Crewe (1858–1945)

Harry, 6th Earl of Rosebery (1882–1974)
m. 1909
Dorothy Grosvenor (1890–1966)
m. 2nd 1924
Eva Bruce (1892–1987)

Neil (1882–1917)
m. 1915
Victoria Stanley (1892–1927)

Nadine (1898–1958)
m. 1919
Adrien Thierry (1885–1961)

Philippe (1902–88)
m. 1935
Elisabeth de Chambure (1902–45)
m. 2nd 1954
Pauline Fairfax Potter (1908–76) — *Issue*

PARIS
James (1792–1868)
m. 1824
Betty von Rothschild (1805–86)

Alphonse (1827–1905)
m. 1857
Leonora de Rothschild (1837–1911)

d

Edouard (1868–1949)
m. 1905
Germaine Halphen (1884–1975) — *Issue*

Gustave (1829–1911)
m. 1859
Cécile Anspach (1840–1912)

d

Robert (1880–1946)
m. 1906
Nelly Beer (1886–1945)

Guy (b. 1909)
m. 1937
Alix Schey von Koromla (1911–82) — s
m. 2nd 1957
Marie-Hélène, Comtesse de Nicolay
(née Van Zuylen) (1931–96) — s

d — **Diane (1907–96)**
m. 1932
Anatole Muhlstein (1889–1957)
m. 2nd 1952
Joseph Benvenuti (1898–1967)

d — **Alain (1910–82)**
m. 1938
Mary Chauvin de Treuil (b. 1916) — *Issue*

Cécile (1913–95)

Elie (b. 1917)
m. 1942
Liliane Fould-Springer (b. 1916) — *Issue*

Edmond (1845–1934)
m. 1877
Adelheid von Rothschild
(1853–1935)

d

Jimmy (1878–1957)
m. 1913
Dorothy Pinto (1895–1988) — *Issue*

Index

Index